Kurt Blaukopf was born in Cernovice in 1914 and is Professor of Music at the Vienna Akademie für Musik und Darstellende Kunst. He has written books on great conductors and virtuosi as well as a fundamental study of the sociology of music and a novel based on the life of Hector Berlioz, the French composer. At present Professor Blaukopf is preparing an International Symposium, sponsored by Unesco, on new patterns of musical behaviour among the young in industrial society. Professor Blaukopf is also musical adviser to the Vienna Festival. His biography of Gustav Mahler is the result of more than twenty years' interest and research.

Professor Blaukopf makes available here many new or hitherto little known facts in a study of Gustav Mahler's life, private and professional, that will be welcomed by all Mahler's admirers.

Kurt Blaukopf

Gustav Mahler

Translated by Inge Goodwin

Futura Publications Limited

A Futura Book

First published as *Gustav Mahler oder der Zeitgenosse
der Zukunft*

First published in Great Britain in 1973
by Allen Lane, A Division of Penguin Books Ltd

First Futura Publications edition 1974
Reprinted 1975

© 1969 Verlag Molden, Wien-Muenchen-Zurich
English translation © Allen Lane 1973

ISBN 0 8600 7034 4
Printed in Great Britain by
Hazell Watson & Viney Ltd
Aylesbury, Bucks

Futura Publications Limited
49 Poland Street,
London W1A 2LG

Contents

Illustrations

ACKNOWLEDGEMENTS

Plates and p. 214: Österreichische Nationalbibliothek
p. 184: caricature by Fritz Schönplug in *Muskete*, 19 January 1907
p. 202: caricature by Schliessmann in *Fliegende Blätter*, March 1901

[1]

Retrospect, 1910

Dr Sigmund Freud was about to start a well-earned holiday by the Baltic. The second congress of the Psychoanalytical Society was over, and his American lectures were ready for the printer. At last he could think of relaxing. He had made complete plans for the summer: Holland, France, southern Italy and Sicily. Why then should Freud be troubled during the holiday season by a colleague trying to interest him in a new patient? The prospective patient's name sounded familiar, although Freud was not very knowledgeable about music. Of all the arts, this one seemed to him positively suspect, because its effect upon his senses could not be as clearly analysed as that of the plastic arts or literature. A doctor specialising in the mind must be chary of abandoning himself to such dubious influences.

He must however reply to the cable of the man from Toblach. After all, this was a man of some distinction, a former director of the Vienna Court Opera, conductor and composer, and now also famous in America. In the previous year Freud had crossed the Atlantic to lecture at Clark University and he must surely have heard of Gustav Mahler's successes over there. In the Old World his name was already well known among music lovers, and connected with a well-defined personality. The *Golden Book of Music*, an encyclopaedia found in almost every musical German-speaking household, had this to say about him: 'M's is a profoundly musical nature; devoted to his profession to the point of self-forgetfulness, he also makes exceptional demands on his collaborators. His originality is manifest, sometimes almost to excess, in his compositions.'

Freud cabled suggesting an appointment: Mahler rewarded this obliging behaviour with a cabled cancellation. He had thought better of it. But Freud, well aware that a patient's resistance begins even before analysis, was not so easily put off. Mahler cancelled two further appointments Freud made for him. At last Freud made it absolutely clear that the next appointment would be the last: he proposed a meeting in the Dutch town of Leiden, which was on his projected holiday itinerary.

The meeting took place in August. Mahler's immediate reason for seeking Freud's advice and help emerges from the memoirs of his wife. That Mahler was undergoing a psychological crisis is confirmed by Freud's notes, reproduced in Ernest Jones's biography of the founder of psychoanalysis. Beyond the immediate motive, however, Mahler's recourse to Freud becomes fully intelligible only if one takes into account all the circumstances that conditioned his behaviour at that time.

All the greetings and good wishes he had received on 7 July 1910 were not purely a source of pleasure to him. He was fifty. Everything points to the fact that he regarded his birthday as a signal – a warning to put his affairs in order, use his American earnings to lead a quieter life in Europe, and sort out his relationships with the people around him. His fiftieth birthday was a moment to take stock. Replying to a greetings telegram from a friend, Mahler wrote: 'At first it is always a tough job to face oneself. Experience is no help at all, alas each time it feels as though you had to be introduced to yourself. But perhaps this only applies to people leading my hectic kind of life, burning the candle at bóth ends.'

Even amid the turmoil of New York that had preceded this more contemplative mood, Mahler had been toying with plans for a quieter future. At times he thought of settling in Paris; at other times he and his wife dreamt of the glories of Capri, Florence or the Black Forest. Yet all the time he hoped that 'in the not too distant future' he would find 'a place somewhere near Vienna, where the sun shines and the grape grows, and never leave it again'.

During the preparations for the first performance of his Eighth Symphony which Mahler was to conduct at Munich in September, he formed a plan to acquire a property in Breitenstein near Sem-

mering. A Viennese lawyer, Dr Emil Freund, his loyal friend since
their youth, was entrusted with the negotiations. At this time more
than ever before Mahler felt the need to share his material success
with others. Arnold Schönberg wrote to him on 2 August 1910
asking for three or four hundred florins ('I am completely penniless
at the moment, and have to pay the rent'): by the next day he had
received the money. Mahler also tried hard to revive his old, though
somewhat intermittent, friendship with Siegfried Lipiner, an awkward follower of Nietzsche who worked in the library of the Vienna
Reichsrat. Mahler's revised contract with his Viennese publishers,
Universal Edition, was being finalised. He hoped at last to clear up
all outstanding tax matters. His pension as former director of the
Vienna Opera had been settled, and his American earnings since
1907 made it possible for him to envisage a tranquil creative period
free from want. Mahler spoke of this in terms that sounded strange
coming from a fifty-year-old artist who had known success on two
continents. America, he said, had offered him not only work corresponding to all his inclinations and talents, but ample rewards which
would soon enable him to 'enjoy the evening of my life with human
dignity'.

It would be wrong to link this urge to settle everything with the
nearness of death. When he was exchanging telegrams with Freud,
Mahler could not possibly have known that he had barely forty
weeks to live. A biographer must resist the temptation to explain
actions by motives known only to hindsight. Moreover, Mahler
was tackling various projects with great vigour. There was his work
on a Tenth Symphony (which in the end he left unfinished), and
another trip to America, where he was to conduct the New York
Philharmonic in sixty-five concerts during the winter season of
1910/11.

What drove him to Freud was not a premonition of death, but
the desire to 'face himself'. This involved, as he must have realised,
a fairer relationship with his wife. He had often said throughout the
previous years that Alma had sacrificed her youth to him. Now at
last he seemed to realise what had been the most painful renunciation for her. Alma had some musical talent, but to please her

husband she had given up composing before they married. In fact, Mahler had strictly forbidden her to compose. Alma Maria Mahler's memoirs show unequivocally how deeply she felt this restriction on her personality. A psychoanalytical study might elucidate how for Mahler erotic experiences were linked with the concept of 'giving birth to music'. A sudden shock may, however, suddenly reveal to the layman what normally only the analysts can see. The shock in this instance came from a letter written that summer of 1910 by a young man who evidently adored Alma from a distance. Protesting that he could not live without her, he besought her to leave Mahler and come to him. The letter reached Toblach in an envelope addressed to 'Herr Direktor Mahler'.

Even without the testimony of his wife, one can readily imagine the effect on Mahler. The crucial part of her account is that she now accused him of having neglected her for years because of 'his monstrous sense of mission'. The frank discussion which ensued disturbed Mahler deeply. In the end he took the decision to consult Freud. A letter of introduction from a Viennese doctor who was a distant relative of Alma's helped him to make the approach.

Mahler went to Leiden for the sake of his relationship with Alma. He sent her a telegram from Innsbruck: 'All good and evil powers accompany me; you sit enthroned above them. Good night, my lyre. I feel only joy and longing.' His stay in Leiden was brief: the conversation with Freud took only a few hours.

The power emanating from Sigmund Freud's words and the effect on Mahler of his own, telegraphically compressed, attempt at complete self-revelation, are reflected in a verse he wrote in the train on the way back to Toblach. He often made use of verse in private communications, when he wanted to underline their significance. Alma Mahler has passed on the communication without, however, explaining that these four lines are a tribute to Freud:

> *Nachtschatten sind verweht an einem mächt'gen Wort,*
> *Verstummt der Qualen nie ermattet Wühlen.*
> *Zusammen floss zu einem einzigen Akkord*
> *Mein zagend Denken und mein brausend Fühlen.*

[Night shades were dispelled by one powerful word,
The tireless throb of torment ended.
At last united in one single chord
My timid thoughts and my tempestuous feelings blended.]

Whatever the more intimate consequences of Freud's 'powerful word', it had a significant effect on Mahler's musical appreciation. He turned his attention to his wife's compositions; singing them to his own piano accompaniment, he exclaimed: 'What have I done? These songs are good. They're excellent! You must work them over and we shall publish them. I shan't rest until you start working again. God, I was narrowminded in those days!'

Oskar Fried the conductor, who was visiting him in Toblach at the time, heard Alma's songs and pronounced them 'gifted' and 'very nice'. Mahler protested against this patronising assessment and defended Alma's creations. This is not the place to decide whether his verdict on the songs – which subsequently were published – was justified. What concerns us is the change in Mahler, the new attitude that emerged from the shock he had had and the brief analysis in Leiden. He had faced himself. In a conversation with Oskar Fried the subject of auricular confession came up. Mahler, born a Jew and turned Catholic only shortly before taking up his post at the Vienna Hofoper, defended it. He had just experienced the comfort of confession, albeit not in a purely confessional sense.

From Freud's notes it appears that he considered mother fixation the crucial factor in Mahler's emotional life. His mother, who suffered from a congenital defect – she was lame – determined his feminine ideal. He tried to find the careworn features of his mother, who had borne twelve children, in the face of his chosen mate. His mother's name was Marie. When he met Alma Maria he wanted to call her Marie, and he wished her face were 'more marked by suffering'.

Any brief analysis, even if undertaken by the most competent psychologist, gives rise to doubts. Freud himself must have felt somewhat sceptical, though he was particularly well equipped for his conversation with Mahler at that time, having recently devoted an essay to the significance of childhood experiences for the psychology of artistic creativity. ('Leonardo da Vinci and a Memory of his Childhood'.) It comes as no surprise that Freud directed his conversation with Mahler towards gaining further insight into the psychology of creative work.

Anyone who has listened to Mahler's music will know how frequently the expression of tragic feeling is interrupted by frivolous turns or simple melodic themes that appear banal. Mahler offered Freud a psychological explanation for this. He spoke of his father's callous attitude to his mother and of the ugly scenes he had witnessed. During one of their painful quarrels he had rushed out of the house. And outside he ran into an organ-grinder churning out the trivial tune *O du lieber Augustin, alles ist hin.* . . . The brutal dissonance of tragic events with the frivolous and commonplace haunted him all his life, dominating him even at moments of maximum inspiration. Because of this he felt that he would never achieve his ideal, never compose music of the highest order.

Mahler's attempt at self-interpretation clearly shows how self-criticism in personal matters extended to his work. Freud could hardly deal with the aesthetic problem that worried Mahler. From Ernest Jones and Alma Mahler we get the impression that, lacking opportunity for a thorough diagnosis, Freud contented himself with a few suggestions to give relief. That he succeeded even in this telescoped analysis in getting Mahler to recall a crucial childhood experience demonstrates not only the skill of the analyst but the cooperativeness of the subject. In a letter to a pupil written almost twenty-five years later, Freud praised Mahler's 'brilliant insight':

I analysed Mahler for an afternoon in Leiden. If I may believe reports, I achieved much with him at that time. . . . In highly interesting expeditions through his life history, we discovered his personal conditions for love, especially his Holy Mary complex (mother fixation). I had plenty of opportunity to admire the capability for psychological understanding of this man of genius. No light fell at the time on the symptomatic façade of his obsessional neurosis. It was as if you would dig a single shaft through a mysterious building.*

Through this shaft light falls on Mahler's childhood.

*Translated by Theodor Reik, in *The Haunting Melody* (New York, 1953), p. 343.

[2]
Childhood

Nearly 60,000 copies of the official *Wiener Zeitung* were printed. The edition was quickly sold out, since everyone who could read wanted to see the *Manifesto* on the front page – the Emperor's address to the peoples of his realm:

In pursuance of My duties as a ruler I propose to conjoin and harmonise the traditions, legal principles and legal claims of My lands and peoples with the present needs of My monarchy and it is with complete confidence that I entrust the happy development and consolidation of all institutions established or reactivated by Myself to the mature understanding and political zeal of My peoples.

Francis Joseph thus broke with the principle of absolutist rule. To be sure, a fully developed democracy and universal suffrage were yet to come. We now know that the Habsburg Empire did not succeed in reconciling the struggle of its member nations for democracy with their separate national interests. And even the first measures of 1860 – summarised in the so-called *Oktoberdiplom*, which the newspaper printed below the Imperial Manifesto – were very soon retracted. Yet a beginning had been made. The Emperor was redeeming his pledge after the battle of Solferino, promising 'improvements in legislation and administration in accordance with the times'. It was a historical process that could be checked but never again wholly halted. Obviously the nations' advance towards greater freedom, the gradual abolition of political tutelage and the propagation of national and political aims in a revitalised press were not solely due to the monarch's voluntary decision. State insolvency at a time of economic prosperity had forced him to consider reforms. The Habsburg Empire, having lost Lombardy in the war of 1859, had to record a budget deficit of 280 million florins. This·

debt could not be settled without the help of the rapidly advancing middle classes. Industrialists and financiers now had to be consulted. Their influence was in proportion to their economic power, which, as the statistics published in the *Wiener Zeitung* showed, was steadily increasing. Coal production had almost quadrupled since 1847, home production of pig iron had risen by 100,000 tons, and the number of cotton and flax mills had increased enormously. The construction of a railway network had only just begun. It was, however, characteristic of the industrial development that the railway lines were more extensive in Bohemia and Moravia than in other parts of the Empire. The principal centres of these two provinces were thus more closely linked with Vienna than, for instance, the Tyrol or Salzburg, which in the 1850s had no better rail connections with the capital than far-off Bukovina, the easternmost province of the Empire. Moravia and Bohemia had moved closer to the seat of power. Road-building, too, had made better progress in Bohemia than in Lower Austria, and with its eleven telegraph stations Bohemia led in the development of the Empire's communications system.

The abolition of internal and external toll barriers and the expansion of trade also benefited those outside the élite of industrial and financial tycoons. For those who could seize the new chances, it was possible with some effort to climb a little way up the social ladder. But it needed the energy of youth. The woman who went from house to house with her basket along the roads and cart tracks of eastern Bohemia, supporting her family by vending ribbons and kerchiefs, could no longer change her way of life. Yet she must have been glad that her son Bernhard showed more initiative. The business she had done on foot he now carried on by horse and cart. Thus he was able not only to offer his own wares but to act as a carrier. There were always some goods the Czech peasants wanted to send for sale to the predominantly German-speaking towns. People knew Bernhard Mahler, and they gave him the friendly nickname of 'the coachbox scholar', because he used to read all sorts of books on his journeys through the hills. They guessed that he had ambitions, for he had even learnt a little French.

The son of Jewish parents, who as a child may have read his Hebrew letters in the prayer-book, speaking German to the towns-folk and Czech with the peasants, he must have been naturally adaptable. He did not stay on the coachbox, but later sought work in various small businesses, and was also employed as a tutor in several households. His goal was financial independence. Before he was thirty he had managed to acquire a house – a modest one, it is said to have had no window-panes – in his home town of Kalist. Here he lived, and here in 1857 he was joined by the daughter of a soap-boiler from nearby Ledeč, a girl not yet twenty at the time of her marriage to him.

'They were as ill-matched as fire and water. He was obstinacy personified, she was all meekness.' That was how Gustav Mahler, many years later, described the relationship between his parents. According to him, Marie did not love her husband, had indeed hardly known him before they were married, and 'would rather have married another man, whom she did love. But her parents and my father were able to break her will and have their way.'

What Mahler says about his father should be considered in the light of Freud's analysis. Otherwise one might misinterpret the fact that, according to his wife, 'he never uttered a word of love for his father'. If Bernard Mahler's character is seen in the wrong light, many of his son's characteristics will be difficult to understand. The carter and subsequent publican's dream of respectability had decidedly beneficial consequences for his son. In later life Gustav Mahler was not pleased to have his humble origins mentioned in print or in any way stressed. When in 1904 Richard Specht drafted a biography of Mahler, then director of the Court Opera, and sub-mitted it for approval, Mahler thought that to describe his father as a 'licensed victualler' was 'somewhat trivial': surely 'business-man' would be perfectly adequate.

In his endeavour to obscure his origins Gustav proved the true son of his father. Bernhard for his part had obliterated, or at least tried to obliterate, his connection with the Jewish tradition – a trail which numerous authors writing about Mahler were eager to

pursue. The indications are that when it came to religion Bernhard
Mahler was a free-thinker and avoided anything at all reminiscent
of Jewish exclusiveness. There is no evidence that religious customs
were strictly observed in the Mahler home, and there was no
question of their shunning the non-Jewish community. There are
hints that even in his childhood Gustav – possibly an occasional
member of the church choir – was more familiar with the Roman
Catholic service than with the ritual of the synagogue, which in
later years he probably never entered.

What the coachbox scholar did hand on to his son was German
culture. The reading-matter which Gustav found in his father's
house scarcely differed from that available to other young people
living in the German-speaking enclave around Iglau. Bernhard
Mahler was drawn towards German culture. At that time the wave
of German liberalism announced by the *Oktoberdiplom* gathered up
many members of the Jewish lower middle classes in Bohemia and
Moravia. The family of Sigmund Freud, who was born at Freiberg
in Moravia, is one example; another is provided by the family of
the musicologist Guido Adler, who was born at Eibenschitz in
Moravia, went to the German primary school at Iglau and later
became a close friend of Mahler's.

The assimilation of the Jewish intelligentsia into German culture
did not, however, lessen the antisemitic backlash. On the contrary:
beside the antisemitism, soon to be put on a 'racial' basis, of the
German-speaking parties and organisations, there was also a Slav
antisemitism based on 'national' arguments. As late as the turn of
the century, a representative of the Young Czechs in the Vienna
Parliament maintained that antisemitic excesses in Moravia were
entirely due to the Jews' identifying with German culture. If the
Jews would change their attitude, the Czechs would leave them in
peace.

As a justification of antisemitic mob rule the argument was unacceptable. Nevertheless it is true that the brightest Jewish minds
in the Slav dominions of the Habsburg Empire all inclined towards
German culture. It is difficult to describe the complex and confusing
interrelations of the various nations of old Austria. We even lack

proper terms of reference. Austria today is a nation state, but in the last century most people considered it a concept of constitutional law uniting various nations under one ruler. Austrians who wanted to stress their national identity – as against Slavs, Magyars and Italians – called themselves 'Germans', irrespective of whether they were loyal to the Austrian state or hoping for a national union within the framework of a greater Germany. Jewish nationalist tendencies manifested themselves only in areas of homogeneous Jewish settlement in the east of the Empire. The further west one went, the more being Jewish became simply a matter of religious denomination. Where even this practical definition lost its meaning, as in the case of Bernhard Mahler, complete affiliation to German culture seemed inevitable. It was not as smooth a transition as the advocates of assimilation had hoped. Since the struggle for admission to the German cultural sphere was soon exacerbated by the violent clash of national interests within the empire and by renewed racialist antisemitism, one can readily understand Gustav Mahler's later subjective comment on this confusion. He was, he said, a threefold exile: a Bohemian among Austrians, an Austrian among Germans, and a Jew among all the nations on earth.

Bernhard Mahler had no inkling of all this in 1860, a year which seemed to promise well. To him social advance meant sharing the culture of the ruling people of the multinational state. Up to this year of the reforming Imperial October Manifesto, social and geographical mobility had been limited. Henceforth citizens of Jewish faith could, like everyone else, enjoy freedom of movement throughout the Empire. In December 1860 Bernhard moved his family – Marie had given birth to her second child, Gustav, on 7 July 1860 – from the confines of the village of Kališt on the fringe of Bohemia to the Moravian town of Iglau, the centre of the German-speaking enclave. Here prospects were good for his small-time brandy distillery – known as 'the factory' in the family circle. Not that we can consult Bernhard's ledgers, but the statistics of the period show a steady increase in the consumption of spirits in Moravia at the expense of wine sales.

Bernhard Mahler had fulfilled a long-standing ambition, but

that was as far as he himself would get. However, as he liked to say, things should be better for his children. German-speaking Iglau offered the education he wanted for them. The town manufactured leather and textiles; it had teachers, doctors and substantial business men. There was even a theatre seating 1200, built more than ten years before the Mahlers' arrival under the patronage of well-to-do citizens. Further culture was represented by a Music Society, founded in 1819, and a Male Voice Choir on the Viennese model, obligatory for all the provinces of the Habsburg empire. After the withdrawal of the regimental band, which had played an important part in musical life, the citizens decided in 1860 to found a municipal orchestra to serve the demands of church music, concert performances and the theatre.

The two eldest Mahler children were born at Kališt; in Iglau Marie gave birth to ten more. It is worth giving their birth dates as this provides some psychologically relevant information.

1. Isidor   born 1858   died in infancy
2. Gustav   born 1860
3. Ernst   born 1861   died at the age of thirteen
4. Leopoldine   born 1863
5. Alois   born 1867
6. Justine   born 1868
7. Arnold   born 1869   died in infancy
8. Friedrich   born 1871   died in infancy
9. Alfred   born 1872   died in infancy
10. Otto   born 1873   committed suicide at the age of
                             twenty-five
11. Emma   born 1875
12. Konrad   born 1879   died in infancy

Lame from birth and with a weak heart, the mother bore the burden of an ever-increasing household. The child Gustav must have seen her as a woman 'marked by suffering' and almost continuously pregnant. Five of the twelve children died in infancy. As Isidor, born at Kališt, was one of these, the role of eldest son devolved on Gustav. The fate of these children seems peculiarly tragic to us today; one is tempted to see the parents as living in a continual state of emotional tension, and the young Gustav as severely affected. The frequently made inference, suggesting a unique psychological quality in the future composer of the *Kindertotenlieder*, is however based on a misconception. In our own age of low infant mortality it is easy to forget how calmly even Europeans accepted the death of an infant until quite recently. To have brought a child safely through the dangers and potentially mortal illnesses of childhood was something to boast of. Towards the end of the nineteenth century the mortality of children under five still amounted to an average of nearly fifty per cent. *The Austro-Hungarian Monarchy in Words and Pictures*, a survey initiated by Crown Prince Rudolf, states with regard to Bohemia: 'One half of all live births die during the first few years of life.' No comment, no expression of regret, no demand for a remedy: the state of affairs thus described was considered inevitable and unalterable.

In pointing out that the infant deaths in the Mahler home were nothing very unusual, we do not wish to rule out their profound impact on the survivors. Indeed, little Justine played at dying, as Gustav well remembered. 'As a child she would stick wax candles round the edge of her bed. Then she lay down, lit the candles, and all but persuaded herself that she was dead.'

Among all his brothers and sisters, Gustav was especially fond of Ernst, who was only a year younger than himself. Ernst was his playmate, his confidant in all those glorious childhood secrets of which the adult merely retains a dim blurred memory. This brother became seriously ill and died after prolonged suffering in the spring of 1874. For days Gustav stayed by the sickbed telling his brother stories. How deeply the fourteen-year-old felt the loss of this much loved brother is shown by his attempt, a few years later, to exorcise the experience by writing an opera called *Herzog Ernst von Schwaben*, which has unfortunately not been preserved. A letter Mahler wrote in June 1879 to his friend Josef Steiner reveals how the figure of his brother merged poetically with the hero of the opera:

Pale figures in my life pass before me like shadows of a long lost happiness and a song of longing sounds in my ears. And once more we walk through a familiar landscape, and there stands the organ-grinder, holding out his hat with a withered hand. And among the discordant strains I hear the voice of Ernst von Schwaben, and he himself steps forth, opening his arms to me, and when I look closely it is my poor brother.

The letters to Josef Steiner, who wrote the libretto for the opera, are among the earliest documents giving an insight into Mahler's psyche. They are remarkable for their rapt tone and for the uninhibited free association characteristic of dreams. There is other evidence that as a child Gustav withdrew into a dream world. Behaviour that adults interpreted as the placidity and passive acceptance of a 'good' child may in effect have been the only form of opposition open to the boy. For instance, when his father told him to keep his desk drawer tidy, polite reminders and scolding proved equally ineffective, because the boy continually 'forgot' – this does seem to suggest the passive resistance of a child refusing to accept the world around him.

Dreams and play are the escape routes open to every child. It is a rare and lucky child, though, whose escape into fantasy earns adult approval. Gustav had this experience at a very early age. He was about four years old when the family paid one of their regular visits to his mother's parents. His grandfather the Ledeč soap-boiler cared for the bourgeois values. The manners of his household seemed 'upper-class' to Bernhard Mahler, who jokingly referred to his father-in-law's family as 'the dukes'. And this more prosperous household owned things which the son of the old pedlar woman would not have considered necessities – like a piano. Gustav discovered it in the attic while the grown-ups were busy with their own affairs. When they called him there was no reply. After a long search they found the little boy strumming on the old instrument. If he had run out into the street to watch other children bowling hoops or flying kites there would have been trouble. As it was, they praised him. And his father – quick as adults are to draw over-

simplified conclusions from fleeting childish whims – decided that
Gustav must become a musician.

The sources of musical talent are a mystery which need not concern us here, but encouragement may well act as a stimulus. It
must have gratified the child that his game with the piano keys was
approved. How could a talented child resist the temptation to
retreat into a world of his own, immune from outside rules, when
such wilful escapism was not merely condoned but positively
fostered?

At school, if reports at second and third hand are to be trusted,
he tended to be 'absent-minded' and 'unreliable'. But he loved
making music. He listened to the songs of the Czech housemaids, to
the dance tunes of Iglau's young people, to the trumpet calls and
drum rolls from the nearby barracks, and he was able to reproduce
them all on his instrument. To begin with he had only an accordion,
but then his father decided to buy a piano. It was, after all, a middle-
class status symbol. The business man who could afford to advertise
in the *Iglauer Sonntagsblatt* had a reputation to keep up. 'The
children shall have a better time of it.' He wanted Gustav to be a
musician, and to be admired for it. Part of this admiration would
surely reflect on the father who had bought the piano. Sladky, who
played the double-bass in the local band, was employed to give
Gustav lessons. Never mind the expense, it was an investment. The
world – Prague, perhaps even Vienna – had been opened up by the
Emperor's declaration, even for the children of a carter from
Kališt. Sladky was succeeded by other teachers; Gustav's father did
all that was in his power. The piano served the dreams of both
father and son.

'From my fourth year on I have always made music, I was composing before I could play scales.' Thus Mahler, at the age of thirty-
six, looked back on his early musical development. There is no
reason to doubt him. Obviously it was not only his father who
considered the boy exceptionally talented, since even the conductor
of the Iglau theatre orchestra was prepared to teach Gustav. While
still at primary school he went on to a piano teacher called Brosch
who soon made a virtuoso of him. In October 1870 the prodigy was

introduced to the Iglau public in a concert held at the theatre; unfortunately we do not know the programme. A short review in the local paper of 16 October shows a definite attempt to make the boy's undeniable talent seem even more remarkable. Gustav was ten, but the paper talks of a 'nine-year-old boy . . . the son of a local business man of the Jewish faith'. The success which 'the future piano virtuoso achieved with his public was great and most creditable to him, though one could have wished that his fine playing had been displayed on an instrument of comparable quality'.

Gustav's musical gifts must have been recognised for some time, since even before his first concert he appears to have given lessons to other children. His career at primary and secondary schools, on the other hand, proceeded less smoothly. Bernhard Mahler seems to have had two reasons for his decision to send the eleven-year-old to Prague: he wanted his son to have better, and perhaps stricter, schooling, and he wanted to place him in an environment that would encourage the development of his musical talent. He therefore boarded Gustav with a Prague family which would also be responsible for his piano lessons. There were two sons in the family, both of whom had great careers: Alfred Grunfeld became a famous pianist, and his younger brother Heinrich became well known as a concert cellist, performer of chamber music and teacher. When Gustav Mahler came to Prague, Alfred was nineteen. It was to be expected that the brilliant student of the Prague Conservatoire would pass on some of his knowledge to the schoolboy from Iglau.

Things did not work out as Bernhard Mahler had hoped. Gustav was left to his own devices, and did badly at school. Bed and board, too, must have been well below the standard expected. Gustav bore it all without complaining, but when his father found out he took the boy back to Iglau. His school report placed him at the bottom of the class.

It does not seem to have worried the absentminded Gustav that he often had to go to bed hungry, or that his clothes and shoes were taken away from him. He accepted it all with the passivity he had already shown at home. 'I thought that was how things had to be,' he commented, speaking of it later in life. He showed more agitation when describing the shock of witnessing 'a brutal sexual encounter between the chambermaid and the son of the house'. Only a psychologist could assess its significance for a boy of eleven. It may well have been a traumatic experience seeing that the adult Mahler felt he had to discuss it with his wife. Some of his difficulties in uniting the sexual and the emotional aspects of love may be traced back to this incident, as may the strengthening of his ties with his mother, and his ideals of purity and renunciation, though these were held in common with other artists of his time. One must admit that hypotheses of this nature are open to suspicion. But in Mahler's case they are supported by other stories about him which are intelligible only in this context, showing how in the young man's mind sensual passion was closely linked with mental and spiritual suffering. A friend of his youth tells of a girl whom the eighteen-year-old Mahler met on holiday. She was 'fascinated by his personality. He rather liked her, and was touched by her innocent responsiveness. But even at eighteen his moral principles would not let him embark on a casual love affair. He behaved warmly and affectionately towards her, advising her as a friend to beware of passion, or she might involve herself in great unhappiness. They parted the best of friends.'

Two years later Mahler heard that the girl had committed suicide. He must have taken this news as confirming his prognosis, and his belief in the fateful link between passion and pain. The sources of this attitude may be found in the experiences of his childhood, of which the Prague episode is only a part.

'Spent my youth at college – learnt nothing.' This brief dismissal of his schooldays, which continued at Iglau after the Prague interlude, sounds exaggerated in view of Mahler's very extensive literary knowledge. But here Bernhard Mahler's collection of books – 'almost a small library' – may have played a more important role than lessons at school. As a student he showed an aversion from any set task; his resistance was due not to any lack of power of comprehension, but to the typical psychology of the daydreamer, a child rejecting the world of reality for the more alluring world of sound. Here he could be his own master, and his skill at the piano brought him more praise than a good school report could ever do. Why should he not enjoy his piano-playing, since all around appreciated it so greatly. The repertoire seemed inexhaustible. There was a music lending library in Iglau from which he could get all the pieces he wanted to study or which others wanted to hear. The operatic repertoire of the theatre, too, was of great interest to a budding musician: *The Marriage of Figaro*, *Don Giovanni*, *Fidelio*, *Il Trovatore*. We cannot simply assume, on the other hand, that he heard all these works performed at that time. It appears that he did not get to know many important operas until he became a conductor.

His approach to theatre music was not primarily determined by the stage performance. For him the music was the important thing, and the action had to fit in with it. We shall see later how his creative activity was conditioned by the Austrian, or rather Viennese, love for 'pure music', how unavailing were his occasional flirtations with operatic projects, and how faithful he remained to the Austrian ideals of the symphony and the sonata. He very soon destroyed *Herzog Ernst von Schwaben*, one of his first attempts at composition, and nothing survives of the early fairy-tale opera *Rübezahl* or of the sketches for *Die Argonauten*.

The musical proficiency of the Iglau prodigy, his piano playing, his gift of improvisation and his attempts at composition became known beyond Iglau soon after his concert debut. Even 'the dukes', the relatives in Ledeč, spoke with pride of the young pianist, and he had to give demonstrations of his skill when he visited them. Acquaintances in the town and the surrounding countryside invited him in order to enjoy hearing him play. Among Gustav's friends at that time was Josef Steiner, who was probably older than himself. In the existing literature on Mahler's youth nothing much can be found about Joseph Steiner, with whom Mahler was to correspond for some time. But from the letter quoted above we know that Mahler shared with him memories of places around Časlau – memories of the dairy farms of Morovan and Ronov, and of a girl's blue eyes, mentioned with feeling.

At Morovan Gustav Mahler met a man who was to have a decisive influence on his future career: Gustav Schwarz, economist and estate manager. Thirty years later Schwarz told the story of these events in the editorial office of the *Neues Wiener Journal* – producing some letters from the young Mahler. Strangely these documents, so important in the history of Mahler's development, have so far eluded research.

The estate manager of Morovan casts new light on Mahler's progress to the Conservatoire in Vienna. Schwarz, himself a music lover, one day discovered among some old manuscripts a few pieces by the famous piano virtuoso Sigismund Thalberg, who had died some years previously. Thalberg's composition presented such technical difficulties that no pianist of merely average ability could cope with them. When Schwarz mentioned his find to a certain Herr Steiner (possibly a relative, or even the father, of Mahler's librettist), the latter said: 'I know a young chap who could sight-read that.' The young chap, 'a thin, awkward boy' as the estate manager described him, was fetched from Iglau to the dairy farm, and lived up to their hopes. 'You must become a professional musician,' they told him. Gustav Mahler confessed that this had long been his secret desire.

Mahler stayed in Schwarz's house as a guest, and the estate manager evolved a plan for getting him to Vienna. He wrote to Gustav's father first, and the two men discussed the matter. The father consented in principle, but seems to have asked for time to think it over, according to the letter Gustav wrote to his patron from Iglau on 28 August 1875:

My dear father is probably afraid that I might neglect or break off my studies, or be corrupted by bad company in Vienna. I think on the whole he is on our side, but please remember that I am struggling on my own against the superior forces of all these 'sensible and steady' people. Therefore I beg you to honour us with your visit this Saturday, 4 September, for it is only you who can win my father over completely.

The letter is revealing not only in its content. Its style, in marked contrast to the effusions of other letters of the period, is sober and judicious, and shows a thoroughly realistic assessment of Mahler's chances. The scruples of the father, who in essence agreed with his son, are not lightly dismissed. For the first time we see the fifteen-year-old as a determined tactician when things are at stake that really matter to him: there is no daydreaming now. All Mahler's subsequent actions in professional matters are characterised by this same purposefulness: he tries to assess his chances dispassionately and to find allies.

The duality of Mahler's character – visionary introspection on the one hand, and cool, purposeful planning on the other – is noticeable at virtually every stage of his artistic and administrative activities. In the battle for supreme command he proves a consummate tactician, yet a moment later he turns into the rapt creator of hitherto undreamt-of sounds. For every situation life throws up he finds the right words, the right stance. To his amazed contemporaries he appears in ever-changing guises. 'I do not believe', thus Richard Specht begins his book published two years after Mahler's death, 'that anyone ever truly knew Mahler.' He was unpredictable. He never fully gave his allegiance to anyone. He never fully exposed himself to anyone. Creative activity was all he really cared about.

The hero-worshippers, though they will never forgive me for saying so, have not understood Mahler. To them he seems like someone coming 'from far away' or 'out of dark depths' – but this was only one of the many facets of his complex nature. The Mahler cult either ignored or tried to suppress any evidence of his worldly wisdom and tactical skill. Certainly he is said on occasion to have run his head against a brick wall. More often, as we shall see, he would avoid the frontal attack and astutely outflank the enemy positions to take the fortress from the rear; patiently biding his time for the major offensive; casting around for allies to help his cause.

The ally in this case being Herr Schwarz of Morovan, it was easy enough for Gustav Mahler to persuade his father one must in common courtesy invite the well-meaning man. Once Herr Schwarz had joined the fray it was no longer necessary to fear the superior forces of all those 'sensible and steady people', for the hitherto vacillating father would finally rally to his son's cause.

Two weeks later Schwarz took his protégé to Professor Epstein in Vienna. On 20 September 1875 a new student enrolled at the Conservatoire of the Gesellschaft der Musikfreunde: 'Mahler, Gustav, from Iglau.'

[3]

The Student in Vienna

It is not easy to reconstruct the impression Vienna made on the young music student. Was he wholly lost in his dream of music, heedless of the surrounding burgeoning vitality of the imperial city? At this time the rising power of the bourgeoisie manifested itself in a spate of new architecture: the Rotunde erected for the World Fair of 1873, the buildings of the Ringstrasse, the railway stations, the high-jet fountain on the Schwarzenbergplatz that commemorated the completion of the aqueducts providing Vienna with water from Alpine sources. He must have seen the parliament house being built; there was the splendour of the newly inaugurated monumental Court Opera House to appreciate. Can the brightly lit rooms of the Conservatoire in the new building of the Gesellschaft der Musikfreunde have impressed him as they did the professors who could still remember the small dark rooms of the old building they had left in 1870?

Two years after his arrival in Vienna, Gustav Mahler sent a letter of thanks to the man who had introduced him to 'the town of promise'. 'It was you', he wrote to Schwarz, 'who opened the gates of the Muses' temple for me and led me into the Promised Land.' Thanks to his patron he had also acquired a powerful friend in Julius Epstein, Mahler's piano teacher for three years, who supported his application for the remission of tuition fees: this was refused at first but subsequently granted, though only for half the fees. Mahler could expect only limited financial assistance from Iglau. It seemed sensible to supplement his slender means by giving private lessons. Epstein evidently considered his pupil adequately qualified to recommend as a piano teacher. He even entrusted Mahler with his own son Richard who later became a capable concert pianist. Possibly this was a tactful way for Epstein to get his gifted pupil a little more money.

In his first year Mahler was taught harmony by Robert Fuchs, a composer known chiefly for his agreeable string serenades which earned him the nickname of 'serenade-fox'. He studied composition and counterpoint under Franz Krenn, a very strict master. It cannot have been easy for talented and impulsive students to submit to Krenn's arid discipline. Mahler's fellow-student Hugo Wolf could not bear it: one day he told the Principal that he wanted to leave the Conservatoire, where he had forgotten more than he had learnt. The ensuing disciplinary action led to Wolf's expulsion. Mahler remained on friendly terms with Wolf – they were almost exactly the same age – and at times shared his modest lodgings with him. Mahler had great sympathy for the hardships of one who lacked a 'powerful friend', and he could also understand Wolf's violent reaction to the inflexible strictness of their teachers, for he himself had once been carried away at the Conservatoire to make certain remarks which he had to retract in a humble letter to the principal, Josef Hellmesberger, on pain of expulsion. Mahler's letter of apology which has been preserved, testifies not only to his occasional rebelliousness but also to his ability to retreat in time. The powers of endurance and perseverance which the boy had developed at home proved useful here too.

Natalie Bauer-Lechner, who took part in orchestral rehearsals during Mahler's student years and who later became a good friend of his, reports a typical incident. There was a composers' competition at the end of every school year, and for one of these events Mahler composed a symphony which was to be rehearsed by the orchestra class under the direction of the principal. As Mahler could not afford to have the parts copied out from the score he had to do this work himself, and during the days and nights of toil mistakes crept in. At the rehearsal these wrong notes emerged as dissonances, which so enraged the principal that he hurled the score at the student's feet. He would have nothing more to do with Mahler's symphony, not even after Mahler had corrected the mistakes in the parts. Natalie Bauer-Lechner, writing many years afterwards, comments: 'I can still see the scene of that boy having to put up with such humiliating treatment.'

Mahler coped as ably with the legitimate demands of his teachers as with their vagaries. Unlike the excitable Wolf, he was determined to complete his studies as smoothly and speedily as possible. He did extremely well in the piano competitions held at the close of each academic year. As early as June 1876 he won the first prize with his performance of a Schubert sonata. His return to Iglau that summer was a small triumphal progress. He brought home not only good reports, but the score of a piano quartet which had earned him first prize in the composers' competition. His parents basked in the tributes paid to their son by the music-lovers of Iglau. In September the prize pupil of the Vienna Conservatoire conducted his own works at a concert in the Iglau Municipal Theatre, where six years before he had been acclaimed as a child prodigy.

Despite this progress in music, his father insisted on his completing his general education. Gustav worked for the final examinations which, as an external student of the Iglau Gymnasium, he passed, not without difficulty, in the summer of 1878. From a letter written during the holidays to his teacher Epstein in Vienna it seems likely that Gustav in the late summer had to retake a paper he had failed at the first attempt.

He concluded his studies at the Vienna Conservatoire rather more brilliantly. He won the composers' contest of 1878 with a piano quintet which was performed at the final concert, Mahler himself taking the piano part. One of the four fellow-students joining him in this performance was the cellist Eduard Rosé, elder brother of Arnold Rosé who became famous as leader of the Vienna Philharmonic Orchestra.

His ties with the Rosé brothers grew even closer afterwards, for his sister Justine married Arnold Rosé and his sister Emma married Eduard the cellist. In addition to the friends of his Moravian days – such as Josef Steiner, or the law student Emil Freund whom Mahler used to visit during the holidays at Seelau – his closest friends were musicians he had come to know in Vienna: Anton Krisper from Laibach, Rudolf Krzyzanowski, organist, pupil of Anton Bruckner and future Court conductor at Weimar, and the explosive Hugo Wolf.

These young men were united by their common ideals and even more by their common worries. They hunted for pupils to make a bit of money, and they were constantly searching for suitable accommodation with landladies who did not charge too much and were tolerant about their loud music, while keeping reasonably quiet themselves. Clearly it was not easy to satisfy all these conditions at once, and it is not surprising that Mahler changed his lodgings in Vienna quite as often as Franz Schubert, whom people had dubbed 'the town vagabond'. We can trace only a few of Mahler's Viennese digs during 1879 and 1880, but his violent objection to noise of any sort is well documented. He complains of 'a maiden leaning on her spinet all day long': on another occasion a baby's crying disturbed him when he was trying to compose. Some 'gay character' was always driving him from one room to the next. Sometimes, however, he was driven away not by other people's noise but by landlords protesting against the full-blooded musical offerings of Mahler and his friends. When Krzyzanowski, Wolf and Mahler got hold of a Wagner vocal score and roared out the parts of Gunther, Brünnhilde and Hagen at the tops of their voices, a furious landlady was only too likely to throw the whole Götterdämmerung crew out, bag and baggage, without benefit of notice.

Everything goes to confirm the student's singleminded devotion to music. Registration at the University after leaving the Conservatoire did nothing to change that. Not that he intended to give all his time to authorised studies. As he later sardonically recalled, he 'studiously frequented the Wienerwald instead of his lectures'. Perhaps we should not take this too literally. Country walks were a necessity to him from his earliest youth, and he was certainly familiar with the Beethoven walks around Heiligenstadt, and with the hills of the southern Wienerwald. But he must also have received intellectual stimulation from philosophy and history lectures, in view of his later familiarity with philosophical texts and problems.

But how did Mahler actually prepare himself, between the ages of fifteen and twenty, for what was to be his profession? How did the composer prodigy turn into a conductor?

The Conservatoire provided training in piano-playing and composing, but specific conducting classes did not yet exist. A 'school for conductors' was only introduced in 1909, when the private Conservatoire became the Vienna State Academy. In Mahler's day an all-round musical training was considered the prerequisite for a conductor: pianistic skill, playing from a score, the ability to compose and improvise. The basis was a thorough grounding in the craft of music, comprising harmony and counterpoint. Beating time – which the general public nowadays tends to consider the be-all and end-all of a conductor's contribution – was of minor importance. What one learnt at the Conservatoire could be summed up as 'a working knowledge of music'. The orchestral rehearsals under Hellmesberger were a part of this; there being no call for his own instrument, Mahler the piano student found himself handling the percussion.

Specialisation in musical training, which is customary today, had barely begun. A conductor who could only conduct, without being able to compose, was unthinkable. At all Austrian and German theatres the conductor's contract contained a clause calling for the occasional original composition: interval music for straight plays, insertions for standard repertory operas, ballet music, accompaniment for *tableaux vivants*, and so on. The Conservatoire qualified musicians to meet these demands, producing people with an all-round working knowledge of music who could also 'beat time'. Thus Felix Mottl who rose to eminence as a conductor at Bayreuth and became director of the Munich Opera had undergone this course of training in Vienna, and by composing opera and chamber music, orchestrating Wagner's *Wesendonck-lieder* and arranging ballet suites, Mottl – a mere four years older than Mahler – gave proof of a musicianship by no means restricted to conducting. Arthur Nikisch, Mahler's senior by five years, may have had early dreams of his future career as a conductor, but Hellmesberger trained him as a violinist, and he played the violin in the orchestra of the Vienna Court Opera before starting his career as conductor in Leipzig. Again, Hans Richter, a young Hungarian, became an efficient horn-player, then from 1875 onwards held the position of Chief Conductor at the Vienna Opera.

Mahler in his turn received this practical training at the Conservatoire. A musical encyclopaedia of the time states that Mahler developed into a masterly conductor 'without ever having had a teacher'. The statement needs modification in two respects. On the one hand there were no professors to teach conducting, consequently Mahler could not become the pupil of a specific teacher; on the other hand, general instruction included everything of importance to a future conductor. If Mahler was a self-taught conductor, so were men like Richter, Nikisch and Mottl. Accuracy to fact does not lessen Mahler's genius.

In a wider historical sense, however, it is true that virtually all the great conductors of that epoch were self-taught. The new concert halls and huge opera houses called for a kind of musical commander-in-chief – someone, as Furtwängler neatly put it, to control the gathering and blending of sound in space. It was the architecture of the modern concert hall – such as the Grosse Musikvereinssaal in Vienna (1870), the Neue Gewandhaus in Leipzig (1884) and the Amsterdam Concertgebouw (1887) – that demanded and established the sovereign authority, indeed the cult, of the conductor. Gradually conductors came to terms with their new role. The best of them mastered it fairly quickly. Among these was Gustav Mahler.

The Conservatoire could not furnish him with rules for coping with the new tasks of a conductor. Still, the training was comprehensive and practical, and there is no evidence that Mahler failed to assimilate anything it offered. Many decades ago Robert Hirschfeld, on the grounds of extensive research, put forward the theory that Mahler had failed in one subject. Hirschfeld's testimony is rendered suspect by his notorious hostility to Mahler; yet the material he adduced in 1912, when he was historian to the Gesellschaft der Musikfreunde, is worth mentioning here as it concerns Mahler's relations with Anton Bruckner.

Bruckner taught harmony and counterpoint at the Conservatoire from 1868 on. Mahler must have had the opportunity to benefit from his teaching, but he expressly stated that he was never formally Bruckner's pupil, although he did describe himself as a successor and disciple of the great symphonic composer. After Mahler's death Hirschfeld, in his semi-official history *Geschichte der Musikfreunde in Wien*, attempted to show the relations of Mahler and Bruckner in a different light.

It may seem strange [he writes] that Mahler's name appears in 1876/7 among the students of the principal counterpoint class, but cannot be found in the final report. The explanation, apparent from the files . . . is that Mahler only obtained a 'Third' in counterpoint. We must conclude that, contrary to current opinion, he was indeed a pupil of Bruckner – the only professor besides Krenn who taught counterpoint – but evidently did not complete the course owing to unsatisfactory progress.

Hirschfeld's intention is clear: he establishes Mahler as Bruckner's pupil in order to deduce that Bruckner gave him a bad mark. The matter would be quite irrelevant, except that the admirable relationship between Bruckner and Mahler, both on the artistic and on the human level, is a matter of musical history. Even as a student, Mahler was one of Bruckner's most faithful followers. Together with his friend Krzyzanowski he witnessed the fiasco of the first performance of Bruckner's Third Symphony in December 1877. The work was received with laughter and demonstrations of disapproval. Many left the hall before the end of the performance. Only a few enthusiasts tried to applaud and to comfort the composer, among them the publisher Theodor Rättig, who even proposed to Bruckner that the work should be included in his publishing list. This was done, and a piano transcription made at the same time by Krzyzanowski and Mahler, with Bruckner's approval, and under the supervision of Mahler's teacher Epstein.

Mahler continued to take an active interest in the fortunes of this symphony, which Bruckner dedicated to his idol Richard Wagner – a fact that remained unknown until Theodor Rättig published his reminiscences in 1936. Rättig relates that some young friends of Bruckner's, among them the brothers Josef and Franz Schalk, advised further revision. Rättig received parts of a revised score which he began to set up in print. Then, Rättig goes on, Mahler happened to visit Bruckner and told him that 'he considered revision entirely unnecessary. Bruckner immediately changed his mind and repudiated the half-finished work.' Later, however, the others did persuade him to a partial revision.

Bruckner's sudden yielding to Mahler's opinion has a more than anecdotal significance. It points to a fundamental accord between the two men. Both claimed a right for symphonies to be diffuse, which, to be sure, worked against their success with a public that preferred romantic musical entertainment; and both were striving for a distinctive melodic and contrapuntal articulation which could not be reconciled with a treatment designed to produce mainly an agreeable blending of sounds. 'Now I don't need the Schalks any more!' Bruckner is said to have explained on hearing Mahler's views. And he showed his appreciation of the latter's understanding by presenting him with the manuscript of the symphony.

Some years later in a letter to Bruckner Mahler emphasised it was one of his aims in life to help Bruckner's music achieve the triumph it deserved. Nor did he stop at mere protestations. In 1886 he introduced the Scherzo of Bruckner's Third Symphony to a Prague audience. In Hamburg he conducted the Third, the Mass in D minor and the Te Deum, the 'powerful structure and sublime thought' of which deeply impressed the audience, Mahler told Bruckner in a letter of April 1892. In 1900 he performed the scherzo of Bruckner's Fourth Symphony at the Paris World Fair. But he made his most moving gesture towards the beloved master at the age of fifty, when his Viennese publisher was planning to take on Bruckner's works. He explained to Mahler this would be financially feasible only if Mahler allowed his almost evenly balanced account to be debited to the sum of 50,000 kronen. 'Mahler found this perfectly acceptable,' Alma Mahler recounts in her memoirs. 'Out of his love for Bruckner he agreed to the new debt without considering for a moment that he was depriving himself of any profits for the next fifteen years.'

We should have liked to quote from the actual business correspondence and ledgers of the Viennese publishing house, but these particular records have not been preserved. We must make do with the information that long after Bruckner's death his account showed various entries connecting it with Mahler's account. This generous adjustment of balance between master and disciple is unique in musical history. Even book-keepers who have not the ear to perceive the evolutions of Mahler's symphonic work from the Bruckner tradition will realise the strong links between the two composers.

Mahler's years as a student in Vienna were marked by the controversies raging around Richard Wagner. To the young disciples of Anton Bruckner who so greatly admired Wagner, the triumphal entry of Wagner's music into concert hall and opera house was an overwhelming experience. As early as 1873 a nucleus of people existed who were to form the *Akademische Wagnerverein*. The young Felix Mottl played a leading role. He received effective support from Albert Gutmann, a music dealer whose premises were a part of the opera house itself (in the frontage under the arcade, now the Operngasse). In effect, though not in name, his shop was a Wagner centre, devoted mainly to creating an interest in Wagner's work and the Bayreuth Festivals that were due to open in 1876. This able businessman and Wagnerian was responsible for the first concert in Vienna, conducted by Hans Richter, which had been arranged by the Wagner Society. As well as the first performance of Liszt's Faust Symphony, the programme included excerpts from *Tristan und Isolde* and *Die Walküre*. A breach had been made in the musical establishment. Two months later the Viennese Wagnerians succeeded in bringing the master himself to Vienna. In March and April 1875 he conducted three concerts in which parts of the recently finished *Götterdämmerung* were given their first hearing. Wagner received fantastic ovations from his ecstatic followers, to which he replied by spontaneously addressing the audience.

Franz Jauner, who had been offered the direction of the Court Opera that spring, had sufficient managerial acumen to sense that the current interest in Wagner's music could benefit the Opera. He had Hans Richter engaged as conductor, revised previous financial arrangements with Wagner to the composer's advantage, and further helped him by releasing some Hofoper singers for the Bayreuth Festspiele of 1876. By means of such material and artistic concessions he secured Wagner's consent to produce *Tannhäuser* and *Lohengrin* at the Court Opera.

Subsequent events excited the curiosity of many who would never normally attend an opera performance. Anyone who thinks that the frantic star cult is an invention of the age of mass media should read eye-witness accounts of 1875 and 1876. Wagner occupied a suite of seven rooms at the Hotel Imperial – a fact known not only to the initiated but spread by assiduous gossip to the farthest suburbs. No one could fail to notice Wagner's fur-trimmed velvet overcoat. Of course the young enthusiasts were also alive to more subtle, aesthetic phenomena. *Tannhäuser* made a huge impression on them. Hugo Wolf, who was standing in 'the gods', wrote afterwards: 'I cannot find words for it . . . I can only tell you that I've gone mad.' The fifteen-year-old concluded: 'I am completely swept away by the music of this great master, I have become a Wagnerian.'

There is no record of such an outburst on the part of Mahler. We may assume that his enthusiasm was less explosive and that he paid more attention to Wagner's work and ideas than to the Wagner cult. However, he seems to have risked losing his lodgings again, with further noisy excerpts from the *Götterdämmerung*. Apart from that, he behaved more diplomatically than his friend Wolf. At that time an immoderate admiration for Wagner was not well received by the stern masters at the Conservatoire – always, of course, excepting Bruckner. Yet Mahler, too, was on occasion inordinately influenced by Wagner's ideas. Through the Academic Wagner Society he must have obtained a copy of Wagner's essay 'Religion and Art' soon after its publication in 1880, for in November of that year he wrote to a friend:

For the last month I have been a strict vegetarian. The moral effects of this regime are immense, owing to the voluntary subjugation of the flesh and the resulting absence of desires. You will appreciate how full I am of this idea when I tell you that I expect it to work the regeneration of mankind. I advise you to change over to a natural way of life, with proper nourishment (wholemeal bread), and you will soon feel the benefit.

The ethical impact of Wagner's doctrines is easily understood.

Mahler's attitude to Wagner's music is more complex. His services to Wagner's work belong to a later period, when he had developed not only the ear of the musician but an eye for the action on the stage. In his youth Mahler was not 'a visual type', to use modern terminology. Nor did he appreciate the beauty of the plastic arts until much later. This is consistent with the psychology of someone 'sleep-walking' through his days, someone who from childhood had sought refuge from an unacceptable reality in a dream world of sound. It may also explain why the young Mahler seldom went to the opera. Guido Adler, a close friend of his for many years, explicitly stated that Mahler did not get to know many of the operas he conducted until he was actually working on them. It is quite conceivable, therefore, that Mahler was not particularly involved with the Wagner vogue at the Court Opera and that he did not struggle to attend the various first nights: *Die Walküre* (March 1877), *Das Rheingold* (January 1878), *Siegfried* (September 1878) and *Götterdämmerung* (May 1879).

Some biographers have put down his apparent lack of early enthusiasm for opera to shortage of funds, saying that he could not afford tickets. Such an explanation is incomplete. Mahler did feel strongly about Wagner's music, but he wanted to apprehend it purely as music. His own compositions provide further evidence. His early attempts at opera emerge as indefinite and indefinable syntheses between some vaguely imagined action on the stage and very precisely realised musical conceptions. The fact that as a mature musician Mahler did not try to establish himself as an operatic composer, though as a conductor with a masterly grasp of stagecraft he might well have done so, is one of those paradoxes in his psychology which a biographer must try to elucidate. There is indeed another interpretation beyond that of the dreamer shutting his eyes to reality. The musical tradition of Austria, and of Vienna in particular, is relevant here. Even Bruckner who so admired Wagner stood in this tradition of absolute music; and however much Eduard Hanslick, the Viennese champion of a pure music consisting of 'shifting sound patterns' might fulminate against him, he can in fact be fitted into Hanslick's aesthetic, and this may even be regarded as the common ground on which Bruckner and Brahms, so often regarded as complete opposites, meet. Bruckner did plan to write operas; but his failure to realise these plans is more significant than the tentative plans themselves. As far as we know, Bruckner did not pronounce on this subject, but the evolution of his Wagner symphony – the Third in D minor – provides sufficient evidence. The first version, which he submitted to the Master of Bayreuth, incorporated musical quotations from *Tristan und Isolde* and *Die Walküre*, but these were excised from the later versions. Thus, his undiminished admiration for Wagner notwithstanding, he drew the dividing line between the German concept of a composite work of art (*Gesamtkunstwerk*) and Austrian symphonic construction.

As a composer Mahler adopted the same attitude to Wagner's music. He assimilated from Wagner's scores whatever might aid his pure musical sound, unburdened by scenic considerations. Even Wagner's 'infinite melody' occurs in Mahler's symphonies, but it is subordinated to the symphonic structure: ecstasy controlled by form.

The young Wagnerians of Vienna followed the Bayreuth master in blind admiration. Mahler's admiration, too, was blind, but in another sense: he would not see the stage, the sound was enough. He studied the piano transcriptions and, enthralled by the printed notes, he achieved what Goethe had longed for, 'hearing with his eyes'. Like Bruckner, then, he became a Wagner admirer Austrian style: an admirer with reservations.

'The fiercest blaze of joyous vitality and an all-consuming longing for death: both reign alternately in my heart, often changing within the hour – one thing I know, it cannot go on like this!'

Such was the mood of Mahler at nineteen, spending the late spring and summer as a private music tutor at Tétény in Hungary. His words recall certain themes of Wagner, Tannhäuser in the Venusberg, or Isolde's identification of 'highest rapture' with bodily death. The close association between sensual passion and physical suffering in the young Mahler's mind has already been noted.

Wagner's art resolved the tension between sensuality and ethics, sexuality and asceticism, in three ways – by isolating it, by setting it aside, and by synthesis, as in 'joyful death'. Nowadays this may appear a calculated and purely aesthetic manipulation. Mahler's words prove its genuine emotional content:

If the abominable compulsions of contemporary hypocrisy and mendacity have actually driven me to self abuse, if inescapable commitment to these conditions of life and art have filled my heart with disgust for all that I hold sacred – art, love, religion – there is no way out save self-destruction.

It is hard for a reader today to accept these words at their face value. It is tempting to see them as the dramatic overstatement of a hypersensitive young man using the trendy vocabulary of his epoch and to forget that by this time his fellow student Hugo Wolf had experienced his 'Venusberg' and already harboured the venereal infection that was to lead to progressive paralysis and death. Mahler's father may have been thinking of such dangers, too, when he feared that his son might be 'corrupted by bad company in Vienna'. In order to comprehend Mahler's attitude to love – significantly named in the same breath as art and religion – one must realise the prevalent tragic connotations which eroticism held for that epoch. Only thus can we understand the constant linking of tragedy and sexuality in the nineteenth century and grasp the social reality underlying the interaction of pleasure, pain and death which is artistically sublimated in *Tannhäuser*, *Tristan* and the figure of Kundry. In *The World of Yesterday* Stefan Zweig has convincingly depicted this reality. Although Zweig is dealing with the turn of the century, his description is equally valid for the preceding decades:

[*Zweig: official translation*]
Unhampered, honest relationships – in other words, all that could have made youth happy and joyous according to the laws of Nature – were permitted only to the very few. And anyone of that generation who wishes to look back honestly upon his first meetings with women will recall but few episodes that he can think about with unmixed pleasure. For in addition to the social pressure, which constantly enforced precaution and secrecy, there

was at that time another element that overshadowed the happiest moments: the fear of infection. Here, too, the youth of that era was neglected in comparison with those of today, for it must not be forgotten that ... sexual diseases were spread a hundred times more than they are today, and that they were a hundred times more dangerous and horrible in effect, because medicine did not yet know how to approach them clinically. Science could not yet cure them quickly and completely as it does today, so that now they are no more than episodes. ... To the fear of infection was added the horror of the disgusting and degrading erstwhile cures, of which the world of today also knows nothing. For weeks on end the entire body of anyone infected with syphilis was rubbed with mercury, the effect of which was that the teeth fell out and other injuries to health ensued. The unhappy victim of a severe encounter felt himself not only physically but spiritually spotted, and even after so horrible a cure, he could never be certain that the cunning virus might not at any moment awake from its captivity and paralyse the limbs from the spine, or soften the brain. Small wonder then that at that time many young people, once the diagnosis had been made, reached for their revolvers because they could not stand the feeling that they were suspected of being incurable. Then there were the other sorrows of a *vita sexualis* carried on in secret.*

That was the oppressive shadow which in those days inevitably fell on the first stirrings of love in a young man's heart, and which every cultural history of the era must needs take into account. Why else should being young have been felt as such a burden? Why should young people have tried so hard to shed this burden by aping the semblance of maturity? Young Mahler sported a beard, which at the age of twenty-six he reduced to a moustache; eventually he dispensed with that too. In a way he grew steadily younger. At twenty he was sometimes an old man weary of life, dismayed by the fate that had overtaken others; familiar with death, which had struck down his most gifted friend, Hans Rott, a favourite pupil of Bruckner's; and oppressed by his own wholly natural emotions, which he had to regard as dangerous.

The 'subjugation of the body' which Mahler exercised for some years by his vegetarian regime was complemented by the suppression

* *The World of Yesterday: an autobiography* by Stefan Zweig, Cassell, 1943, pp. 75-6.

of his emotions. This needed true self-restraint, since he was very much alive to female charm. At nineteen he wrote: 'A new name is graven in my heart – a mere modest whisper, yet no less powerful for that.' A few months later he reveals the force that drew him, reluctantly, into violent love: 'For the first time the world has really taken hold of me, and the feeble commonplaces of hackneyed love affairs, to which I used to listen with a pitying smile, have now, like so many water sprites, drawn me into their round, and I am out of my depth.' At the age of twenty-three he was caught up in a painful relationship with a singer, and at twenty-five he wrote: 'I go from one folly to another. In this short space I have once again landed myself in a mess that will take some while to clear up.' A year later, for all his good intentions, he reports to a friend: 'I have found a beautiful girl – I must tell you frankly, the sort one can get into trouble over. You understand my friend? But this time I will be careful, I don't want to suffer like that again.'

All the documents – down to the letters written by the thirty-year-old opera conductor in Hamburg to Anna von Mildenburg – leave no doubt of Mahler's intense capacity for love. Far be it from me to try and refute the theory of Mahler's 'chastity'. It may well be correct, although no biographer can ever prove that. What can be stated with certainty is that Mahler's sexual feeling had a strong and healthy side. With increasing age he gradually extricated his emotional life from the doomed, sultry atmosphere that weighed down his generation, and became ever younger, though he could never quite free himself from his mother-fixation, subsequently transferred to his sister Justine. At twenty he still felt oppressed by a society which attempted to ward off the perils of eroticism by banishing it to the Venusberg, brothel of the pagan gods. The call of the sirens ('Blissful compassion shall still your desires')* was admitted only in secret – or, transfigured by music, on the stage of *Tannhäuser*. And even here polite society, as represented at the Wartburg, was bound to come out against the minstrel of sensual enjoyment.

* *Tannhäuser.*

* * *

It was *Tannhäuser* that unleashed the young generation's enthusiasm for Wagner. Sixteen-year-old Hugo Wolf, home for the holidays, thumped out the *Tannhäuser* Overture for his parents with such force that he broke four piano-hammers. It was not only the music, the romantic story also enthralled him. This is shown by the subject he chose for his first attempt at an opera: the fable of King Alboin, who is murdered by his wife because he had forced her to drink from the skull of her father. In conversation with Mahler, Wolf once had the idea of writing a fairy-tale opera. They discussed many subjects and eventually agreed on *Rübezahl*.* One night Mahler began to write a libretto which on the following day he showed to his astonished friend. Wolf, too, had started on one, but he was 'so enraged by this surprise attack that he immediately abandoned the whole idea'. Outwardly Wolf and Mahler remained friends for some time yet, but, says Alma Mahler, 'they no longer sought each other out'.

Mahler did not complete his *Rübezahl* project. But he stuck to the idea of setting a fairy-tale to music. He chose *Das klagende Lied*, a tale he found in Ludwig Bechstein's *Neues deutsches Märchenbuch*, modifying to some extent this story of 'the singing bone'. A wandering minstrel finds a human bone in the forest and fashions it into a flute. As he begins to blow, the bone itself sounds forth, accusing the King his brother of having murdered him in order to get his bride and his crown. When the minstrel plays at the King's wedding, the accusation rises above the sound of wedding revelry. The King and Queen are exposed, the throng of guests scatters, the candles go out, and the castle walls come crashing down.

Mahler himself wrote the text of this ballad. In the musical setting, the words are sung by three soloists (soprano, alto and tenor) and a mixed chorus. The piece is scored for a large orchestra plus an off-stage orchestra consisting of wind instruments, percussion, kettle-drums and harp. Mahler began to write the text in 1878. Composition of the music came later. It was a lengthy task, constantly interrupted by the necessity of giving lessons to make his living.

*A benign through mischievous spirit popularly supposed to haunt the Riesengebirge on the Bohemian-Silesian border.

Theodor Rättig, Bruckner's publisher, advised Mahler to get out of this difficult situation by consulting a theatrical agent to find him an engagement as a conductor. The influential agent Gustav Lewy, whose business premises on the Petersplatz included a music shop, was prepared to act for Mahler if the latter would sign a contract giving Lewy five per cent of his total earnings as a conductor over the next five years. On 12 May 1880 Mahler put his signature to this document, which bound him to the theatre.

A few weeks later he was acting conductor of the small summer theatre in Bad Hall, in Upper Austria, at a monthly salary of thirty gulden plus fifty kreuzer 'performance money'. For this he had to conduct operettas, provide the musical accompaniment to farces, put up the music-stands and try out the orchestral parts. In his spare time he took the bandmaster's infant daughter – Mizzi Zwerenz, who became a popular operetta star – out in her pram. He discharged all his duties conscientiously, except that he would not go on stage as a super – a refusal he regretted in later life when he had become really interested in all aspects of the theatre. In Bad Hall, however, he still considered theatre work unmitigated drudgery, only to be borne for the sake of the money. Yet he appreciated the steady income, and wrote to his agent from Bad Hall, offering him fifty gulden if he could find him a better post for the autumn. But his hopes were not to be realised so soon. Mahler returned to Vienna and resumed work on *Das klagende Lied*. On 1 November 1880 he was able to report: 'My fairy-tale play is finished at last – a true child of woe at which I've laboured for over a year. My next step: to bring about its performance, by any conceivable means.'

Bold words, as is shown by a glance at the score, the realisation of which demands vast resources. How could an impecunious musician, eking out his living with music lessons while waiting in vain for an engagement as a conductor, hope to get such a work performed? What gave him the courage even to voice such a wish? To be sure, there was the Beethoven Prize, recently instituted by the Gesellschaft der Musikfreunde. Mahler went in for it, thinking that the prize money of 600 gulden might relieve him of his most pressing financial worries for almost a year, and enable him to return to his *Rübezahl* project. The jury dashed his hopes. Still he would not give up his plans. He was determined to conquer this town. And after all, we know the outcome, we know that Mahler did in the end conquer Vienna. But one must put oneself in the place of all those ambitious firebrands who during the nineteenth century came up from the provinces to conquer the capital cities. Even thus did the young Romantics fight for Paris; thus did Berlioz – the completed mammoth score of his Requiem in his bottom drawer – wait for some great general to die, and give occasion for his pre-composed funeral music. Such were the manoeuvrings of Lucien de Rubempré, Balzac's imperishable symbol of a fighter in the great city. Everywhere the young provincials pressed on to the alluring strongholds of the metropolis, intending to take them by storm. There were innumerable casualties, but history remembers only those whose *idée fixe* proved victorious. Yet there was no real difference between Berlioz's unrealistic plans and the ludicrously farfetched ambitions of Richard Wagner who in 1850 – before he had written one single note of the *Ring* – first mentioned his *Festspiel* project that became a fact twenty-five years later. Wagner's success seemed to make all the wish-fulfilment novels come true: perseverance wins.

Mahler at twenty had no reason to think otherwise. He knew that he had found a form for his creative work. 'The first work in which I really found myself as a composer was a fairy-tale for chorus, solo-ists and orchestra: *Das klagende Lied*! I call that work my Opus 1.' Thus Mahler wrote many years later in a letter to Max Marschalk about the work whose performance he meant to 'bring about by any conceivable means'. The first version of *Das klagende Lied* has been wrongly described as 'an opera'. In fact it was always meant to be 'a fairy-tale for the concert hall'. Originally it consisted of three parts. Mahler eventually excised the first part. For the rest, as Donald Mitchell has shown, the new version published at a much later date retained the basic structure of the original. There is no question here of an opera. Mahler's conception, though certainly influenced by Wagner in sound, aims not at the multivalent *Gesamt-kunstwerk* but at music suited to the concert hall. An essential feature of Mahler's later orchestral technique anticipated here is the use of 'spatial sound' in the form of an off-stage orchestra, which Mahler wanted to be so placed that 'the musicians blow fortissimo, but are only heard piano'.

Mahler did not give up his plan to have the work performed; his youthful rage worked on in him long after he had written more mature scores. He waited more than twenty years to realise the dream of his penniless and powerless youth. In February 1901, as director of the Vienna Court Opera, Mahler assembled the Singakademie, the Schubertbund, the orchestra of the Opera, an additional wind orchestra and solo singers of renown in the Great Philharmonic Hall for a 'Concert of 500', as it was called on the posters. The critic Max Kalbeck summed up his impressions thus: 'What is interesting to the musician about this work is its technique. Shuddering, we duly register our respect.' The composer Richard Heuberger wrote: 'Here and there – not often – we hear some genuine, moving music. . . . It is a pity that everything else seems calculated to produce unmusical effects by unmusical means.' Another critic says of the work's powerful conclusion: 'Compared with the collapse of the castle in this ballad, the twilight of the gods is a purely local event.'

Mahler's strategy in promoting this early work (and remembering his unalterable resolution of 1880, we can see his point) was praised with unmistakable irony in the Vienna *Reichswehr*'s review:

As a composer, Herr Mahler enjoys an advantage given to few others: he has the power of entrusting his creations to the best conceivable hands: his symphonies to the best orchestra in the world, the Vienna Philharmonic; his songs to the most celebrated singers, and his intentions to one of the shrewdest conductors of all time – Gustav Mahler. These are helpful factors indeed, and under such auspices budding immortality does not do too badly.

In this way Mahler realised his dream after more than twenty years – 'by any conceivable means'. It shows the intensity of his resolution of 1880, the obsession of a genius who recognised in this first, admittedly imperfect, work the mould of his entire creative output: the birth of symphonic composition out of song, the

crystalline articulation of orchestral counterpoint, and the organisation of a hitherto unheard and unheard-of spatial sound.

In the autumn of 1880 all this was audible only to Mahler's own
inward ear. The next few months saw no improvement in his
situation. He changed lodgings continually, stayed at inns, in an un-
heated holiday cottage in Vienna (which was cheap in winter); he
struggled with *Rübezahl* ideas, looked for pupils and tried to damp
down his 'metaphysical fire'. All this time he was busily corresponding with Anton Krisper in Laibach. When hopes of the
Beethoven prize came to nothing, he was glad to find an engagement at Laibach. He seems to have owed this engagement not to the
zeal of his agent but to the influence of his Laibach friend (who
belonged to a prominent merchant family). 'Had I been granted the
Beethoven Prize of 600 gulden for *Das klagende Lied*, my whole life
would have taken a different turn.' Perhaps we should not accept
Mahler's remark – addressed to Natalie Bauer-Lechner – at face
value. Ultimately he regarded theatre and concert work as essential
'supplementary exercises' for a composer, and though the money
that went with the prize would certainly have been useful to him,
in the end his creative work undoubtedly benefited from the much
maligned experiences in the theatre. In the autumn of 1881 Mahler
finally became a theatre conductor. It did not stop him dreaming of
other things, and certainly did not stop him composing. The
chimera of his youth assumed a more practical shape, but he still
loved fairy-tales.

[4]

The Conductor

Laibach, now Ljubljana in Yugoslavia, was the capital of the
Austrian duchy of Krain. The Austrian geography textbook which
Mahler probably read at school states that the population of this
Habsburg province belonged 'mainly to the Slovenian race'.
Nevertheless, cultural life in the centre of the region was still largely
maintained by German and Italian elements. The artistic character
of the little town was based on German plays, Italian operas, and
concerts of the Philharmonic Society. At the Ständetheater (theatre
of the estates) built in 1765 and renamed Landestheater (county
theatre) in 1862, there was at the time of Mahler's arrival the core
of a small orchestra, consisting of eighteen men who might on
occasion be augmented by instrumentalists of the Philharmonic
Society. The choir had fourteen members; there were also a few
local soloists. They did not, however, carry the main burden of the
repertoire, for this, according to established usage, was undertaken
by visiting theatrical troupes and guest singers, both men and
women, on short contracts. The theatre conductor, on the other
hand, was busy all the time. At the opening performance of the
1881–82 season, a play by Bauernfeld, Beethoven's *Egmont* Overture, played as a curtain raiser, was – according to the *Laibacher
Zeitung* – given 'an accurate performance under the lead of the
conductor Gustav Mahler'.

Thus the young conductor's work extended not only to operas,
operettas, *Singspiele* and fairy-tales with songs, but also to plays.
Mahler did not take these less seriously, as can be seen from a
review praising a performance of Goethe's *Egmont* with Beethoven's
music. Throughout his life Mahler frequently complained of the
dreary routine of provincial theatres, and some biographers have
too readily assumed this included Laibach, but it should be said at

this point that the Landestheater at Laibach was rather well run. The distinguished Slovenian music historian, Dragotin Cvetko, who has studied the situation at Laibach in Mahler's time in the light of the relevant documents, concludes that the level of operatic performance during this period was well above the provincial: 'It approached, and on some occasions equalled, the standard at important musical centres.'

Among the works Mahler conducted here – many of them freshly rehearsed – were *Ernani*, *Il Trovatore*, *The Merry Wives of Windsor*, *Martha* and *The Magic Flute*. Moreover, the theatre director under whom he worked was keen on new works. Mahler found himself conducting Lecoq's operetta *Giroflé-Girofla*, and in 1882 he was rehearsing Johann Strauss's *Der lustige Krieg*, first performed in Vienna only a few months before.

Every day was brimful of musical tasks, as he was the Landestheater's sole conductor. Reactions to his work have to be culled indirectly from the rare and by no means expert reviews in the Laibach daily paper. At first we read merely that the orchestra 'did well' under his direction, but soon the appreciation increases, and at last becomes glowing approval: the orchestra positively caught fire playing Verdi; Mahler had conducted some operetta 'with great verve'; the chorus in Mozart's *Magic Flute* had revealed 'unsuspected powers'.

The young conductor also enjoyed social popularity, which brought him an invitation to take part in a concert of the Philharmonic Society. This institution had a venerable tradition. Haydn and Mozart had been proud to be made honorary members of the society, which by the beginning of the century enjoyed a great reputation even beyond the confines of the duchy, on account of its well-chosen musical programmes. Mahler did not appear as a conductor at the Philharmonic Society concert of March 1882, but as a pianist. He played three pieces from Schumann's *Waldszenen*, the Polonaise in A flat major, Op. 53 by Chopin – of which his 'bravura rendering' was commended – and Mendelssohn's *Capriccio brillante*, in which he proved himself a pianist who 'possessed a brilliant technique and knew how to apply it'.

Two weeks later Mahler had his great moment at the theatre, the benefit night which, by custom of the day, was one of the conductor's privileges, serving both to honour him and to secure him the evening's takings. For his benefit night he chose Flotow's opera *Alessandro Stradella*. When he appeared, the orchestra greeted him with a fanfare, the public acclaimed him, and the administration presented him with a large laurel wreath decorated with elaborate bows. The reporter of the *Laibacher Zeitung* was obviously expressing the general view when he wrote that such appreciation was 'well deserved by this highly trained musician who takes his difficult task most seriously and has given much hard work and care to it throughout the season'.

Mahler must have been a happy man, and to cap it all the Philharmonic Society decided two days after the benefit concert to pay him a fee of twenty gulden for his appearance as a pianist. He had no financial worries now. Socially, too, things seem to have gone well, although we have no data about his contacts with the citizens of Laibach. Anton Krisper's parents probably took him under their wing. His friendship with Krisper, who had once also wanted to be a composer, was as firm as ever. It is likely that Mahler was responsible for getting an opera of Krisper's performed at the *Deutsche Theater* in Prague a few years later, during his own time there, but the work failed to please. Krisper then gave up composing, led a restless life as a student, first of philosophy and later of mining, and eventually succumbed to an incurable mental illness. He was one of the many who fell by the wayside and whose fate grieved Mahler.

For Mahler the short Laibach season had been both a success and a real advance. He had proved himself in the theatre. Orchestra, chorus and soloists had been willing to accept the authority of the hard-working young man, who impressed them by his tireless zeal. The running of a musical theatre had lost its terrors for him. The memory of forced labour at the summer theatre in Upper Austria was effaced. He could reasonably look forward to a similar, or even better engagement; leaving Laibach at the end of the season, he could not foresee what a vile theatrical slough lay ahead of him.

In nearly every conductor's biography there is a hackneyed moment when he 'steps into the breach'. Some maestro has thrown down the baton in anger, or suddenly been taken ill, and the young hero has the chance to deputise for him. He proves equal to the task, wins all hearts, and henceforth never looks back.

Towards the end of 1882 Gustav Mahler waited in Vienna for his chance. Enquiries from Herr Lewy, the theatrical agent, produced no results. Not until 10 January 1883 was there a glimmer of hope. The director of the theatre in the Moravian town of Olmütz was sending calls for help in all directions, telegrams urgently requesting someone to replace his conductor who by some unspecified action during an evening performance had unloosed a scandal. The theatre itself was in dire straits, technically, financially and artistically. The stage fittings were in such bad repair that there were accidents, while the dismal financial situation gave rise to constant quarrels between the artistic personnel and the director. Finally at a performance of Meyerbeer's *L'Africaine* that scandal involving the conductor had occurred, which had only been stopped by the intervention of the police.

Such was the chance that offered itself to Mahler when he answered the Olmütz director's cry for help. It seemed a real chance nevertheless, for everywhere else the season had started long ago and Mahler could not expect anything but occasional short-term engagements until the summer.

The Olmütz director had been told about Mahler's purposeful approach to work. It appears that Lewy in Vienna had also sounded a warning that the zealous young man might not fit too easily into the charged atmosphere of an under-subsidised theatre. Jacques Manheit, a baritone then with the Olmütz theatre, tells of the director briefing his staff shortly before Mahler's arrival. He said he had found a young conductor who had the reputation of being a genius, but also somewhat eccentric. The director, Raul, begged everyone to treat the newcomer with the utmost consideration.

The man who turned up for the first rehearsal was odd-looking indeed. He had bristly hair, a black beard and a sharply projecting nose, emphasised by horn-rimmed pince-nez. After the first session the choristers complained that Mahler's demands had already made them hoarse. He began his rehearsal with the soloists without introducing himself. One can readily imagine the antipathy he aroused. He took no notice of openly expressed disagreement, but calmly and firmly insisted on absolute compliance with his orders.

At the inn where the singers met in the evening, he invited ridicule by drinking water instead of wine or beer. Refusing meat, he asked for spinach and apples, and loudly declared his allegiance to Richard Wagner's vegetarian principles, throwing in a plea for woollen underwear for good measure. The citizens of the little town were agreed that he was a very queer specimen. Mahler spurned the food they offered him, and went hungry for the sake of his convictions.

The first performance he conducted got bad reviews. But after ten days – starting with the performance of Auber's *La Muette de Portici* – there was a gradual change, and the première of Verdi's *Un Ballo in Maschera* on 3 February 1883 was a great success. As the singer Manheit noted:

Gradually the little town got used to the peculiarities of the young conductor, whom the musical fraternity had learnt, if not to love, at any rate to fear. He had such a decided way of making demands and giving orders that nobody dared oppose him, particularly as under his direction performances improved tremendously. Strange to say, Mahler knew hardly any of the operas, he learnt them as he went along. He did not seem to care that he was not popular, he merely insisted that everyone should do his duty.

Mahler's singleminded devotion to his work might lead one to think he was insensitive to the reactions of people around him. Nothing could be further from the truth. He was greatly depressed by the general situation, so different from that in Laibach. He wrote to a friend in Vienna: 'From the moment I crossed the threshold of the Olmütz theatre, I felt like one awaiting the wrath of heaven.' He could not help feeling 'soiled' by it all. It was a small mercy that he had to conduct mainly Verdi and Meyerbeer. By desperate scheming he managed to avoid Mozart and Wagner, as 'I couldn't bear to rattle off *Lohengrin* or *Don Juan* in this place'. Singers and players bowed to his command, perhaps partly because they felt sorry for this obsessional idealist. When their frequent lack of understanding threatened to paralyse him, his enthusiasm revived him: 'Only the feeling that I am suffering for my great masters and that I may yet be able to cast a spark of their fire into the souls of these poor people, keeps my courage up – and then in my happier moments I vow to persevere lovingly – even against their scoffing.'

This passage from the much-quoted letter which he wrote after a month at Olmütz shows a new motive emerging: 'the feeling that I am suffering for my great masters'. It is the first known manifestation of Mahler's artistic philosophy as a conductor. On the rostrum he considered himself the composer's representative, carrying out the master's will, and this attitude was fundamental to all his future work as a conductor: to the reconstruction of the composer's original intentions as laid down in the score; and also – though this may sound paradoxical – to the alterations the mature Mahler was to make in the scores of the great masters.

Asked as a child what he wanted to be when grown up, he is said to have replied, 'a martyr'. Now for the first time he became one, suffering for the 'poor people' who mocked him and into whose souls he hoped to cast some spark. Such a state of mind was hopeless for composing. Indeed, there is no record of any composition dating from Mahler's Olmütz period. He could not serve the great masters as a conductor and at the same time follow his own musical inspiration, much though he wanted to do both. The high degree of concentration he attained in all his activities forced him to devote himself exclusively to one or the other at any given time. If he was going to be a conductor he had to become a 'holiday composer', practising self-denial in a good cause. There is, of course, another type of composer – Richard Strauss was a good example – who can switch from one activity to the other at a moment's notice.

Between 11 January and 17 March 1883 Mahler directed twelve opera performances – among them Bizet's *Carmen* – and two repeats, as Dagmar Kučerová has shown by research into the surviving documents. This artistic achievement on the part of a man not yet twenty-two cannot therefore be dismissed as one of the many legends that have sprung up about Mahler. Karl Überhorst, producer-in-chief of the Dresden Court Opera, who was on the lookout for singers, attended Mahler's benefit, a performance of Méhul's opera *Joseph and his Brethren*. His description of Mahler rehearsing shows a conductor in complete command of the stage. Mahler leapt from the rostrum clear across the double-bass players on to the stage, where he simultaneously produced, directed and conducted. Afterwards Überhorst commented: 'One can only marvel at the man who created such a performance.' When, however, someone suggested to this influential man that Mahler might like to go to Dresden, he answered: 'No, no, that figure, that appearance, quite unsuitable for Dresden . . .'

For all his appreciation of Mahler's artistic powers, Überhorst could not visualise the impetuous youth with his wild mop of hair and the bespectacled nose jutting out from his bearded face as conductor of a Court Theatre. Yet he realised that something should be done for the odd unkempt young man, and he was prepared to do it.

Mahler's work at Olmütz finished in the spring. The town council debated the question of subsidies for the needy theatre, but without concrete results. The director terminated his contract and peremptorily ended the season. Mahler was glad to leave his lodgings in the Michaelergasse: whenever he had tried to study a score, he had been disturbed by neighbours strumming on the piano. In 1934 a plaque was affixed to this house in memory of his brief (though, for his future career, crucial) stay at Olmütz. The plaque was taken down in 1939 during the German occupation. In 1962 the civic committee passed a resolution giving Mahler's name to the street where he had lived.

Mahler had managed to avoid performing Wagner in Olmütz – the image of the master must not be sullied by inadequate staging. His veneration for Wagner was of an almost religious nature. When news of Wagner's death (13 February 1883) reached him, he wandered in tears about the streets of Olmütz, and that summer he decided he would at last make the long-planned pilgrimage to Bayreuth. But first he returned to Vienna to look for a new job. An Italian opera troupe doing a short season at the Carlstheater needed a musician to rehearse the chorus, work that Mahler took up in March and continued till the beginning of May. There was no long break, as Gustav Lewy's agency had received an enquiry from Freiherr von und zu Gilsa, director of the Royal Theatre at Kassel, who was looking for a second conductor, to work mainly with the chorus. Lewy could wholeheartedly recommend 'this well qualified, conscientious musician' who had made a success of his appointments in Laibach and Olmütz.

From Mahler's personal file at Kassel – fortunately extant – it seems that Mahler did not wholly rely on his agent, since he also asked the Dresden producer Überhorst, whom he knew to be well disposed toward himself, for a recommendation. It was dispatched to Kassel on 14 May, and describes Mahler as a conductor 'of quite exceptional distinction' and as 'a highly skilled score-reader and pianist'. Überhorst's letter contains a paragraph that dwells lovingly on the Olmütz conductor's virtues: 'Not only did he produce the operas with fine discrimination and great precision, despite the limited talent available, but as a conductor he succeeded, by dint of hard work and tact, in welding the rather feeble means at his disposal into one harmonious whole.'

The mail must have been more efficient than it is now, for the letter reached the director at Kassel on the following day, and he at once sent a telegram to Mahler, believing him to be still in Olmütz: 'Are you interested in post of royal musical and choral director starting October? If so request curriculum vitae by return. Details by letter. Von Gilsa.' The cable came back from Olmütz the same day, marked 'addressee unknown'. Mahler, longing for news in Vienna, had no idea how urgently he was being sought. Von Gilsa asked in Dresden if Mahler could be traced; at the same time he forwarded his conditions of employment to Lewy in Vienna. The agent insisted on a new contract which not only secured him five per cent of Mahler's earnings but stipulated that this amount should be held back by the management every payday and paid directly to Lewy. The agent's caution proved justified. One gathers from Mahler's personal file at Kassel that he was often short of cash; the tax authorities had to recover certain very trifling arrears by distraint – a fact which in view of his contractual salary of 2100 marks per annum is surprising.

The contract was signed in Kassel on 31 May 1883. Mahler had come early for the obligatory trial rehearsals, which included the musical direction of the dress rehearsal of *Hans Heiling*. He acquitted himself to the director's satisfaction and was to take up his post as musical and choral director on 1 October 1883. His travelling expenses were refunded, and he was able to fit in a visit to Iglau, to tell his parents of his latest success.

At home spirits were low. His mother was ailing as usual, and now his father too was ill. Gustav's twenty-year-old sister Leopoldine was about to get married. The fate of the younger children who still lived at home (Alois, Justine, Otto and Emma) must have worried Mahler, who could see that his invalid parents could no longer provide as well for them as they had done for him. In comparison with the glamour Kassel held out, his home now seemed 'so poor, so dull'. Mahler tortured himself with self-reproach for being 'hard and cruel' to his parents, though he felt for their 'poor tormented hearts'. We do not know whether it was at this point that the salaried musical and choral director decided to support his brothers and sisters. Later on he certainly assumed responsibility for both his sisters and his younger brother Otto, and one reason for his lack of funds during the Kassel years of 1883–85 may have been his support of the Iglau household.

During the summer Mahler escaped from these confines and visited Bayreuth where *Parsifal* was the only work on the programme. We do not know the cast on this occasion, but that season the alternating conductors were Franz Fischer and Hermann Levi; in the role of Parsifal, Mahler may have seen and heard either Heinrich Gudehus or Hermann Winkelmann; Amalie Materna and Therese Malten shared the part of Kundry, and Titurel was sung by either Anton Fuchs or Theodor Reichmann. The producer was Emil Scaria, a native of Graz, who in the previous year had appeared as the first Gurnemanz under Richard Wagner's direction. The intensity of Mahler's emotional experience is conveyed by a single sentence: 'As I left the Festspielhaus, incapable of speech, I knew that I had undergone the greatest tragic experience of all, and that I would carry it unprofaned through life.'

Returning to Iglau he found a request from Kassel to go there for rehearsals in August if possible. He agreed to go, although it cut short his time for 'proper preparations'. It appears from correspondence in the Kassel file that his parents wanted to fit him out rather more stylishly.

On 21 August 1883 Mahler held his first orchestral rehearsal. It was brought home to him at once that his position was nothing like as dominant as at Laibach or Olmütz. The service agreement he had signed subordinated him in every respect to the principal conductor, and regarding the use of the chorus he was also answerable to the chief producer. The regulations obliged him to make cuts only with the management's consent, to 'give notification' of breaches of discipline, to write daily reports on rehearsals, and to rehearse with individual female members of the company only in the presence of a third party, for the sake of propriety. Besides this, he had the task of rearranging scores that demanded more than the available number of players, and he was expected to orchestrate any vocal insertions and supply compositions 'as required by the management for special occasions'.

Thus Mahler wrote the music for a representation of Scheffel's *Der Trompeter von Säckingen* in seven *tableaux vivants*. The score, which was used successfully soon afterwards by other German theatres, has not survived. In a letter Mahler says the music had none of Scheffel's affectations, but 'far surpassed the writer's work'.

Mahler's operatic work included operas by Lortzing, Flotow, Donizetti, Rossini, Delibes and Adam. Court conductor Wilhelm Treiber saw to it that none of the major classics came his way. This made for friction. Treiber called Mahler, who showed his usual persistence in musical matters, 'a most pig-headed young man'. He may well have felt some jealousy of the hard-working, highly skilled young conductor. When Mahler, for musical reasons, added a violinist to the orchestra without having asked permission, he found himself in trouble. His self-willed action was recorded in the file, and he was forced to pay the player's honorarium out of his own pocket. Lateness at rehearsals, of which he was sometimes guilty, was severely punished. His impetuous habit of keeping singers and players in time by stamping his heels was entered in the black book. Mahler felt all this as a degrading restriction on his freedom. Before long he determined to use the first opportunity to break out of this prison.

An opportunity seemed to offer itself in January 1884. The occasion was an orchestral concert given in Kassel by the Director of Court Music at Meiningen, that great pianist and conductor Hans von Bülow. Von Bülow's complex relations with Wagner, who had enticed away his wife Cosima, were as widely known as his historic services to Wagner's music – he had given *Tristan und Isolde* and *Die Meistersinger* their first performance.

Mahler was enthralled by the concert von Bülow conducted on 25 January 1884. Here, he felt, was the escape route from the slavery of the theatre into pure art. He resolved to become von Bülow's pupil, to be guided by him to greater artistic achievements. It is hard to see how Gustav Mahler, an officially appointed music and choral director with a three-year contract, could have been so naïve as to believe that he could change his life with one gushing, almost hysterical missive to the worldly-wise Freiherr von Bülow. Yet try he did.

I am a musician wandering without a lodestar through the desolate night of contemporary music, exposed to all the dangers of doubt and confusion. When at yesterday's concert I saw my highest hopes and dreams realised, it dawned upon me – here is your native soil, this is your master – now or never your journeying shall cease. And now I come to ask you: take me with you – in whatever capacity – let me be your pupil, even if I have to pay for it with my own blood. I am twenty-three years of age, studied at the University of Vienna, learnt composition and the piano at the Conservatoire, and after the most ill-starred wanderings find myself employed as second conductor at the local theatre. – Whether this futile bustle can satisfy a man who with all the love and longing in him believes in art, yet sees it maltreated everywhere in the most abominable manner, you yourself will best be able to judge. — I put myself completely in your hands, and if you would accept this present, there is nothing that would make me happier. If you give me an answer, I am ready to do whatever you have in mind. Please, do at least give me an answer. In expectation,

Gustav Mahler.

The Director of the Meiningen Court Orchestra knew what was due to his colleague at Kassel, Herr von und zu Gilsa. It was not von Bülow's custom to involve himself with ambitious young men and thereby prejudice correct relations with his colleagues in office. Besides von Bülow could not have known anything of the letter-writer's musical abilities: the letter merely betrayed an unruly character. He did not deign to answer, but handed the missive to Mahler's immediate superior, Court Conductor Treiber, who passed it on to the director. The latter seems to have been all too familiar with Mahler's outbursts. Though he rather liked the young musician, Herr von und zu Gilsa realised that he would not be able to keep him for long. He did the kindest thing possible in the circumstances: he had the letter filed away.

The management at Kassel were now aware of Mahler's intentions. They would not oppose the premature termination of his engagement, if that was what he wanted. But Mahler stayed on till the summer of 1885. It needed time to find some place where art was not 'maltreated' and where the freedom of a conductor was less limited.

His letters from Kassel to Fritz Löhr in Vienna show that Mahler was deep in an unhappy love affair with a young actress. Löhr, Mahler's confidant in many intimate secrets, notes on one of these letters dated September 1883: 'Affairs of the heart at Kassel have embarked on their extravagant course, nor will the passionate young soul escape now.'

The precise difficulties of this relationship are unknown, but may be divined from the text Mahler was setting to music at that time: *Lieder eines fahrenden Gesellen* (Songs of a Wayfarer). The close connection between this text and Mahler's personal experience is confirmed by a letter to Löhr in which he says: 'I have written a cycle of songs which are all dedicated to her. She has not seen them. What could they tell her that she does not know already?'

'What she knows' can be read in the very first lines of the poem:

> *Wenn mein Schatz Hochzeit macht,*
> *fröhliche Hochzeit macht,*
> *hab' ich meinen traurigen Tag!*
> *Geh' ich in mein Kämmerlein,*
> *dunkles Kämmerlein!*
> *Weine! Wein'! Um meinen Schatz,*
> *Um meinen lieben Schatz.*

> [My darling's wedding-day
> joyful wedding-day,
> will be my day of mourning.
> I shall hide in my chamber
> my dark little chamber,
> weeping, weeping for my darling.
> for my dearest darling.]

Most reference books state that Mahler wrote the lyrics of the *Songs of a Wayfarer* himself. But as early as 1920 and 1921 Siegfried Günther and Paul Bekker showed that these texts stem to a marked degree from the collection *Des Knaben Wunderhorn*. In this collection we certainly find the model for Mahler's first song:

> *Wann mein Schatz Hochzeit macht,*
> *Hab ich einen traurigen Tag,*
> *Geh' ich in mein Kämmerlein,*
> *Wein' um meinen Schatz.*

> *Blümlein blau, verdorre nicht,*
> *Du stehst auf grüner Heide ;*
> *Des Abends, wenn ich schlafen geh',*
> *So denk' ich an das Lieben.*

> [My darling's wedding day
> Will be my day of mourning.
> I will hide in my chamber
> Weeping for my darling.

[61]

Do not wither, little blue flower,
You are on a green heath.
At night when I go to sleep
I think of my love.]

Mahler has made various minor alterations, and also inserted a contrasting section which gives him occasion for a musical 'central episode':

Vöglein süss! Vöglein süss!
Du singst auf grüner Heide!
Ach! Wie ist die Welt so schön!
Ziküth! Ziküth!
Singet nicht! Blühet nicht!
Lenz ist ja vorbei!
Alles singen ist nun aus!

[Sweet bird! Sweet bird!
Singing on a green heath!
Ah, the world is beautiful!
Ziküth! Ziküth!
Sing not! Blossom not!
Spring is past and gone,
All the singing ended.]

The statement that the *Songs of a Wayfarer* were written to 'original texts' by Mahler – still found in H. F. Redlich's contribution to the eighth volume (1960) of the encyclopaedia *Musik in Geschichte und Gegenwart* – therefore needs amending, since the 'original text' is based on the *Wunderhorn*. Our view seems to be contradicted by Paul Stefan's assertion, made in Mahler's lifetime, that Mahler did not come across the *Wunderhorn* collection until he was twenty-eight – long after the first Kassel draft of the *Songs of a Wayfarer*. But the contradiction is only apparent. *Des Knaben Wunderhorn* contains many texts of old folksongs which survived in oral tradition for many years, in some cases to the present day. Why then should Mahler not have heard these songs sometime between Iglau and Kassel? This seems even more likely in that Kassel was the place where, some eighty years before Mahler's coming, the compilers of *Des Knaben Wunderhorn* produced the volume containing *Wenn mein Schatz Hochzeit macht.*

The cycle originally consisted of six songs, but we know it in a later version of four sections which was first performed in Berlin in 1896. Both text and music are conceived in the folk idiom. Just as the mood of the poems alternates between deepest grief and the soothing solace of Nature, so the harmonic structure vacillates continuously between major and minor. The Wayfarer tries to escape from suffering by taking refuge in Nature (no. 2 of the cycle).

> *Ging heut morgen übers Feld*
> *Tau noch auf den Gräsern hing . . .*

> [Walked this morn across the fields,
> Dew still clinging to the grass . . .]

He is painfully reminded that for him 'happiness will never bloom'. The desperate outburst of no. 3 ends with the cry: '*Ich wollt', ich läg' auf der schwarzen Bahr', könnt' nimmer, nimmer die Augen aufmachen!*' [O that I were laid on the black bier, and could never, never open my eyes again.]

The last song brings consolation with a sort of folk tune:

> *Auf der Strasse stand ein Lindenbaum,*
> *da hab' ich zum ersten Mal im Schlaf geruht!*

> [By the road stood a linden tree
> Where I found rest for the first time.]

In the dying cadence, 'all is well again, all, all! Love and pain, and world and dream!' ('*Alles wieder gut! Alles! Alles! Lieb' und Leid! Und Welt und Traum!*').

Mahler's letters at that time underline the autobiographical character of the work. They show that his love did not remain un-requited; it was external circumstances that worked against the couple's union. The world of nature with its stylised bird calls was as real an experience to Mahler as the Wayfarer's flight across meadows and fields. From his window Mahler looked out on the slow-flowing Fulda; he enjoyed the panorama of hills and forests; and, nostalgically remembering walks in the Wienerwald and excursions around Iglau, he tramped through the Habichtswald, to look down upon Kassel from the summit.

There is yet another sense in which the *Songs of a Wayfarer* are autobiographical. From this point on we can clearly trace the progress of Mahler's thoughts and feelings through his compositions. Even if we had no other data about his life than the musical notes he wrote down, we could still discover from them the important traits of the composer's make-up. One dominant feature is the obsessional tenacity with which he clings to his musical prototypes. The history of *Das klagende Lied*, composed in 1880 and performed in 1901, was an example of this. With the *Songs of a Wayfarer* his persistence takes a specific musical form: he retains two themes for use in a symphony that he was already planning while at Kassel. The D major song, *Ging heut morgen übers Feld*, reappears in the first movement of this symphony; the linden tree theme becomes part of the third movement. The persistence of a well-defined intellectual content in the symphony, despite the absence of text, points to Mahler's desire to be considered ultimately a creator of absolute music.

Any attempt to build up a picture of Mahler's personality from his compositions alone is necessarily incomplete. Posterity has the right to concern itself exclusively with Mahler the composer, since it cannot receive the impact of Mahler the conductor and man of the theatre. But such uncompromising selection distorts the likeness. We see merely the romantic, high-flying dreamer, the wayfarer of music, living in his imagination without regard for the outside world. Certainly this is one aspect of Mahler. In his letters to his friends he manifests this ecstatic side, soaring above the constraints of reality. At times, under the influence of especially intense musical experiences, he reveals it on the wrong occasion – as when hurling at von Bülow a thoroughly misjudged outburst of enthusiasm which must have struck the recipient as a laughable attempt at familiarity.

But in general Mahler had complete command of himself. That was the other side of his character: coolly calculated tactics in the struggle for positions to conquer. While still at Kassel, he sought contacts with other musical centres. During the holidays he went to Dresden, not only to attend a performance of *Tristan* conducted by Ernst von Schuch, but also to sound the benevolent producer Überhorst about the chances of an engagement. When he left Kassel he had a contract for Leipzig in his pocket, and had begun negotiations with Prague. But before saying farewell to Kassel, Mahler wanted to make people talk about him. In this he succeeded remarkably well: for years the people of Kassel would remember the splendid *Musikfest* at the infantry barracks – and the scandal that hung thereby.

The festival was planned for the end of June 1885. With the permission of the Court Theatre Director, Mahler had taken over the mixed choir of the Münden Choral Society the year before, rehearsing with it every week. Three other choral societies were to take part in the festival as well. The chief event was to be a performance of Mendelssohn's oratorio *St Paul*, and the music-loving citizens put Mahler in charge of this; there were strong hopes of the theatre orchestra. But the idea did not appeal to Mahler's superior, Court Conductor Treiber. Objections from distinguished people who happened to be friends of Treiber reached the director, who tried to persuade Mahler to exercise magnanimity by stepping down in favour of the Court Conductor. Mahler flatly refused, although he knew that this would 'finish him' at the theatre. But he did not care any more; he considered his Kassel period over anyhow, and the confirmation of his engagement at the Leipzig Stadttheater helped to stiffen his resolution. Here at last was the great chance to lead a chorus of four hundred and a vast orchestra. Among the soloists, besides a local baritone, was Herr Gudehus of Dresden, a tenor who two years before had appeared as Parsifal at Bayreuth under Wagner's own guidance. There was also a young singer from the Vienna Court Opera, Rosa Papier, who was said to have a glorious voice. How could Mahler have forgone such an occasion? He dismissed the director's proposal as 'preposterous'.

The countermovement inspired by Treiber did not give up. They succeeded in getting the theatre orchestra to refuse to participate. Peacemakers from the choral societies worked for a compromise whereby Chief Conductor Treiber would take over the orchestral rehearsals and another conductor the rehearsing of the chorus, but Mahler would be in charge of the whole. This was the signal for an antisemitic newspaper to mount a frontal attack. The Jew Mahler was usurping the limelight, although there were better and more deserving conductors about. If the proposed compromise were accepted, the Germans would have all the work, 'the Jews the kudos'.

Mahler did not throw in the sponge. He could do without the Kassel orchestra. Musicians were brought from Weimar, Meiningen and Brunswick, and augmented by the band of an infantry regiment. The performance took place. The critic of the *Casseler Tageblatt* assured the conductor in his review that he was a 'talented musician' and had 'an enterprising character'.

The day this review appeared, 1 July 1885, also saw the end of Mahler's contractual obligation to the Kassel theatre. Herr von und zu Gilsa could not decide on the premature termination of the contract without the agreement of the government department in Berlin, but this was readily granted when they read in Berlin what the director had recorded in Mahler's dossier:

I take leave to inform you that this young man, who at the beginning of his engagement gave rise to the highest hopes, has now, by negotiating an agreement with Leipzig and by his ambition to shine as a festival conductor, wholly lost his grip on himself, and on account of various breaches of discipline and omissions figures regularly in the book of fines. He has consequently lost his standing with the chorus as well as the orchestra.

Mahler himself saw things differently: 'I have become positively popular, a sort of man of the moment.' The Kassel music festival had brought him ovations, honours, a laurel-wreath, a diamond ring and even a gold watch, which last came in very handy as his own had recently been confiscated, apparently for tax arrears. All the organising he had done had cost a lot of money. He had to disappoint the hopes of his family in Iglau; indeed, he was lucky to get off as lightly as he did. Financially he had 'suffered shipwreck', but he was pleased about his work. 'I am, as you might say, on my way up.'

The contract with the Stadttheater in Leipzig hardly justified this remark, for there was another year to go before he took up that post. What should he do till then? Mahler did not just sit and brood. Wherever he scented a vacancy for a conductor, he offered his services. Von Bülow, who wanted to retire from Meiningen, had only to hint as much to his closest friends to find himself deluged with applications, including letters from Zumpe of Hamburg, from Nicolé in Dresden, and from the twenty-two-year-old Felix von Weingartner, as well as an offer from the importunate letter-writer at Kassel. Meanwhile, however, Mahler had heard that the German Theatre in Prague would shortly have a new lessee and director.

⌐5⌐

The Struggle for Freedom

The Emperor's Manifesto in the year of Mahler's birth had opened up the world to the son of the coachbox scholar turned brandy distiller. To the peoples of the Habsburg empire it acted as a spur in the development of their national identities. This had its due effect on the theatrical life of Bohemia, and its capital, Prague. The demand, first raised during the revolution of 1848, for the Germans as well as the Czechs to have 'free and independent theatres within a free state' gradually led to a separation of the nationalities. In 1862 the Czechs created their 'Interim Provincial Theatre' whose company moved at the beginning of the 1880s into the proud edifice of the *Národní Divadlo* (National Theatre), which still exists. The unchallenged supremacy of the German element in the theatrical culture of the Bohemian capital had ended. The Royal German Provincial Theatre was now exposed to strong competition from the Czech musical theatre, which attracted a considerable section of the public. The financial crisis this caused at the German Theatre took on such menacing proportions in the spring of 1885 that a great effort was made to find a rescuer, in the form of a well-to-do and imaginative director for the theatre. They succeeded in securing a man whose previous commercial and artistic successes gave cause for optimism. Angelo Neumann, who had started his career as a lyric tenor and had sung for some years at the Vienna Court Opera, was installed as director of the German Provincial Theatre at Prague. Subsequently he had become well known for his skilful management of the Leipzig theatre, and particularly for his enthusiastic championship of Wagner, whose works his travelling company had taken as far afield as England, Spain and Russia.

Angelo Neumann was so impressed by the letter of application he received from the unknown musician at Kassel that he wrote a more than courteous reply and eventually called Mahler for an interview. He quickly recognised the talent of the 'young Hotspur'. The first assignment he gave Mahler was the direction of Cherubini's opera *Les Deux journées*, though he had some doubts about putting him in charge of the special performance for the Emperor's birthday (18 August). Mahler was 'too fidgety' at the rostrum, his manner reminded the director very much of Hans von Bülow. In those days impulsive gestures did not coincide with the accepted idea of a conductor's beating. With a man of von Bülow's stature allowances could be made for such eccentricity, but the second conductor of the Prague Theatre should be self-effacing, as befitted a musician. However, Angelo Neumann took the risk, and Mahler's debut passed off smoothly. He was engaged at the German Theatre for a year. He was even entrusted with Wagner's works. To begin with Anton Seidl was still there; he had long collaborated with Angelo Neumann as a conductor, and it was he who conducted the opening première (*Lohengrin*) of the Prague season of 1885–86. But Seidl, who with Neumann's travelling company had taken the *Ring des Nibelungen* (in a practicable, ruthlessly cut version) all over Europe, soon went on to the New York Metropolitan Opera, where he presented his potted digests of Wagner's stage works to the public in the guise of American premières.

With the departure of Seidl, Mahler became the resident Wagner-conductor. In December 1885 he produced *Das Rheingold* and *Die Walküre*. Nominally Mahler was second conductor, but in practice he had the field to himself. The chief conductor, Slanský, though Mahler's superior, was content with less demanding tasks. When Neumann offered him the direction of Mozart's *Don Giovanni*, in compensation, as it were, for the Wagner operas he had missed, Slanský turned down the offer on the grounds that the people of Prague had never cared much for this opera. Thus *Don Giovanni* also fell to Mahler's share, and he, in collaboration with his producer-director, achieved a performance that moved the public to ecstasy and the press to enthusiastic acclaim.

Mahler also distinguished himself as a concert conductor in

Prague. A performance of Beethoven's Ninth Symphony made such a powerful impression on the listeners that a group of academics headed by a university professor presented Mahler with an address bearing numerous signatures and expressing their gratitude and admiration for the twenty-five-year-old conductor. Mahler revelled in this social recognition. He could now dispense with the beard that was meant to make him look older and more respectable. In February 1886 he reduced it to a moustache. From that month, too, dates a poem he wrote for the third anniversary of Richard Wagner's death. Perhaps he intended to set it to music; nothing is known about that, but the verses have survived. His ideas on Wagner come out clearly in the penultimate stanza:

> *Was wir ersehnt in unbestimmtem Drang,*
> *Hast du zu festen Formen uns gestaltet,*
> *Der deutschen Bühne gabst du ihre Macht*
> *Zurück, wo fremde Melodie gewaltet.*
> *Du zeigst uns, was wir immer noch gesehen,*
> *Was wir geahnt, gefühlt in mächt'gem Glühen,*
> *Du liessest eine morsche Welt vergehen,*
> *Schufst eine junge Welt von Melodien.*

> [All that we longed for, all that undirected urge,
> You gave it solid shape and definition;
> You gave back power to the German stage
> Where foreign music had become tradition.
> You showed us all we ever wished to see,
> All that we dreamt of, sensed in hopeful passion,
> The world's decay you stripped away,
> Creating a new world of melody.]

Whatever the literary merits of this poetic effusion, the nationalist German emphasis is unmistakable. It would be wrong, however, to see in this a more than incidental affinity with the chauvinistic aspects of the Wagner-cult. In the German chord that was first struck in 1848 there still sounded a fundamental libertarian note which by no means precluded harmony with other nations. This, and no other, construction must be put on the Wagnerian creed of the conductor at the German Theatre: its effect was not restrictive but universally receptive. The contribution of the Czechs, and of Slavs in general, to the musical theatre excited Mahler's deep interest. He frequented the *Národní Divadlo* to hear the operas of Glinka, Dvořák and Smetana. We do not know whether *The Bartered Bride* was among these works. Smetana's masterpiece was not then known outside Bohemia. Not until six years later did it set out from Vienna on its triumphal progress round the world. But what Mahler heard of Smetana's music struck him as 'very remarkable'. So much so that he wrote to his future chief, the director Staegemann at Leipzig: 'Though Smetana's operas will never be part of the repertoire in German, it would be highly worth while to acquaint an educated public, like the one at Leipzig, with such a truly original and independent musical mind.'

Mahler's affection for the great Bohemian composer was lasting. In Prague, then, Mahler's musical horizon was enlarged in two ways: the world of Wagner, hitherto the dreamland of a passionate vegetarian, became the spiritual dominion of the second conductor (now undeniably wielding the first baton); Slav music on the other hand spoke to him in a language familiar from his childhood.

He would have liked to stay on in Prague, where it was perhaps possible to be 'German' in a sense devoid of nationalistic overtones; where the music of his native Bohemia was heard; and where – a thing scarcely intelligible today – he might still remain an Austrian. Leipzig was in another country. The Leipzig Stadttheater was dangerous territory, for there Mahler was once again to take second place, and the chief conductor was not as lazy as old Slanský in Prague. The Leipzig first conductor was Arthur Nikisch. Five years older than Mahler, he was also a product of the Vienna Conservatoire and had been at Leipzig since 1878. 'A jealous and powerful rival', whom Mahler would have cause to fear. There would have been no obstacles for Mahler in Prague. But the Leipzig director insisted on keeping him to the contract: he had no intention of losing this young man who had by now made a name for himself.

In the circumstances it is not surprising that work at Leipzig began amid tension. Mahler had expressed the wish to conduct *Tannhäuser*, and this was granted, along with *Rienzi*, *Der Freischütz* and *La Juive*; but Wagner's *Ring des Nibelungen* was pre-empted by the director for the more experienced Nikisch. Mahler protested. He 'could not possibly remain in a position' where he was excluded from such tasks. After a few months he asked to be relieved of his post. Staegemann, who appreciated Mahler's talent and wanted to prevent him from making a rash decision, persuaded him to stay. Though Mahler calmed down outwardly, he still went on looking for a new job. By December he had received an offer from the impressario Pollini in Hamburg, the chance of a place at Karlsruhe (as successor to Felix Mottl), and 'a most advantageous offer' from Angelo Neumann, who wanted him back in Prague.

Public and press noted the differences in style between Nikisch and Mahler: the former was controlled and regal, sparing of movement, the latter full of emphatic gestures, never satisfied at rehearsals, wanting every *piano* to be softer, every *forte* stronger. All Mahler's instructions to singers and orchestra were directed towards clarity. This led to modifications of the basic tempo which ran counter to tradition. The method was criticised by some, praised by others as a means of enriching expression. Some members of the orchestra protested: they did not need Herr Mahler from Prague to teach them what was soft and what was loud. But Mahler also had his supporters in the orchestra. Among the few 'capital fellows' he singled out was a young Dutchman called Henri Petri. Mahler praised Petri – who was leader of the orchestra, a pupil of Joachim and father of the pianist Egon Petri of future renown – as a musician 'of true warmheartedness, who can read the most enigmatic convolutions of my stick and turn them into music'.

In January 1887 Mahler's hopes for an improvement in his position revived, for Nikisch was toying with the idea of going to Hungary. The Royal Opera at Budapest, which had opened three years ago, offered him a tempting appointment. Mahler was pleased by the prospect of his powerful rival's departure. 'Nikisch and I,' he wrote to Löhr in Vienna, 'have got much closer during this last phase and are behaving like good comrades.'

Nikisch was unable to realise his plan; illness forced him to go on long leave. Thus the role of chief conductor devolved on Mahler, at least temporarily and *de facto*. He was at last able to conduct *Die Walküre*, remarking with pride that this had put him in a very strong position, and soon after he produced *Siegfried*. He could now await the return of his rival with equanimity: 'With the recent turn of events I have in fact become Nikisch's equal in every respect, and can face a fight for supremacy with confidence; I shall win, if only because of my stronger constitution. I think Nikisch will not stick it much longer with me around, but will sooner or later decamp.'

This is not a very generous way of putting it, but it has the virtue of honesty. During the season of 1887–88, Mahler threw all his physical reserves into the struggle for supremacy. In 214 performances he conducted no fewer than fifty-four different works. Nor was this the sum total of his activities. He also undertook the editing of an unfinished work by Carl Maria von Weber. He had plans for a Weber cycle on the lines of the Wagner cycle, and Weber's posthumous opera *Die drei Pintos* was to be a part of it.

Mahler had discovered this fragment at the house of the composer's grandson, Captain Carl von Weber. He fell in love not only with the score, but also with the captain's wife. Frau von Weber, who appears to have returned his feelings, is probably the subject of those passages in his letters from Leipzig which refer to folly and getting into trouble. The heat of this passion we can only guess at; but the fire it kindled in Mahler was that raging creative conflagration from which the First Symphony was to spring.

The completed and thoroughly re-edited comic opera *Die drei Pintos* was performed on 20 January 1888 at the Leipzig Stadttheater. Mahler's version – rejected today by orthodox connoisseurs and admirers of Weber's music for its improper hybridisation of Weber's style with Wagnerian elements – not only drew much applause but also roused the interest of other opera houses. Hamburg, Dresden and Vienna put on *Die drei Pintos*. Richard Strauss, at that time a faithful disciple of von Bülow, got to know both the opera and Mahler himself. In contrast to von Bülow, he was enthusiastic about the score and its arranger, although eventually, under von Bülow's influence, he noted various reservations.

Mahler's zeal for work knew no bounds. The mental and physical burden of his daily duties, his work on the Weber opera and the preparation of the Weber cycle, seemed negligible compared to the emotional tension of his relations with the Webers. We know little about his relationship with Frau von Weber. Whether she really intended to leave her husband and children and run away with Mahler is beside the point. What matters to us is the process of transmutation of latent erotic energy into kinetic creative force. It would be presumptuous to speculate about this change, did we not have evidence of Mahler's creative turmoil. To his friend in Vienna asking for news, he sent an evasive reply, a few sentences each ending with an exclamation-mark: 'Trilogy of passion and whirlwind of life! Everything within me and around me unfolds! Nothing is! Just give me a little longer! Then you shall hear all!' The reader may surmise a love story behind these words. But it was more than that, it was a very epic of love. Mahler had succumbed to the symphony.

The passion that now chained Mahler to his desk and his manuscript paper made him neglect his duties. The theatre director warned him to mend his ways. Mahler openly admitted that he had ceased to carry out his duties as Staegemann had come to expect; in a note to the director he hinted that the latter would judge him more leniently if he knew the cause of his dereliction. He would not actually name this cause, but pleaded for indulgence: 'Let another two months pass and you will find me my old self again.'

Two months later he wrote a letter to Löhr in Vienna beginning: 'There! My work is finished!' The symphony, which 'rushed out of him like a mountain torrent', was completed in its essentials. But there was still much to be done. Whenever he found time, Mahler went back to the score. The death of the German Emperor in May 1888 came opportunely, for official mourning was declared and the theatre had to close for ten days. That time could be used at the desk in tracing and correcting the course of the mountain torrent.

Though Mahler admitted eight years afterwards that his First Symphony in D major had been inspired by a passionate love, he stressed that 'the symphony begins where the love-affair ends; it is based on the affair which preceded the symphony in the emotional life of the composer. But the extrinsic experience became the occasion, not the message of the work.' In his mind the 'extrinsic experience' of Leipzig coalesced with the unhappy Kassel romance, just as the melodies of the Kassel period are incorporated in the symphony. The *Lieder eines fahrenden Gesellen*, though significant enough in themselves, now acquire the character of a preface to the First Symphony. The theme of *Ging heut morgen übers Feld* appears in the first movement of the symphony; the folk tune of *Auf der Strasse stand ein Lindenbaum* turns up in the third; the theme of the second movement is derived from another song written in Kassel, *Hans und Grete*.

Here in a musical context is that element of continuity which is as characteristic of Mahler's art as it is of his attitude to life. What he has experienced is never lost: a casual affair, unrequited love or a consuming mutual passion – together they form a synthesis, love itself. Melodic material, taken either from a single unassuming song or from a song cycle, loses its connection with the text and becomes 'music itself'.

It is not the aim of this book to train the tools of formal analysis on Mahler's symphonies, yet we must draw attention to the quite extraordinarily novel and volcanic force of the First. In both its original five-movement and its subsequent four-movement form it is designed to give maximum effect to the finale. This purposeful approach towards the last movement is apparent even at first hearing. One of Mahler's devices – here as in the later symphonies – is to diversify and develop his ideas progressively as they recur throughout the work. In this he resembles the representative of French Romanticism, Hector Berlioz, whose technique of thematic development has rightly been called a method of 'varied repetition'. In this sense the themes may be compared to the characters in a novel, whose appearance changes with their experiences in the course of the story. Adorno* applies the term 'technique of variants' to this. He produces an incisive analysis of the process:

* Theodor Wiesengrund-Adorno. German aesthete and sociologist.

At times Mahler's themes assume the role of the joker in a pack of cards — whose ornamental stylised images are altogether not unlike the images in Mahler's music, which does occasionally have the air of playing-card kings. The variants of such joker motifs may easily be taken for granted, as though they were accidental, and indeed, an element of randomness in their sequence is as much a part of their meaning as is accident in games of chance. Yet even here the patient observer will discover a logic in the composition.

What is astonishing is that this irresistible logic flowed out of the twenty-eight-year-old composer like lava from a volcano — and apparently without lengthy preparation. All aspects of this symphony written for a large orchestra (3 flutes, 3 oboes, 4 clarinets, 3 bassoons, 7 horns, 4 trumpets, 3 trombones, tuba, tympani, percussion and strings) demonstrate Mahler's principles of composition which, though he was to vary and develop them, he never abandoned.

At one time he named the symphony *The Titan*, but finally decided against this. In books on Mahler it is still asserted that this has no connection with the sort of hero suggested by Beethoven's *Eroica*, but refers to Jean Paul's novel of that title. Mahler knew and loved the writings of Jean Paul, but anyone who has ever read any of the latter's work must conclude that there is no trace of his mannered style in Mahler's symphony. Natalie Bauer-Lechner relates in her memoirs that Mahler in this composition meant to portray a 'vigorous, heroic man', his life and sufferings, his struggle and defeat. Her statement that Mahler's Second Symphony should be seen as the 'true, higher solution' of the First is borne out by a letter from Mahler to Max Marschalk in 1896 in which he speaks of the hero of the First Symphony being carried to his grave at the beginning of the Second.

Here too we see the continuity of Mahler's creative process. None of the symphonies stands by itself. Each belongs to a total cycle which should be conceived as a musical counterpart to Balzac's *Comédie humaine*. With this in mind one can understand a saying of Mahler's that has a presumptuous ring to it. Beethoven, Mahler once remarked, had composed only one Ninth, but of his own symphonies every one was a 'Ninth'. This is not in fact arrogance, but the statement of a psychological truth about Mahler's creative work: every symphony has its fundamental philosophy, and the symphonies without words (the First, Fifth, Sixth, Seventh and Ninth) reveal even more of it to the perceptive listener than do those that use a text.

The programmatic interrelation of musical creativeness with the emotion of love – in both the widest and the narrowest sense of the word – is stressed in one of Mahler's earliest songs, *Erinnerung*:

> *Es wecket meine Liebe die Lieder immer wieder!*
> *Es wecken meine Lieder die Liebe immer wieder!*

> [My love ever awakens my songs;
> My songs ever awaken my love.]

The music expresses this even more strongly than the words; as for instance in the song's middle section, where the sharply dissonant suspended notes accompany the phrase *So kommen meine Lieder zu mir mit Liebesklagen* ('My songs turn to me with plaints of love').

Those psychologists who consider chastity the vital factor of the creative artist's powers might find Mahler's conduct at Leipzig evidence for their thesis – not a generally tenable one. The process of sublimation which resulted in the D major symphony affected not only his feelings towards the female sex but his attitude to his whole surroundings. Hence the temporary neglect of his professional duties and a sudden proneness to 'sleep-walking'. Contemporary reports mention time and again how Mahler would change in a trice from a stimulating conversationalist to a man whose thoughts were patently elsewhere. His sensitiveness to noise, too, is the mark of an abstraction which he not only experienced passively, but actively sought. Even so, one should beware of picturing him as an artist removed from this world and chaste in the trivial sense of the word. Where he could further his aims by grappling with reality he did so unhesitatingly. He had no truck with the sickly common or garden romanticism fashionable among young composers. Even the programmatic idea underlying the First Symphony was to his mind far removed from the whole suggestion of tone poems. In this he differed from Richard Strauss, his junior by four years and much given to tone poems. Titles of the kind used by Strauss (*Aus Italien*, 1887, *Don Juan*, 1888) would have been unthinkable for Mahler. He would simply call his production 'Symphonic Work', if it came to a performance. For a time he permitted the name *Titan*, to please his friends, but later insisted the work should be taken as a manifestation of absolute music. Tone-painting for its own sake was an abomination to him. Once at a private gathering in Leipzig, when a young composer of programme music played a work entitled *Im stillen Tal* ('In the tranquil valley'), and those present were hard put to it to find words of appreciation, Mahler burst out mockingly: 'Very good! Absolutely true to life! I know that valley – at least I think I recognise it – it is situated in Styria.'

The score of the First Symphony was completed. Mahler might have picked up the strands of his Leipzig job, but he found it difficult to regain his equilibrium in everyday matters. Staegemann had presumably been enlightened as to the causes of the temporary upset. But what good was the news of a finished symphony to him? He needed a disciplined conductor who was willing to support Nikisch. Mahler was no longer prepared to do this. The news from Iglau was depressing. His father was seriously ill, there was little hope for him. Justine, now twenty, was in charge of the household, which had become too much for their sick mother. Alois was to go into business. Otto, now fifteen, showed signs of musical talent that should be fostered. And there was the future of thirteen-year-old Emma to be considered.

No real change in his fortunes could be expected from a performance of his symphony in some 'beer concert', as Mahler called it. He had to find a new field of activity. Perhaps Pollini in Hamburg might be prevailed upon to renew his offer. It might be worth sending a letter to New York to ask about engagements. After all, Anton Seidl had won both fame and money there. And seeing that Nikisch had negotiated with Budapest, Mahler might try his luck there, too. The great thing was to overtake Nikisch, who obviously had no intention of 'decamping'. Mahler served his ties with

Leipzig, not without difficulties. In the summer of 1888 he sought relaxation at Bayreuth. *Parsifal* and *Die Meistersinger von Nürnberg* were on the programme. After that he had to undergo a surgical operation, the nature of which is not known.

In September, after the briefest of negotiations, his goal materialised: Budapest. Mahler became artistic director of the Royal Hungarian Opera, with a ten-year contract. His annual salary of 10,000 gulden gave him the necessary sense of security in view of the approaching, unavoidable period of pressing family commitments. In Budapest he did not have to fight for supremacy, he was 'the chief'. Surely he could also find a hall, an orchestra and a public for his symphony. An opera director did not have to look to 'beer concerts' for his symphonic productions.

Mahler had a right to be proud. Nor did he think of Leipzig with resentment. He dispatched parcels of 'real Magyar specialities' to Staegemann from Budapest. By such gestures, however friendly the intention, Mahler as it were placed himself on an equal footing with his former chief. It was a correspondence between directors, lords of the theatre, who might recommend singers to one another, or entice them away from each other. Maybe Mahler was even on a higher rung. Staegemann was in charge of a provincial Stadttheater, whereas Mahler led the Royal Opera House of a proud nation.

[6]

Campaigns

The Royal Hungarian Opera at Budapest, opened in 1884, had difficulties during its early years both in finding its artistic identity and in establishing a firm financial and administrative basis. By the autumn of 1887 the first artistic and financial crisis had arisen. A government commissioner was appointed to improve matters. Ferenc von Beniczky, who took office in January 1888, was no autocrat, but sought the advice of experienced artists. The head of the Budapest Academy of Music and Drama was Ödön von Mihalovich, a cultured musician who as a young man had gone on pilgrimage to Munich to hear *Tristan und Isolde* and had established relations with Wagner and von Bülow. This Hungarian Wagnerian was among those Beniczky consulted when it came to appointing a new director for the Opera. Other artists were also drawn into the enquiry, among them the cellist David Popper, a native of Prague, who taught at the Budapest Academy of Music.

On behalf of a group of Budapest musicians Popper approached the well-known musicologist Guido Adler for information about Mahler. He received the reply that 'Mahler as an artist and as a man was wholly suitable for the position of operatic director, and that he would certainly develop the necessary administrative ability'. Adler, who was a friend of Mahler's, had followed the latter's career attentively. He had been a professor at the German University of Prague during Mahler's time there. Himself a convinced admirer of Wagner, he could unreservedly recommend to the Wagner-lovers of Budapest a musician noted for his enthusiastic promoting of the *Ring*. Moreover, Guido Adler had been among the signatories to the address of thanks presented to Mahler for his performance of Beethoven's Ninth Symphony.

It is pure conjecture that this chain reaction of enquiries and testimonials was set off by Mahler himself; yet his behaviour on other similar occasions would support the assumption. No doubt it was the success of *Die drei Pintos* which impressed the government commissioner most. This arrangement of Weber's opera, which had been produced by various theatres and had now appeared in print, would carry more weight than Mahler's fundamental concerns – the techniques of rehearsal, or the coordination of music and stage action, not to mention his own symphony in D major, which was of course quite unknown except to his closest friends.

Beniczky was much struck by Mahler's enthusiasm about his future work. Mihalovich, the director of the Academy and a friend of Count Albert Apponyi, one of the leading politicians of the Hungarian nationalist opposition, added his recommendation, and thus encouraged the government commissioner could risk giving Mahler a long-term contract. He liked, too, the latter's readiness, laid down in the contract, to learn the Hungarian language. This promise Mahler, as even his friends admit, never kept; but he responded to the demand for a 'national opera' in a much more effective manner, by the 'Magyarisation' of the theatre. In his first official utterance in a Hungarian newspaper on 7 October 1888 he expressed disapproval of the custom whereby singers were permitted to use different languages (sometimes as many as four) in one single performance; he was amazed that Hungary was not intent on creating a national opera.

This emphasis on national character evoked widespread sympathy and made Mahler's position easier, even with those who objected to 'certain entries on his birth certificate' – his German affiliations even more than his Jewish origins. The opera house, for the opening of which Ferenc Erkel, the founder of the national school of opera, had written his *King Stephan*, and where a work by the Hungarian nobleman and amateur composer Geza von Zichy had been mounted a few months before Mahler's arrival, must not be lost to Hungarian culture. In these circumstances Mahler's support for all things Hungarian was a good tactical move. Yet it was not a mere ruse, for it conformed to his great artistic principle – clarity of communication. The musical theatre must be intelligible to the people, and the linguistic confusion of the guest stars was detrimental to comprehension. Splendid voices and brilliant orchestral playing were not enough. If Wagner's *Ring* was to conquer this public – and Mahler was determined that it should – one must dispense with foreign singers. The task now was to discover members of the ensemble who were capable of singing *Das Rheingold* and *Die Walküre* in Hungarian. Mahler, whose grasp of the language after a year's stay did not go beyond reciting a memorised speech of welcome, engaged an actor of the Hungarian National Theatre as 'elocution master', his job being to check the diction of the singers and supervise the translation of Wagner's texts.

Mahler devoted himself to this Wagner problem with all his zeal. He left to others the new productions of the autumn of 1888, including *Carmen*. On 26 January 1889 he conducted *Das Rheingold*, and on the following day *Die Walküre*. He deflected the clapping and shouting of the public on to the orchestra and the singers, among them the first Brünnhilde to sing in Hungarian, Mme Arabella Szilágyi, a member of the ensemble who had received scant attention until now. The fact that the 'German' opera director did not engage an experienced Wagner-soprano but went to the trouble of preparing a Hungarian Valkyrie for her task with dozens of rehearsals shows how seriously he took his responsibilities as head of a Hungarian national institution.

If ever in the history of the Dual Monarchy there was a man of the musical theatre who might justifiably be called an Austro-Hungarian artist, it was Gustav Mahler. He really extended the meaning of the 1867 settlement, which had granted rights to the Hungarian nation alone and ignored the claims of the Slavs. His German culture – as was shown in Prague – did not lessen his interest in the operatic merits of Smetana and Dvořák. His faith in the German art of Richard Wagner did not prevent his fostering the development of an autonomous Hungarian operatic culture. After the Wagner, Mahler produced a work by Ferenc Erkel, *Brankovics György*. Then it was Mozart's turn. *Le Nozze di Figaro*, in the repertoire since 1886, was musically and scenically refurbished.

The result was acclaimed by the press: never yet in the history of the opera house 'had an opera been given such an exemplary performance'. Mahler then did the same for *Don Giovanni* – this was the production which drew a famous quote from Brahms. Visiting the Hungarian capital during Mahler's tenure, he was invited to attend a performance. He did so reluctantly, believing that an educated musician would get greater pleasure from just reading this score, since no performance could do it justice. Mahler's interpretation convinced him of the contrary. To hear 'the true *Don Giovanni*', said Brahms, one had to go to Budapest.

For his second season (1889–90) Mahler announced works by Marschner and Nicolai and the continuation of the *Ring* cycle. Even the press which approved of him considered this 'too sharp a turn towards the German side'. Also, Mahler's attempt, welcomed at first, to build up a homegrown Hungarian team of singers, eventually met with the objections of a public that was not at all willing to go without its 'feast of beautiful voices'. He was told that there were 'gaps in the ensemble' – as though he did not know! What, then, did people want – a united Hungarian effort, or international stars, whose engagement must mean the loss of national character?

He had made the mistake of taking the national pretensions too seriously. The opera-going public and most of the critics would have been content with a few pro-Hungarian policy statements and the occasional performance of an opera by Erkel, for the rest happily wallowing in an Italian-German-Hungarian mishmash, provided this was put across by brilliant voices. No one appreciated the sacrifice Mahler was making, or that the 'Magyarisation' he pursued with such moral conviction was in fact a torture to him. 'If only I could hear a word sung in German again!' His longing for this was 'almost unbearable'. It seemed to him he had forgotten how to speak. Nor could he get down to composing, nor even to playing the piano, 'for what I'm doing here is all petty detail, and I can't concentrate on important things'.

In November 1889 he made his debut as a composer in Budapest. In the second subscription concert of the Krancsevics String Quartet the soprano Bianca Bianchi sang three songs by Mahler, with him at the piano. One of the songs was *Es wecket meine Liebe die Lieder immer wieder*. Mahler's accompanying was praised. The brief samples of his music could give no idea of what the performance of the D major Symphony on 20 November would reveal. That concert of the Philharmonic Orchestra under Mahler's direction gave the composer the long-desired opportunity of hearing how his orchestration sounded; and indeed, he thoroughly retouched the score during rehearsals. On the whole, this venture did Mahler more harm than good. The critic of the newspaper *Egyetértés* was 'infuriated' by the work. Its main defect, he said, was its 'endless length'. The symphony, which in its later, definitive form takes about fifty-five minutes, was at that time even lengthier. Between the first movement and the scherzo there was an andante, which Mahler subsequently took out.

Some reviewers linked their dislike of the symphony with criticism of Mahler's operatic activities: 'This composition', wrote the critic of the *Pesti Hirlap*, 'is as confused as Mahler's policy for the Opera.' Beniczky, who in the autumn of 1889 had been made Director in addition to being Government commissioner, was not put off by these opinions. The statement of accounts of 31 December 1889 showed that Mahler had even been financially successful – he had increased the annual receipts by 20,000 gulden. As long as Beniczky was in office, Mahler could feel secure. Even parliamentary criticism of 'foreign rule' at the opera house could not harm him, for he had at least one influential sponsor in the *Magnatentafel* (the Hungarian Upper House): Count Apponyi, a close friend of the leading figures in the Academy of Music. The cellist David Popper, the violin virtuoso and composer Jenö Hubay, and the director of the Academy, Ödön von Mihalovich, were all friends of Mahler's. In the autumn of 1890 Mahler conducted excerpts from Mihalovich's opera *Toldi* in a concert which also included a performance of Liszt's *Festklänge*; he conducted from memory. This sent up his stock again, but he was by now wary of relying on the favour of the Budapest public. His contacts with Pollini in Hamburg, which had never entirely lapsed since the Leipzig days, were resumed. The result was a financially satisfactory offer, not to mention the comforting prospect of hearing 'a word sung in German' once more.

His future thus secured, Mahler could face any untoward turn of events in Budapest operatic politics with equanimity. Certain influential circles were obviously trying to oust Beniczky from his position, which would in turn have jeopardised Mahler's. The instigator of this movement was the one-armed pianist and pupil of Liszt, Geza von Zichy, 'an overbearing nobleman', as some contemporaries described him, and a composer of sorts. This group was certain to find allies: nationalist critics who wanted to see Mahler replaced; orchestral musicians who could not come to terms with his demanding work schedules; opera-goers who did not care for Wagner's works either in German or Hungarian, but preferred a pleasing *bel canto* every time.

However, as yet the anti-Mahler front had not prevailed – the direction of policy was still his. At the end of 1890 he decided to put on a work that was bound to strike Budapest as daring. The playbill announced it as *Parasztbecsület*. Only the initiated knew that this opera had been first performed in May at the Teatro Costanzi in Rome. The composer's name, Pietro Mascagni, was unfamiliar even to educated music-lovers. And the original title, *Cavalleria rusticana*, meant as little to the Budapest public as does *Parasztbecsület* to those unfamiliar with Hungarian.

Mahler had got to know the score that summer. He was as enthusiastic about it as Verdi, who had greeted it with the exclamation: '*Non è vero poi che la tradizione della musica Italiana sia finita!*'* The performance on 26 December 1890 became a theatrical event of international significance. Arabella Szylágyi, the Hungarian Brünnhilde of the uncompleted *Ring* cycle, now became the Hungarian Santuzza. Not only press representatives from abroad but also directors of foreign opera houses attended the première. In Budapest began the worldwide success of the Italian composer who until then had made a modest living at an Italian provincial theatre. Mascagni, three years younger than Mahler, owed to him the beginnings of fame and wealth.

In January 1891 the united opponents of Beniczky and Mahler

* 'It's not true, then, that the tradition of Italian music is finished!'

struck the decisive blow: Beniczky was removed from office, and Count Zichy was appointed director. His first statement to the press could only be taken as a declaration of war against Mahler. Zichy said that the role of director should not be a purely administrative one. In artistic matters, too, he must have the final say. To be sure, Zichy's intentions were blocked by the wording of Mahler's contract, but he tried to get round that by introducing a new set of regulations. These contained a paragraph (no. 40) dangerous to Mahler, giving the director power to exercise some or all the rights of an artistic director. Not surprisingly this led to some sharp scenes between the two men, in the course of which Mahler tended to get carried away. The minister of the interior issued a directive reproving the opera director 'for his unseemly behaviour towards the chief director' and threatening him not only with suspension from his duties but with disciplinary action on future occasions.

On the whole, however, Mahler behaved diplomatically, although he knew that Zichy had gone so far as to offer his post, before it even fell vacant, to Felix Mottl, Court Conductor at Karlsruhe. Mottl refused to stab his colleague in the back, but forwarded Zichy's letter to him so that he might be aware of what was happening.

Fortified by his contract with Pollini in Hamburg, Mahler moved carefully. He was not willing to withdraw without some financial recompense. He realised that Zichy would like to rescind his ten-year contract of 1889, and therefore suggested drawing up a new two-year contract whose provisions would be in agreement with Zichy's new regulations. In recognition of his willingness to allow this redrafting and limitation of status, Mahler asked for an indemnity of 25,000 gulden to be paid to him on expiration of the new contract. Geza von Zichy saw his chance. He got the ministry to agree to pay the indemnity, and then informed Mahler by telephone of his readiness to terminate the existing contract by payment of the requested sum – not in two years' time, but immediately. Mahler consented, but asked for immediate disbursement of the money by the treasury. On receipt of the indemnity, which was paid out at once in cash, Mahler's contract ended. He wrote a farewell letter to the press, concluding with the words: 'I leave my post in the knowledge of having faithfully done my duty, and with the sincere wish that the Royal Opera may flourish and prosper.'

The 'overbearing nobleman' had achieved his purpose. Had he been cleverer, he might have saved the treasury 25,000 gulden. For Mahler had long been resolved to leave Budapest and to take up his post in Hamburg by 1 April 1891 at the latest. But he had kept this secret. It did not matter to him that the Budapest public, including some of his friends, would believe that he had been driven away against his will. A little touch of martyrdom would not come amiss. At his departure, Mahler received a gold baton from Count Apponyi, and a group of admirers brought him a laurel wreath decorated with a bow in the Hungarian national colours. Even Jenö Rakosi, one of the most nationalistic, indeed chauvinistic, Hungarian journalists declared that 'this German Jew' had been 'the only man capable of transforming the hitherto polyglot Hungarian opera into a unified national institution'.

The great power Mahler had enjoyed as director of the Budapest opera, the position in society he attained and the financial means at his disposal should have made him a happy man. He was even able to get away from the drudgery of the theatre. His periods of leave were ample, but they bore no creative fruit. During the Easter holidays of 1889 he was visited in Budapest by his friend the archaeologist Fritz Löhr, to whom he played on the piano fragments of the 'second symphony growing within him'. But some time was to pass before this took solid shape. Real musical creation was out of the question for Mahler at this time, despite his success. In 1889 he suddenly became a paterfamilias, responsible for the wellbeing of three children. News reached him in February that his father had died. His mother died in the autumn. His brother Alois at twenty-two was a ne'er-do-well who could not succeed in his business career and again and again fell back on Gustav's assistance. (In the end he fled to America, apparently for good reasons.) Leopoldine, married and living in Vienna, was gravely ill. She too died in this year of mourning. The responsibility for his younger sisters, Justine and Emma, and for sixteen-year-old Otto now rested on Gustav alone. Though Justine was old enough to look after herself, her health had been affected by the strain of nursing her sick and dying parents.

Mahler hurried from Budapest to Iglau, took Justine to Vienna for a medical examination and tried to revive her spirits. Fortunately Fritz Löhr and his wife were ready to help. He was able to lodge Otto and Emma with them, sending money from Budapest for their keep, for warm winter clothing and for the private tutor engaged for Otto. Mahler took Justine, now twenty-one, to stay with him in Budapest for a while. To her he transferred all the love he had given his mother. When the business in Iglau was sold and the modest affairs of his parents settled, he took some time off for a journey to Italy with Justine. From Florence, where they stayed in May 1890, he wrote to his friend in Vienna: 'Justine is thriving.'

The journey, which took him to Florence, Milan, Bologna and Genoa, was in no sense a cultural trip. Löhr commented, years later, on the letters he received from his friend: 'Any expectations of getting Mahler's impressions of Italy will be disappointed. Quite apart from the short time available, which did not favour extensive correspondence, Mahler lacked the mainspring of most travellers in Italy: enthusiasm for the incomparable art treasures.' This naturally struck the archaeologist as odd, but he understood the cause: Mahler was possessed by one art alone, by music. 'He did not visit any art collections, even the most famous, either in Florence or later in Paris . . . his own predilections were solely for the charms of Nature, which never failed him.'

Mahler once summed up the relationship of the musician to the plastic arts – or rather, his own view of it: 'It is perhaps intensely significant that the musician evinces scant interest in the plastic arts: it is his nature to explore things in depth – *beyond* their external appearance.'

This statement needs some qualification, for if it were taken literally, his subsequent achievement as a stage producer would remain inexplicable. Even people in whom the visual sense does not predominate are capable, in the musical theatre, of gauging the adequacy and meaningfulness of gestures and movements, since events on the stage, their setting and the light that illumines them, are determined by the music. Mahler, who knew how to learn from others, was indebted to Löhr for many flashes of insight. Löhr, for his part, must have been sensitive enough to realise that Mahler's 'optical reactions' were more readily stimulated by philosophical reflections than by simple visual perception. He drew Mahler's attention to the diaries and letters of Sulpiz Boisserée, the great scholar of medieval German art. From here further vistas opened into the life of Goethe. Mahler was struck 'in the strangest way'. He felt tempted to 'eat his way through a sizeable chunk of Goethe literature'; moreover, he gained an insight into the Romantic view of the Middle Ages, as well as into German Romanticism itself.

Mahler's first contact with the works of the Romantic writer Clemens Brentano had also come through Löhr, with whom he discussed the stageworthiness of Brentano's comedy *Ponce de Leon*. When Mahler later turned to the collection *Des Knaben Wunderhorn* by Brentano and Achim von Arnim, he was mentally well prepared for it.

In 1891, at the time when Mahler left Budapest, Nietzsche irrupted into his world. The first impetus came from a prominent member of his circle, Siegfried Lipiner, author of *Der Entfesselte Prometheus* (*Prometheus Unbound*), whom Nietzsche had called 'a veritable genius'. Lipiner, who came from Galicia, was employed as librarian at the Reichsrat (Parliament). The power of his mind and the brilliance of his exposition captivated everybody. Richard Wagner had taken a liking to him and brought him to Bayreuth for a short while. Lipiner is remembered now as the translator of the great Polish poet, Adam Mickiewicz. His dramas are forgotten. Together with Mahler he planned a trilogy on the life of Christ intended for the musical theatre; this occupied him throughout his life.

Lipiner was devoted to the plastic arts. What attracted Mahler to him was the enthusiasm he radiated. On the other hand, he was alienated by Lipiner's fragmented mode of thinking, his progress by leaps and bounds which more often than not prevented him from achieving perfection, or even completion. Similarly ambivalent was Mahler's reaction to Nietzsche, whose fiery language he admired even when he could not agree with its intellectual content. Bruno Walter noted a most revealing 'musical' objection of Mahler's against Nietzsche: the master of the large symphonic form was characteristically irritated by Nietzsche's aphoristic style.

Mahler's concern with structural cohesion seems a crucial tenet of his aesthetics. That he took Goethe for his model in this does not alter the fact that Mahler's art was embedded in the Austrian tradition of form which can be traced from the Viennese classics to the school of Schönberg. The structural severity of Schönberg's works (except for the erratic boulders thrown up by his expressionist phase), the transplantation of sonata form into opera undertaken by Alban Berg, Anton Webern's philosophy that defines life as 'preserved form' – all these bear witness to an impulse, irreversible since the quartets of Haydn, towards the supremacy of soundforms which created their own laws.

Vienna, the town that was subject to this musical law, was to be Mahler's home. Here too lived the friends he cared for, and his brother and sisters. In the autumn of 1891, when Mahler was already working in Hamburg, Löhr told him that he was going on a study course to Italy and that it was time to make a permanent home for Justine, Emma and Otto. An apartment was taken in a house in the Breite Gasse – no. 4. Here Otto and Emma grew up, looked after by Justine and supported and supervised from a distance by Gustav. The sisters, Mahler thought, would find husbands sooner or later; he would not have to do more than augment from his own means the scanty dowries of their Iglau inheritance. Otto, on the other hand, was to be educated as befitted what Mahler believed to be his musical talent. He thought Otto was a gifted composer. We know nothing of his works. All we know is that Otto Mahler at the age of twenty-two took a revolver and shot himself. He left a note saying that he had had enough of life and was returning his ticket of admission.

Of Bernhard and Marie Mahler's twelve children, eight had died by 1896. Alois, who had given his brother nothing but trouble, had disappeared. There remained Gustav, Justine and Emma, a united family. Even though he earned his living in Hamburg at the time, he felt Vienna to be his home. Iglau was forgotten. A single piece of furniture Mahler took to Hamburg reminded him of his parental home: an old arm-chair with torn linen covering, which had been used by his sick father and was now Mahler's favourite chair. Without having married or had children of his own, he had become a father.

Even after the war of 1870, in the German Empire which had emerged from the victory over the French, Hamburg, the most powerful German city, was able to maintain its special position. Only after prolonged hesitation did the citizens agree to a customs union with the new empire. At the beginning of this era Hamburg wanted to enjoy the fruits of German predominance as well as the advantages of economic independence. The Hamburg theatre, too, flourished in these empire-building days. In 1873 a man was installed as lessee and director of the Stadttheater who had shown himself an efficient manager in more than one European town. Pollini, as Bernhard Pohl of Cologne called himself, had begun his career as a tenor and had then travelled with an Italian opera troupe, as their impresario. In 1865 he settled at Lemberg as a theatrical director. Soon he was wealthy enough to take over the management of the Italian opera in St Petersburg and Moscow. Then in 1873 he became the ruler of the Hamburg Stadttheater, where he invested the profits he had made in Russia. A few years later he enlarged his dominions by incorporating the Stadttheater of Altona and the Thalia Theatre. Pollini, whom singers and conductors nicknamed 'Mono-Pollini' because of his commanding position, had many financial and artistic successes in Hamburg. As early as 1876 he staged Verdi's *Aida*, following this in 1878 with Wagner's *Ring des Nibelungen*. *Carmen* reached the Hamburg stage five years after its première (1880), and in 1888 Pollini presented the first German performance of Verdi's *Otello*.

The manager of the Hamburg theatre was equally famous as a

talent scout and an unscrupulous exploiter of his personnel. He contrived to obtain some of the best singers of the age – among them the Wagnerian dramatic soprano Rosa Sucher and the baritone Eugen Gursa – and then to employ these stars in a way that guaranteed a high return on the capital invested. The cost of new rows of boxes provided with anterooms, of the new colonnaded portico fronting the Dammtorstrasse, had to be recovered. The brilliant effect of the red and gold auditorium had to be reflected in equally brilliant box-office takings. And in 1891, when Mahler came to Hamburg, Pollini was making renewed efforts to modernise his theatre. A new heating system was installed and battery-powered electric lighting introduced. While in the nearby Altona Stadttheater a recklessly gesticulating conductor might still burn his fingers on the hot cylinders of the gas lamps placed by his desk, at Hamburg conducting was done by electric light.

The Stadttheater was a paying enterprise, highly up to date as befitted a town even then building its first electric tramway. But operatic production itself was still untouched by the revolutionary new ideas that had emanated from Bayreuth. Everything still revolved around the vocalist: the staging was left to the whim of the singer, to accident or to precedent; the function of the orchestra was merely to provide an accompaniment. The art of operatic production in those days, so Bruno Walter said, looking back in sorrow, was ninety per cent resignation.

Mahler was faced with the task of gaining control over the stage from the rostrum. That was not so easy here as in Budapest. As director of the Royal Hungarian Opera he had carried far more authority. In Hamburg he was tied to a theatre manager used to considering every artistic project from the angle of its profitability. An old hand like Pollini could not be won over by purely artistic considerations. The new concept of the union of music and stage had to be realised by constant, persistent attention to detail.

In numerous rehearsals with individual singers, himself accompanying at the piano, Mahler sought to bring out the emotional content predetermined by the music, in order to achieve a better scenic realisation – without the cooperation, even against the will, of the official producer. Pollini was not keen on all this. The main thing, to his mind, was the beauty and strength of the voices; everything else was unimportant. When Mahler called for expressiveness and sensitive acting, Pollini thought this eccentric. However, he gave Mahler, whose talent he clearly recognised, a free hand in pursuing his ideas, as long as they did not interfere with his commercial projects.

One of these projects was the German première of Tchaikovsky's *Eugène Onegin*, to be conducted by the composer himself. Tchaikovsky came to Hamburg at the beginning of 1892. During rehearsals it became clear that the German version of the libretto presented some difficulties. Changes had to be made with which Tchaikovsky was unable to cope, and in the end he became so agitated that he refused to conduct the opera. Mahler grasped the baton and his opportunity. On 19 January 1892 he conducted the première, which the composer thought 'quite marvellous'. In a letter to his nephew Tchaikovsky wrote: 'The conductor here is not of the usual kind, but a man of genius who would give his life to conduct the first performance.'

Mahler also appeared as concert conductor. In April 1892 he conducted a performance of Bruckner's *Te Deum*, which, he wrote to the composer, deeply moved the audience.

In spite of all his reservations, Pollini was well satisfied with his vigorous Chief Conductor. He recommended Mahler to Sir Augustus Harris, the impresario of Covent Garden, as the most important conductor for a season of German opera in London. Mahler was accompanied to London by such singers as Rosa Sucher, Theodor Reichmann, Max Alvary and Katharina Klafsky, and also by a section of the Hamburg orchestra which Pollini, with three theatres at his disposal, could afford to release on favourable terms. Pollini's opposite number in London must have been gratified by the success of the season. Applause for the *Ring* knew no bounds. 'Yours truly was tops again!' Mahler wrote slangily to a friend, and this is borne out by the reviews that appeared in *The Times* and the *Morning Post*. In a review of *Tristan*, 'only the word "perfect" could do justice to the orchestra, which worked wonders under the direction of Herr Mahler'. The *Sunday Times* critic forty years later still remembered Mahler's technique of individual rehearsals and the impression of unity between the orchestral and vocal strands, which surpassed any previous Wagner performance.

There were also some dissenting voices, which were no less revealing. They were raised against the first London performance of *Fidelio* ever to be given in German. Incredible as it seems today, Beethoven's opera had hitherto always been presented in Italian in England, with specially composed Italian recitatives replacing the German dialogue. Something of an Italianate manner had apparently rubbed off on to Beethoven's music. Mahler's interpretation, and in particular his version of the *Leonora* No. 3 Overture (which was played before the second act, and not, as Mahler subsequently used it in Vienna, as 'transformation music' before the last scene), utterly baffled some of the critics. With what justification, asked the reviewer of the *Daily Telegraph*, did the Hamburg conductor begin the allegro at a moderate tempo, only to follow this with an accelerando? The alteration of basic tempi, which Mahler made into a principle of musico-dramatic expression, in accordance with Richard Wagner's teaching, evoked the opposition of those music-lovers whose taste was formed partly by Italian opera, partly by the Mendelssohn tradition. Evenness of tempo and a persistently fast pulse in an allegro, however, seemed insensitive to Mahler. His modifications of tempo had already earned him the acclaim of the young in Leipzig and the Wagnerians in Budapest. He disliked nothing more than to be put on a level with an 'elegant conductor of the Mendelssohn school'. Even in purely instrumental music (such as the *Leonora* No. 3 Overture), expressiveness was enhanced by the method derived from Wagner's music dramas, of varying the basic tempo.

This contradicted the belief that the tempi prescribed by a composer were to be strictly observed for as long as they were valid, a belief held by some of Mahler's London reviewers. The performance of *Fidelio*, Mahler wrote to a friend in Hamburg, 'has been violently attacked and opposed by half the critics here. The public, on the other hand, granted me absolution for my blasphemy by a positive

storm of applause. After every act I have to appear at the footlights –
the whole house just goes on shouting "Mahler" until I appear.'

His London success and the subsequent new productions in Hamburg strengthened Mahler's position. In the 1893–94 season he
produced two important new works: Puccini's *Manon Lescaut*, first
performed in Turin only in February 1893 and now presented in
Hamburg with the composer in the audience; and Verdi's *Falstaff*,
the beauty of which had kindled the enthusiasm of German opera
experts soon after its Milan première of February 1893, though the
general public, then as today, was slow in giving this masterpiece
its due.

Mahler now had the satisfaction of receiving appreciation from
the great musician whose interest he had tried to arouse with that
importunate letter when he was a young conductor in Kassel. Von
Bülow now recognised his genius: the interaction between stage
and music achieved in Mahler's productions pleased Bülow so
much that he had a laurel wreath presented to Mahler – probably at
a benefit night – bearing an olive-green bow with the message:
'*Dem Pygmalion der Hamburger Oper* (To the Pygmalion of the
Hamburg Opera) – *Hans von Bülow*.'

Von Bülow had seen the transformation wrought by Mahler.
His admiration for the 'Pygmalion' who had brought the stage to
life by the strength of his baton was manifested on suitable and
unsuitable occasions. Mahler attended the concerts arranged in
Hamburg by the Berlin agency Wolff, which were conducted by
von Bülow. The esoteric ways in which von Bülow showed his
esteem for Mahler at these concerts struck the latter as 'comical'.
He wrote to Löhr:

He [von Bülow] makes eyes at me (I'm sitting in the front row) at
every beautiful passage. From the rostrum he hands down the scores of
unknown works for me to follow during the performance. The moment he
catches sight of me, he honours me ostentatiously with a deep bow. Sometimes he talks to me from the platform. . . .

Mahler inevitably felt tempted to convert this good will to his
own purposes. Here was a chance to entrust the D major Symphony,

which in Budapest had not found the recognition it deserved, to the hands of a master-conductor. But von Bülow was not interested in Mahler as a composer, despite his admiration for the conductor. Once when some orchestral songs of Mahler's were on the programme of a Wolff Agency concert, von Bülow asked the manager to invite Mahler to take over that part of the programme as he himself found these songs 'much too strange'.

Mahler tried to interest him in an orchestral work in C minor which he had sketched out long ago: the *Totenfeier* (Obsequies) of the First Symphony's hero, which was later to become the first movement of the Second Symphony. Von Bülow declared himself ready to hear the composer play this on the piano. But after a few bars he stopped up his ears in horror, eventually exclaiming: 'If this is still music, I know nothing of music!'

Mahler's relation to von Bülow was ambivalent: he admired him, yet felt the master's rejection of his compositions as a hostile act. When von Bülow fell ill and there was a possibility that Mahler would deputise for him, he declared himself ready 'to take up the contest with von Bülow'. The reverence he evinced towards the master had a double meaning. He wanted to follow his example, and also to follow him in the sense of replacing him. The history of the Second Symphony in C, long since begun and now in the doldrums, tells us something about the relationship between the two men. It was not only his everyday tasks at the theatre that kept Mahler from working on it, but also some inner resistance. This was only removed by the news of von Bülow's death (he died on 12 February 1894 in Cairo where he had sought a cure for a serious illness) and after the great conductor's funeral in Hamburg. In his psychoanalytical study *The Haunting Melody*, Theodore Reik has even put forward the theory that Mahler in his heart of hearts desired the death of the man who refused to recognise him as a composer. Though we may not go as far as this, there is no denying that von Bülow's death removed at one stroke all the obstacles that had blocked the completion of the Second Symphony. Three years after von Bülow's death Mahler himself described the effect of the funeral on his own creative work:

I had long considered the idea of employing a chorus for the last movement, only the fear that this might be seen as a superficial imitation of
Beethoven made me hesitate time and again. Then von Bülow died, and I
went to his funeral. My mood as I sat there thinking of the man who had
died, was wholly in tune with the work that was growing in my mind.
Suddenly the choir chanted from the organ-loft the Klopstock chorale
Auferstehn! It was like a flash of lightning – the whole work now stood
clearly before me!

We have confirmation from another source of the creative energy
released by that experience. The composer J. B. Foerster in his
Erinnerungen an Gustav Mahler, published in 1920, tells us that
shortly after von Bülow's funeral he found Mahler busy working
on the last movement of his symphony. Hitherto the possible
significance for Mahler's *Totenfeier* of the funeral rites in the
Hamburg Michaelis church has been considered only from the
literary aspect. Theodor Reik has, however, revealed the creative
dynamism behind it: the birth of the Second Symphony from the
experience of death, from Mahler's relationship to von Bülow, the
paternal model he wanted, in two senses of the word, to 'follow'.
Reik might have adduced further evidence of ambivalent feelings
towards a father-figure by referring to the chair which Mahler had
brought along from Iglau and in which he, the supporter of the
family, now sat. The paternal throne, to elaborate this theory,
was now augmented by von Bülow's insignia of power. Mahler
treasured the laurel wreath and its bow that von Bülow had given
him. Foerster noted the bow on the wall above the simple bedstead
in Mahler's first Hamburg dwelling; Bruno Walter was to see it,
later still, in Mahler's Hamburg studio.

But instead of pursuing these psychological speculations, let us
return to the effect of von Bülow's obsequies on Mahler's creativity.
We shall see that Klopstock's text was to be no more than a
starting-point. The composer of the Second Symphony could
justly claim that in the Finale he had been forced to fashion
his own literary mould for his thoughts and emotions. Klopstock's
ode inspired him to write his own different, more comprehensive
text.

*   *   *

Mahler's fear that his Second Symphony might be taken 'as a superficial imitation of Beethoven' is understandable. A composition that demanded solo voices, chorus and orchestra, and suddenly after an hour's duration, broke out into a concluding chorus, was bound to conjure up memories of Beethoven's Ninth. Mahler's C minor Symphony is related to Beethoven's last symphonic work in yet another respect. The philosophical nature of the symphony – which Beethoven expressed only once, in his setting of Schiller's *Ode to Joy* – for Mahler became a creative principle, an attempt to 'build a world' in every symphony. For Mahler, the text is more than a subject which he sets to music. He begins with a musicophilosophical idea, and then looks for a suitable text. 'The last movement of my Second Symphony really obliged me to search through the whole of world literature, including the Bible, in order to find the liberating word. . . .' If the search is successful, Mahler goes on to arrange the literary material in his own way. J. B. Foerster in his Hamburg reminiscences quotes from the programme of von Bülow's funeral the text of Klopstock's ode as sung on that occasion. It is instructive to compare this text with Mahler's version:

Klopstock's Auferfsteh'n
(Text according to the programme book of February 1894)

Aufersteh'n, ja auferfsteh'n wirst du
mein Staub, nach kurzer Ruh',
unsterblich's Leben
wird, der dich schuf, dir geben. Halleluja!

Wieder aufzublüh'n, werd' ich gesä't;
der Herr der Ernte geht
und sammelt Garben
uns ein, die starben. Halleluja!

Tag des Dank's, der Freudenthränen Tag!
Du meines Gottes Tag!
Wenn ich im Grabe genug geschlummert habe,
erweckst du mich.

[Thou shalt arise, yea, rise,
dust of my body, after a brief rest;
immortal life shall He
who made thee, give thee, Alleluia!

Again to blossom am I sown;
the Lord of Harvest goes forth
collecting sheaves:
we who have died. Alleluia!

Day of thanksgiving, day of joyous tears!
Day of my God!
When I have slumbered in the grave awhile
Thou shalt awaken me.]

Mahler's version

Aufersteh'n, ja aufersteh'n wirst du
Mein Staub, nach kurzer Ruh!
Unsterblich Leben
Wird, der dich rief, dir geben.

Wieder aufzublüh'n, wirst du gesät!
Der Herr der Ernte geht
Und sammelt Garben
Uns ein, die starben.

O glaube, mein Herz, es geht dir nichts verloren!
Dein ist, ja dein, was du gesehnt,
Was vergangen, aufersteht!
O glaube: du wardst nicht umsonst geboren,
Hast nicht umsonst gelebt, gelitten,

Was entstanden ist, das muss vergehen,
Was vergangen, auferstehen!
Hör auf, zu beben!
Bereite dich, zu leben!

O Schmerz, du Alldurchdringender,
Dir bin ich entrungen!
O Tod, du Allbezwinger,
Nun bist du bezwungen!

Mit Flügeln, die ich mir errungen
Werde ich entschweben!
Sterben werd' ich, um zu leben!

Aufersteh'n, ja aufersteh'n wirst du,
Mein Herz, in einem Nu!
Was du geschlagen,
Zu Gott wird es dich tragen.

[Thou shalt arise, yea, rise,
dust of my body, after a brief rest.
Immortal life shall He
who called thee, give thee.

Again to blossom thou art sown.
The Lord of Harvest goes forth
collecting sheaves:
we who have died.

Have faith, my heart, for nought is lost to thee.
All that thou longed for shall be thine,
what is gone shall rise again.
Have faith: thou wast not born in vain,
Thy life, thy suffering were not in vain.

All that has grown must perish,
what perishes will rise again.
Be not afraid!
Prepare thyself to live!

All-pervading Pain,
I have escaped thee!
All-conquering Death,
Now thou art conquered.

On wings that I have won
in ardent toil and love
I shall soar to the light
that never eye has seen.

On wings that I have won
I shall rise up again.
I die, to live again.

Thou shalt arise, yea, rise,
My heart, instantly.
Whatever strength was thine
shall carry thee to God.]

Mahler has transformed the pious resignation of the original text into an incantation against the power of death: 'Be not afraid! Prepare thyself to live!' The earthly grave has vanished from Mahler's poem. Death does not extinguish life, for resurrection is certain. All the toil of earthly life is meaningful. The creed is: You were not born in vain, nor have you suffered in vain.

Henceforth his friends called Mahler a 'God-seeker'. The Second Symphony rather stamps Mahler as a man who has found God. Mahler's long persevering struggle with the Finale of this symphony can only be understood if one remembers his profound sense of mission. He was obsessed by the idea that his compositions were in the truest sense indestructible; nor was he afraid to assert that art and humanity would be the poorer without his C minor Symphony. it is true, of course, that lesser musicians have created their lesser, works in the same belief. Without creative illusions, artistic labour is not possible even at a lower aesthetic level. In Mahler, however, this philosophy is relevant to his work as a composer. It becomes a concept of workmanship, ensuring creative continuity. Mahler links the movements of his symphonies with thematic references; he steers towards the finale from the very beginning; he even connects one work with the next – strains of the *Wayfaring lad* appear in the First Symphony, and the hero of the First is in the Second borne to his grave – towards resurrection, rather.

The four movement pattern, preserved in the First Symphony, is cast aside in the Second. After the symphonically developed funeral march (first movement) the score requires 'a pause of at least five minutes'. This is to prepare for the memory of 'a blissful moment in the life of the dear departed': an andante moderato (second movement) in the form of an Austrian Ländler, played by a reduced orchestra in which the strings predominate. The third chapter in this symphonic novel expresses the 'spirit of unbelief'. 'World and life', explains the composer, 'become a dismal noise.'

The music here harks back to an earlier orchestral song, *Des Antonius von Padua Fischpredigt* (St Anthony of Padua's Sermon of the Fish) from the collection *Des Knaben Wunderhorn*. Here again, as in the First Symphony, Mahler evolves a symphonic structure out of the pre-existing song. Freed from the text, the music in this symphonic version unfolds its latent energy, extending its form beyond that of the orchestral song and building up to a violent climax of despair. The fourth movement begins with the solo of the alto voice: '*O Röschen rot, der Mensch liegt in grösster Not, der Mensch liegt in tiefster Pein, je lieber möcht' ich im Himmel sein!*' [O red rose, man is sorely troubled, man is sorely tried; I wish the more I were in heaven!] Mahler took the text from *Des Knaben Wunderhorn*, finding in it 'the touching voice of naive faith'. With a wild outburst – so the score demands – the Finale breaks into the dying fall of this fourth movement, and the composer sets out its programme in the following words:

There sounds forth the voice of the caller: the end of all living creatures is come; the Day of Judgment is at hand, and all the terror of the day of days has broken out.

The earth trembles, the graves open, the dead arise and march in unending array. The great and the small of this earth – kings and beggars, just and godless – all throng forward – the call for pity and mercy sounds dreadfully in our ears. Ever more horrible are the cries, all our senses falter, consciousness fails us at the approach of the Holy Spirit. The Last Trump sounds forth – the trumpets of the Apocalypse blare; in the midst of the dreadful silence we seem to hear a far, far away nightingale, like a last trembling echo of earthly life! Softly begins a choir of the saints and the blessed: 'Thou shalt arise, yea, arise.' Then the glory of God is revealed. A wonderful gentle light pierces us to the heart – all is still and blissful. And lo, there is no judgment – there are no sinners, no just, no great – and no small – there is no punishment and no reward. An all-powerful loving kindness fills us with joyous knowledge and life.

In this fifth and final movement, an offstage orchestra is employed, in furtherance of Mahler's concept of 'spatial sound' as already manifested in *Das Klagende Lied*. In this respect, too,

Mahler broke with formal conventions, The established confrontation of the source of sound and the public no longer satisfied him. The sound should not only reach the listener from the concert hall platform, but must be omnipresent. To this purpose Mahler veils the distant sound by mixing it with a plainly audible cantilena coming from the instruments placed on the platform. There is, moreover, an explicit direction for the stereophony of the Last Judgment. The score prescribes that the four trumps of the Apocalypse must 'blow from opposite directions'.

The chorus of the saints and the blessed ('Arise') begins unaccompanied after the last nightingale call of the piccolo. This form was suggested to Mahler by the boys' choir of the Michaelis church, as well as by the chorales of Bach which he studied in Hamburg.

The influence of Bach's music on Mahler is shown not only by the chorale-like entry of the Resurrection Chorus, but by other parts of the Second Symphony showing Mahler's preoccupation with Bach's counterpoint. The encounter with Bach, vital for all Austrian masters from Mozart to Webern, leading as it did to a modified incorporation of counterpoint into the structure of sonata and symphony, duly enriched Mahler's style. Coming home from the Stadttheater, he would take up the works of Bach and play them on the piano. What he particularly admired was the purity of the workmanship. 'This cleanses me,' he once told his friend Foerster, 'in this Castalian spring I can wash off the dirt of the stage.'

Mention of 'the dirt of the stage' once more underlines the hostility towards the theatre felt by Mahler the composer, who is so different from Mahler the theatre conductor that one is tempted to speak of split personality. True, he takes over all the craftsmanlike technical devices of the musical theatre which can be useful to his symphonies, but he is always aware of the 'definitive parting of the ways between symphonic and dramatic music'.

The symphony, as he sees it, must guard its autonomy. It may, however, assimilate whatever technical advances have been made in other fields of creative music: the classic Viennese sonata, the polyphony of Bach, the orchestral mixtures and tempo modifications of Wagner, the alienation of sound produced by the unusual handling of instruments, the 'true to nature' tolling of bells as well as the assorted noises of tomtoms, cymbals and whips. In this sense, too, Mahler set out to 'build a world'. His striving for synthesis laid him open to the reproach of eclecticism, levelled against him in his own time as it still is today.

Synthesis is the essence of Mahler's philosophy in his symphonies, combining in a uniquely personal manner philosophical concepts, ecstatic confessions, expressionist outbursts, and the poetic innocence of *Wunderhorn* Romanticism.

By the time he was at Leipzig (but probably even earlier) Mahler had discovered *Des Knaben Wunderhorn*, the collection of old German songs made at the beginning of the nineteenth century by Achim von Arnim and Clemens Brentano. Of the fourteen songs with pianoforte accompaniment which Mahler published in 1892 and which are now known to us as *Lieder und Gesänge aus der Jugendzeit*, nine are settings of texts from the *Wunderhorn* collection.

The piano part of these early songs already shows Mahler striving for complexity of sound texture. The frequent direction *Mit starkem Pedalgebrauch* ('With much pedal') aims at a dense flow of sound. At times Mahler requires the piano to imitate other instruments. Trills in the left hand are meant to represent muted drum-rolls; the word 'Schalmei' (shepherd's pipe) accompanying a simple tune suggests the shepherd boy referred to in the text. It is the sort of colouring that demands orchestral realisation. As a song composer, Mahler gradually emancipated himself from the piano. How intent he was on shaking off its fetters may be seen from the advice he gave to a musician friend of his Hamburg days, the critic and composer Max Marschalk (the future brother-in-law of Gerhard Hauptmann). He told him that 'mood-music was a trap': the composer should not conceive his work in terms of pianoforte sound and then transcribe it for orchestra in a necessarily inhibited, pianoforte-conditioned manner, but should from the first think in plastic, orchestrally inspired ideas. Mahler admits that in his early days as a composer he himself was far too tied to the piano.

This critical self-assessment came at a time when he was making real progress as a song composer, witness the ten songs with orchestral accompaniment on texts from *Des Knaben Wunderhorn*. The dating of these songs seems to present some difficulties. According to H. F. Redlich, they date from the years 1888–99, while E. Ratz in his catalogue gives 1892–95. On stylistic grounds the songs may with some certainty be placed in the Hamburg period (1891–97). Difficulties of dating are partly due to Mahler's working methods. Between the first conception and publication he subjected his compositions to many modifications. This certainly happened with the *Lieder eines fahrenden Gesellen* which were written in the Kassel period (1883–85) but, according to Natalie Bauer-Lechner, were cast in their orchestral form only in 1896 – the same period that produced the orchestral songs on *Wunderhorn* texts.

What was the reason for Mahler's fascination with this romantic folksong collection? Comparing texts previously written by Mahler himself with the *Wunderhorn* poetry of his orchestral songs, there seems a close relationship. Bruno Walter thinks that the discovery of the *Wunderhorn* must have struck Mahler as a spiritual homecoming.

There he found everything that stirred his emotions, presented in the same way as he felt it: Nature, piety, longing, love, parting, death, the spirit world, soldiering, youthful high spirits, children's games, whimsy – all this lived in him as it did in those poems, and so his songs poured forth. The happy union of native poetry with a deeply kindred music produced a series of enchanting works of art which revealed the now fully formed personality of a self-sufficient man of powerful originality.

This view, convincing as it may seem at first, is not wholly satisfactory, since it ignores the criticism Mahler exercised on his chosen texts. The sound itself may be taken as an instance of this criticism. The harsh abruptness with which Mahler lets the major mood clash with the minor in the orchestration of the *Wunderhorn* militates against any naive confrontation of 'grave' and 'gay'. Harmonic relationships characteristic of folk music are exploited by Mahler, and at the same time superseded. A cheerful phrase may be given an ominous and sombre setting, while a word like *traurig* (sad) – at the close of the first song, *Der Schildwache Nachtlied* – may land on a major chord, only subsequently negated by a minor.

Mahler adapts the lyrics to his own particular use. Among hundreds of songs he chooses those that approximate to his mood. He handles the *Wunderhorn* collection like a chapbook, and indeed it was as a chapbook, for everyday or inspiring occasions, that Goethe had recommended the anthology, which Achim von Arnim and Clemens Brentano had dedicated to him. In his famous review of 1806 Goethe wrote:

> By rights, this little book should be found in every house where un-spoilt people live, lying by the window, or under the mirror, or wherever song and cookery books are kept, so that people can open it at a moment's notice, in good or in bad moods, for sympathy or stimulation, though it may be necessary to leaf through a few pages to find it. The best place of all, however, would be on the piano of the amateur or practised musician, so that full justice can be done to the songs, either by means of their well-known traditional tunes or by fitting them to suitable airs. Or, God willing, they may give rise to grand new melodies.

Mahler was certainly inspired by those songs. Whether he found in them sympathy, or at times merely stimulation, they made demands not only on his musical powers but on his literary gift for changing or developing. One of Mahler's most beautiful orchestral songs owes its origin to a radical departure from the original words. It is based on a song which in the *Wunderhorn* collection bears the title *Unbeschreibliche Freude* (Indescribable Joy). Mahler rejected this title. In his study the verses which speak of blissful sensual love were turned into a melancholy orchestral song. This is the original text:

'*Wer ist denn draussen und klopfet an,*
Der mich so leise wecken kann?' –
'*Das ist der Herzallerliebste dein,*
Steh auf und lass mich zu dir ein.'

Das Mädchen stand auf und liess ihn ein
Mit seinem schneeweissen Hemdelein,

Mit seinen schneeweissen Beinen,
Das Mädchen fing an zu weinen.

'Ach weine nicht, du Liebste mein,
Aufs Jahr sollt du mein eigen sein;
Mein eigen sollt du werden,
O Liebe auf grüner Erden.

Ich wollt', dass alle Felder wären Papier,
Und alle Studenten schrieben hier,
Sie schrieben ja hier die liebe lange Nacht,
Sie schrieben uns beiden die Liebe doch nicht ab.'

['Who is out there, knocking at the door?
Who wakens me up so gently?' –
'It is your own heart's darling,
Rise up and let me in.'

The girl arose and let him in,
All in her snow-white shift,
With legs of snowy white,
The girl began to weep.

'O do not weep, my darling,
Next year you shall be mine,
My own love you shall be,
My love on this green earth.

I wish all the fields were paper,
And the students all writing thereon,
They could write the whole night through,
And never write our love away.']

Mahler deleted the last stanza. In the second, he eliminated the snow-white shift and snowy white legs that gave a trivial physical sensuality to the lovers' meeting: instead their union is symbolised in a new verse by the song of a nightingale. Additional lines transform the pure love song into a story with a sad ending. What the ghostly muted horns and trumpet hinted at the beginning is borne out by Mahler's text and finally confirmed by the dying fall of the minor close. The 'indescribable joy' of the *Wunderhorn* poem has turned into an orchestral song which does not preserve even the basic mood of the textual original. The new title is *Wo die schönen Trompeten blasen.*

'Wer ist denn draussen und wer klopfet an,
der mich so leise, so leise wecken kann?'—
'Das ist der Herzallerliebste dein,
steh auf und lass mich zu dir ein!

Was soll ich hier noch länger ste'n?
Ich seh' die Morgenröte aufgeh'n,
die Morgenröt', zwei helle Stern.
Bei meinem Schatz da wär' ich gern,
bei meinem Herzallerliebe.'

Das Mädchen stand auf und liess ihn ein;
sie heisst ihn auch willkommen sein.
'Willkommen, lieber Knabe mein,
so lang hast du gestanden!'

Sie reicht ihm auch die schneeweisse Hand.
Von ferne sang die Nachtigall;
das Mädchen fing zu weinen an.

'Ach weine nicht, du Liebste mein,
aufs Jahr sollst du mein Eigen sein.
Mein Eigen sollst du werden gewiss,
wie's keine sonst auf Erden ist!
O Lieb auf grüner Erden.

Ich zieh' in Krieg auf grüne Heid',
die grüne Heide, die ist so weit.
Allwo dort die schönen Trompeten blasen,
da ist mein Haus, mein Haus von grünem Rasen.'

['Who is out there, knocking at the door,
who knows to wake me up so gently?'
'It is your own heart's darling,
rise up and let me in.

Why should I longer stand and wait?
I see the red dawn rising,
the red dawn, and two bright stars,
with my darling I long to be,
with my own heart's darling.'

The girl arose and let him in,
she also made him welcome:
'Welcome, my dearest lad,
so long you had to wait!'

She offers him her snow-white hand.
Far away the nightingale sang.
The girl began to weep.

'O do not weep, my darling,
next year you shall be mine,
My own you shall become for sure
as none other is in this world,
O love on this green earth.

I go to war on a green heath,
a green heath far away;
where the bright trumpets blow,
there lies my house, my house of green sward.']

Mahler, far from merely fitting notes to pre-existing words, created and shaped his text according to the musical conception in his mind. Once he had got the words, he developed the vocal line from the diction. Even his instrumental music betrays its origin in songlike conceptions, which gives his symphonic works an almost linguistic quality. The tuneful, diatonic form of his symphonic themes contrasts notably with the oppressive chromatic indeterminateness set up as a goal by many of his composer contemporaries (and attained by some in masterly fashion). It is difficult to deduce from Mahler's symphonies his veneration for the composer of the agonised music of *Tristan*, bleeding from all its harmonic wounds. The world Mahler creates in every one of his symphonies derives its coherence from a groundplan firmly based on natural structure and buttressed by trumpet-calls, fanfares, vocal lines resembling folk music and harmonic cadences.

The *Wunderhorn* continued to interest him; 1899 produced the songs *Revelge* and *Der Tamboursg'sell*. However, the significance of the *Wunderhorn* settings goes beyond the individual compositions. The songs are not simply self-contained works, but also the germ

cells from which the symphonies grew. Mahler's idea of the in-
destructibility of human effort, his theory, propounded in the
Second Symphony, that 'nothing is ever lost', applied to his
technique of composition. In every new work he critically re-
examined the preceding ones. The hero of the First Symphony has
his funeral rites in the Second, the Third presents a philosophy of
nature in six movements: summer, flowers, animals, man, angels
and love. In the third movement, *Was mir die Tiere im Wald
erzählen* (What the beasts of the forest tell me), Mahler goes back
to an earlier *Wunderhorn* song, *Ablösung im Sommer*, casting it into
an instrumental form; for the fifth, *Was mir die Engel erzählen*
(What the angels tell me), he uses women's and boys' voices in setting a new *Wunderhorn* text; but for the fourth movement, *Was mir
der Mensch erzählt* (What man tells me), he turns to a quotation
from Nietzsche's *Also sprach Zarathustra*.

The gigantic score of the Third Symphony – with a playing time
of over an hour and a half it exceeds the length of the preceding
symphonies – was written during the summer holidays of 1893–96
at Steinbach on the Attersee. Mahler's homage to Nature – his
Pan Symphony, as he sometimes called it – was completed in
August 1896. In this work Mahler, who loved the mountains and
lakes of the Salzkammergut above all else and found peace in this
landscape, created a symphony which, together with the First and
Second, he ranked among his major works. A few months later he
wrote: 'A man who is chained to the theatrical gallery cannot produce piles of music like the current champion composers. He can
only write on his days of rest. But at such times his inner life will
concentrate itself on *one* work. I cannot do otherwise than give
myself *wholly* and *fully* in *every* new work.'

In June 1894 at Weimar Mahler was able to conduct his First
Symphony, which in Budapest had failed to please the critics,
before a German audience. The symphony was received partly with
furious hostility, partly with approbation. The clash of opinions
pleased the composer: 'When the hounds bay, we know we are in
the saddle.' In Weimar, too, Mahler attended a performance of

Hansel und Gretel which delighted him. Richard Strauss, who for some years now had been working here as the Grand Duke's chief conductor, had staged Humperdinck's opera in December 1893. Strauss had also given his symphonic poem *Don Juan* and his opera *Guntram* their first performances at Weimar. Mahler renewed his friendship with Strauss, who showed interest in the Second Symphony which, he said, he wanted to perform the following year in Berlin. Mahler received this somewhat sceptically, although plainly there was much common ground between the two men on many fundamental musical questions.

At that time a concert in Weimar had stronger repercussions than performances in any other town of the German empire. The work of Richard Strauss, the many first performances at the opera house and in the concert hall and the exemplary preparation these enjoyed, had made Weimar a centre of musical life. News of events here carried much weight in other towns. Thus a young man not yet eighteen who was engaged as coach at the Cologne Stadttheater, at a monthly salary of one hundred marks – Bruno Walter – read the conflicting reports on the performance of Mahler's First Symphony, and longed to meet the composer. He imagined Mahler as 'a new Berlioz', a musical firebrand worth emulating.

That same year Bruno Walter succeeded in entering Mahler's world. He was engaged by the Hamburg Stadttheater. More than forty years after this first encounter, Walter described the powerful impression made on him by Mahler's personality:

Past experience, gathered in a middle-class environment, had taught me that one may meet genius in books and scores, in the enjoyment of music and drama, in the art treasures of museums, but that the living man was more or less ordinary, and real life a sober affair. And now I felt as if a higher realm had opened up to me – Mahler, in looks and behaviour, struck me as a genius, a demon: life itself had suddenly become romantic. I cannot better describe the elemental power of Mahler's personality than by saying that its irresistible effect on a young musician was to produce in him, in the shortest space of time, an entirely new attitude to life.

This life-enhancing change in Walter was not solely due to his professional contact with Mahler: he was fortunate in getting to know the composer on a human level. Mahler introduced him to the world of Schopenhauer and Nietzsche, and philosophical conversations intensified the spiritual bond between the young musician and the mature artist sixteen years his senior. Eventually Mahler even discussed his creative projects with Walter.

Walter's account also reveals the working atmosphere at the Stadttheater, with increasing tension between Mahler and the director, Pollini. In 1895 Mahler was already trying to sound out his chances of an engagement in Vienna. He dreamed of 'being summoned to the god of the southern regions', as he used to put it. But so far this was merely wishful thinking. Mahler realised that the desired move from Pollini's commercial theatre to a musical theatre of nobler standing was blocked by one great obstacle: 'In the present state of affairs, my Judaism bars the way to any Court theatre. Neither Vienna nor Berlin nor Dresden nor Munich is open to me. The same wind blows everywhere.'

No less daunting was the prospect of coming up in those 'southern regions' against a practical tradition of music that ran counter to all his beliefs. He had no illusions on this point:

Suppose I did get to Vienna: given my particular views, what would happen to me there? The moment I tried to impart my conception of a Beethoven symphony to the famous Philharmonic orchestra, trained by honest Hans (Richter), I'd find myself in the midst of a most unpleasant battle. Have I not experienced that even here, where the unstinted appreciation of Brahms and von Bülow have made my position unassailable? The storms I evoke whenever I depart from routine and try out some original idea of my own!

Even more important to Mahler than his search for a post more worthy of his work as an opera conductor was his fight for recognition as a composer. Of the five movements of the Second Symphony, Strauss wanted to perform the purely instrumental movements, numbers one to three, at a concert in Berlin. The artistic risk attached to this was hardly less than the fortune of being performed at all. What guarantee did Mahler have that the sound-picture he had embodied in the score would correspond to his mental image of it? Unlike the more fortunate Strauss, who was always able to test his scores in performance, Mahler had to be content with the written signs he had committed to paper. The more critically he looked at these, the less they seemed to do justice to his original musical conception. He would not put up with mere approximations. The only way of testing the score of the Second Symphony in practice was by performance in a rehearsal. Luckily he had like-minded friends in Hamburg who were able to help him achieve this. Hermann Behn, a pupil of Bruckner and an active Wagnerian in his home town of Hamburg, assisted Mahler in a practical manner by making an arrangement for two pianos of the Second Symphony, which the two of them played to a group of their friends. An orchestral rehearsal of the first three movements was also arranged. Only a few friends sat in the auditorium, among them Hermann Behn, the composer J. B. Foerster, his wife Bertha Foerster-Lauterer (who was a soprano in Mahler's ensemble), and a well-to-do citizen of Hamburg called Wilhelm Berken, who deserves to be remembered for the financial support he gave to Mahler's endeavours. Foerster has left a description showing the workmanlike character of the rehearsal:

Mahler conducted, the gallant Stadttheater orchestra played. Behind Mahler's desk stood the faithful old Weidlich with his indispensable note-book, carefully noting down every remark, every hint of the composer's: slight nuances of tempo, expression marks, changes of instrumentation. To us listeners it all sounded wonderful; only Mahler was dissatisfied.

This report is instructive for the light it throws on Mahler's methods of working. The formal structure of his symphonies was hardly ever subjected to changes in the course of such studio rehearsals. What concerned him were details of instrumentation, unambiguous expression marks, unmistakable clarity with regard to modifications of tempo, and distinctness of melodic articulation. The rehearsal was a laboratory experiment by Mahler the orchestral expert on the work of Mahler the composer. Even in the absence of contemporary accounts one could reconstruct this experiment, since the printed scores provide data. Thus at the very start of the Second Symphony the score contains instructions that emphasise Mahler's fear of slovenliness and banality. He may trust the cellos and double-basses to make their first entry with sufficient power, but at the change to mezzoforte there is the danger of losing distinctness. Therefore Mahler writes over the eighth bar *Immer wuchtig* (Always powerfully). The first and second violins are provided with bowing-marks (up-bow and down-bow) to ensure the desired increase and decrease of volume. The trumpets are told at the first climax, *Schalltrichter in die Höhe* (With bells raised). Moreover, there are many instructions for the conductor. These refer not only to the 'gradual and imperceptible' changes in tempo, but contain warnings against familiar imprecisions Mahler wishes to eradicate. 'Celli and basses rhythmical, do not play triplets' is written above one passage. A harp must come through 'very distinctly': elsewhere the tomtom and the large drum are to 'fade until inaudible', while in another passage the first violins should 'enter almost inaudibly', to reach, by way of a crescendo, a maximum volume that still must not exceed pianissimo!

One reason for the exceptionally detailed performing instructions was doubtless to make Mahler's intentions quite clear to Strauss so that the Berlin performance should achieve the desired effect. Strauss kept his word: in March 1895 the three instrumental movements of the Second Symphony were played at a Berlin concert. Mahler never forgot this generous act of friendship. Strauss freed him from the secret fear of seeing score after score disappearing into desk drawers. He realised, too, that Strauss's achievements as a composer had smoothed the path for his own work:

Quite apart from the fact that my works would be regarded as monstrous if Strauss's successes had not cleared the way for me, my chief joy is to have found among my contemporaries such a friend and comrade-in-arms.

In the spring of 1895 Mahler could justifiably hope that his compositions would now find a wider hearing. His daily life was made easier by the fact that Justi, as he called his sister Justine, was able to leave Vienna and come to run his household in Hamburg. He could think of concerts, and even of composing, a luxury normally reserved for holidays by the Attersee. But events at the theatre ruined his plans. The second conductor of the Hamburg Stadttheater was inveigled by an offer from America into breaking his contract. He left, together with his wife, the soprano Katharina Klafsky. In her, Pollini lost a dramatic star, a distinguished interpreter of Brünnhilde and Isolde. He had to look for a replacement. But he did not worry about a successor to the faithless second conductor. Let Mahler make up for the loss by working harder. 'So I'm actually conducting every day,' Mahler wrote to a friend. He was a galley-slave again, as in his Leipzig days. But then he had, by dint of intensive efforts, worked his way up to authority, whereas now he was burdened with all the routine tasks that could bring him neither profit nor honour.

Pollini showed no understanding for Mahler's plight. The lack of a second conductor seemed unimportant to him compared with the embarrassment caused by the departure of the dramatic Wagner heroine. Scouting for young talent was Pollini's forte. He seized it where he could find it: preferably in Vienna.

For the last few years a teacher had been working at the Vienna Conservatoire who had herself been a famous singer of Wagner roles. Pollini was not unfamiliar with the name of Rosa Papier. A pupil of the famous Marchesi, she had reached the Vienna Court Opera at the early age of twenty-two. Her range was the dramatic contralto parts – Ortrud, Brangäne, Erda. But in her enthusiasm for Wagner, she wanted to 'rise higher', to the young soprano heroines of the Wagnerian stage. The roles of Sieglinde (*Die Walküre*) and Elizabeth (*Tannhäuser*) ruined a voice that had been highly praised in its time. 'Her Sieglinde', wrote the music-dealer Gutmann in his memoirs, 'was a masterpiece, but the part was above her range – catastrophe was inevitable.'

Mahler had met Rosa Papier in 1885, when she took part in the performance of Mendelssohn's *St Paul* which, Mahler, to the annoyance of his opponents in Kassel, had given at the infantry barracks. It is therefore conceivable that he encouraged Pollini to contact her, in case some pupil of hers might be suitable for the Hamburg vacancy. Rosa Papier could sincerely recommend a certain pupil who had been under her care for some time and seemed cut out to be a dramatic singer. Staegemann, the director at Leipzig, had already signed a contract with the twenty-two-year-old singer – a thin, somewhat gawky, but vocally highly gifted girl. Nevertheless, Pollini, who was taking the waters at Karlsbad, asked Frau Papier to visit him with her protégée. An audition was held at the Karlsbad Stadttheater. The great arias of Donna Anna and the Queen of the Night, Ortrud's curse and Brünnhilde's war cry went so well that Pollini that same day made a deal by telegraph with his rival Staegemann for the young singer. Pollini declared himself well satisfied with his acquisition. 'But she must put on weight,' he said to Frau Papier, 'a Valkyrie needs substance.' Soon afterwards, Anna von Mildenburg – this was the stage name the young singer had chosen – found herself in Hamburg with her new director, who could not wait to exploit this vocal goldmine. In her very first week she was to sing the parts of Brünnhilde, Elisabeth and Fidelio. She felt terrified by the thought of the unaccustomed tasks ahead. Worse, her new colleagues filled her with fear of the chief conductor. Mahler, it appeared, was a tyrant; it was impossible to please him.

A piano rehearsal at last brought her face to face with Mahler, and broke the spell.

From the first Mahler's manner gave me a confidence that released me from all my doubts and anxieties. A boundless sense of security came over me in that first hour of being with him. The bustle of theatre life had amazed and frightened me. I was in a foreign country and felt utterly alone and abandoned. And then suddenly there was this man speaking to me with true human kindness – the very man I had most cause to fear, the chief conductor.

When the rehearsal was over, the young singer's tension resolved itself in a flood of tears. Mahler comforted her. She had done well. There was no cause for tears. 'The time to bawl is when you've succumbed to the universal messiness of theatre routine. But no one bawls then!'

Anna von Mildenburg did not succumb. Instead she became what she had certainly not been to start with, a great singer of Wagner. She knew how deeply she was indebted to Mahler for this. Their relationship did not remain on a purely artistic level: Anna von

Mildenburg and Gustav Mahler became engaged, or so, at any rate, Ludwig Karpath states in his book, published in 1934. Anna von Mildenburg, who died in 1947, knew this book – Karpath was a friend of hers – and though she objected to many statements contained in it she did not deny the story of the engagement. Documentary proof of formal betrothal is irrelevant; what matters to us is the influence of this relationship on Mahler's thoughts and actions during the years 1895–97. In consideration of his subsequent marriage and also of Anna von Mildeburg's marriage to Hermann Bahr (in 1909), the significance of this relationship has been suppressed or distorted in many biographical accounts. Indeed, strange legends about this 'affair' existed even in Mahler's lifetime.

One such legend was current in Prague around 1905. Wilhelm Ritter, the first and most passionate of French Mahler enthusiasts, noted it in his *Études d'art étranger*:

I reproduce the legend as I heard it and without vouching for its correctness. Mahler, before his Vienna appointment, was director of the Hamburg Opera and married its foremost singer. When she stood on the stage as Isolde while he led the orchestra, Wagner's score really took fire. . . . She died. Since then, this man has sung of joy and the coming of the superman.

These few sentences contain many errors. Mahler was not director of the Hamburg Opera, but its first conductor. He did not marry Anna von Mildenburg, and she had not died by 1905. All the same, the story thus handed down conveys the emotional state of affairs more truthfully than the available sources; it enables us, in fact, to interpret the sources correctly.

From the moment Anna von Mildenburg entered Mahler's life, his struggle for recognition as a composer gained a new impetus. She was, so far as we can tell, the first woman he considered his intellectual equal. He trusted her, as hitherto he had trusted only men. At last he could tell all that he had expressed in conversations with Foerster and Behn and in his letters to his friend in Vienna to a sympathetic woman whom he doubtless loved with his whole heart. This emerges from the letters and notes he sent her, often full of detailed artistic advice or the 'post mortem' of a performance. By December 1895 the formal *sie* had given way to the familiar *du*.

She knew all about his battles on behalf of the Second Symphony. The fragment Strauss had revealed in Berlin was no longer enough, he had set his heart on a complete performance. That needed money. But he had friends who were ready to help him. The physicist Arnold Berliner lent him money as his own means were insufficient to mount a performance in the German capital. The Berlin concert agency Wolff – which had acted for von Bülow and now counted Strauss among its stars – was put in charge of arranging the concert. The hire of the hall, orchestra and choir took a great deal of money, but Mahler was ready to stake everything. How carefully he prepared for this concert in Berlin can be seen from a letter he wrote to Anna von Mildenburg from Berlin on 8 December 1895:

As you know, at the end of the last movement of my symphony (the Second) I need bell-sounds which cannot, however, be produced by any known musical instrument. I have long thought that only a bell-founder could help me in this. At last I have found one; to reach his workshop one must take half an hour's train journey out of town. It is situated in the Grunewald district. I set off early in the morning, everything covered in crisp snow, and the frost revived my somewhat lowered vitality, because again last night I had very little sleep. When I arrived at Zehlendorf – that is the name of the place – and made my way through the snow-covered fir trees – all quite countrified, a pretty church sparkling gaily in the sun – my heart grew lighter again and I realised how free and happy man feels as soon as he leaves the unnatural, restless turmoil of the big city and returns to the peaceful realm of Nature. You too grew up in a small town, and will understand. After prolonged search I discovered the foundry. A homely old gentleman received me, with white hair and beard and calm, friendly eyes – I felt transported back to the age of master craftsmen. It was all so pleasant. I talked to him – true, in my impatience I found him a bit slow and long-winded. He showed me some marvellous bells; amongst others, a huge powerful one he had made to the Emperor's order for the new cathedral. The sound was of a mysterious power. It was something like that I had in mind for my work. But the time is still far off when only the most precious and splendid will be deemed good enough to serve a great work of art. Meanwhile I chose some bells – more modest, but still serving my purpose – and after a stay of about two hours took my leave from the lovable old man. The way back was again marvellous. But now for the general management: back to waiting upon their lordships! Those faces! Those bone-dry people! Every inch of their countenance bearing the marks of that self-tormenting egotism which makes all men wretched. Always I, I – never you, you my brother!

The performance of the Second Symphony on 13 December 1895 in Berlin laid the basis of Mahler's fame as a composer of symphonies. Bruno Walter, who was present at the performance, called it a decisive day: 'To be sure, there was hostility, misunderstanding, belittlement, scorn. Yet the work left such a deep impression of greatness and originality, of the force of Mahler's personality, that one may date his rise to fame as a composer from that day.'

In March 1896 Mahler again presented himself to the Berlin public with a concert devoted exclusively to his own works. It began with the first movement of the Second Symphony, then came *Lieder eines fahrenden Gesellen*, a first performance with the Dutch singer Anton Sistermans as the soloist, and finally the First Symphony. The breakthrough had been achieved. Weingartner asked for Mahler's scores. Not only Berlin, but Dresden and Leipzig also offered performances. Often they preferred to do a single movement. Mahler, who always wanted to 'build whole worlds' in his symphonies, might have been expected to demur. The dismemberment of what he had painstakingly welded into a whole was an abomination to him. But he agreed to such disfigurements as readily as 'Marsyas about to be flayed'. Though he did not abandon his principles, he was prepared to make compromises when it was a question of being performed and heard. 'What else can one do?' he asked with apparent resignation.

Actually he was far from resigned. It was time to get on with the Third Symphony, long since begun. The recognition currently accorded to his work must be put to good use. Moreover, he had at last found a companion who understood him. Whatever he might henceforth accomplish would be done for her sake as well.

In his Third Symphony Mahler used texts from *Des Knaben Wunderhorn* and Nietzsche's *Also sprach Zarathustra*. He had doubtless been introduced to Nietzsche's ideas earlier on by his friend Lipiner. In the 1890s, however, Nietzsche's philosophy became downright fashionable, and musicians were not insensible to this influence. While Mahler was working on his Third, Richard Strauss in his symphonic poem *Also sprach Zarathustra* made the singular attempt of translating a philosophical tract into music.

Whether Nietzsche stood in need of orchestration is not an entirely irrelevant question. Nietzsche once asked himself in what category *Zarathustra* should be placed, and came up with the answer, 'I rather think among the symphonies'. That is a remarkable admission. It points to the ringing and resounding message contained in *Zarathustra*, the stream of language swollen into cataracts, the absence of logical deduction, debasement of words to be merely the conveyors of a mood. Nietzsche's writing anticipates film techniques: tracking, zooming, fading, angling, cutting. Some of his camera-angles produce breathtaking pictures; some statements strike home by their aphoristic power. But the sum total – the portrayal of the 'superman' – is of a floating vagueness that confounds any attempt at orderly analysis. Strauss does not analyse. He designs mood-music of genius on a symphonic basis, an orchestral poster, as indicated by the subtitle he originally meant to give it 'Symphonic optimism in fin-de-siècle form, dedicated to the twentieth century.'

It was the Nietzsche vogue of the nineties as much as Strauss's orchestral technique that made this work so successful. The belated popularity of Nietzsche – long silent, and by now mortally ill – was part of a movement that ranks among the most embarrassing and yet forceful manifestations in the history of German culture. In respectable treatises on the German cultural life of that time one will look in vain for the name of the leader of this movement. Julius Langbehn, well known in his day as the author of a muddled and ludicrous publication called *Rembrandt als Erzieher* (Rembrandt the Educator), is today written off as a curiosity. His book ran into dozens of editions. Hundreds of thousands of people professed his pseudophilosophy, a mixture of Germanic chauvinism, hostility to science, irrationalism, contempt of technology and antisemitism. Langbehn's diatribe against the democratic spirit, which he called 'levelling down', expressed the mood of a nation that had not yet overcome the misery of its historical provincialism, a nation that had been created not on its own soil but in the Hall of Mirrors at Versailles. Such provincialism found confirmation of its national status not in democratic government but in the power of the sword. Berlin, since 1870 the swiftly rising metropolis of the new realm, seemed to this anti-intellectual movement the incarnation of modernity, technology, science and all that was evil. Langbehn writes: 'We must mobilise, play off and incite the provinces against the capital, politically as well as spiritually.' It is hardly surprising that this precursor, in suitably anticapitalist disguise, of the most hellish movement of the next century also anticipated the latter's fulminations against 'degenerate art'. Even Richard Wagner was marked down by Langbehn as a secondrate artist, and rebuked for being 'nervous' and 'making others nervous'. But the chief target of Langbehn's exceedingly popular anti-aesthetic campaign was Naturalism. With loathing and contempt he inveighed against Emile Zola, who based his novels on sociological research and medical discoveries. German art should shun the scientific spirit and social consciousness. Its salvation lay in peasant simplicity.

Nowadays we can hardly imagine the enormous impact of this disastrous ideology. Reading the periodicals of the nineties, one is dismayed to see that the German intelligentsia honoured Langbehn's turgidities with well considered reviews, showing appreciation as well as reservations. 'No one will regret having made the acquaintance of this distinguished eccentric,' wrote Georg Brandes, an expert on Nietzsche. His article appeared in the journal *Freie Bühne für Modernes Leben*, edited by Otto Brahm, the champion of Ibsen and Hauptmann! There was apparently a widespread inability to distinguish between the puerile outpourings of Langbehn and the word symphonies of Nietzsche. Of course the derivation was undeniable. Nietzsche in his essay of 1874, *Schopenhauer als Erzieher* (Schopenhauer the Educator) campaigns, with a better grasp of language than of subject matter, against specialisation and pure science; Langbehn in his book *Rembrandt als Erzieher* acts as a vulgarised echo: 'The professor is the German national malaise.'

Langbehn rendered down the ideas that were in the air, ready for mass consumption. Nietzsche's 'superman' – the result of an exercise of creative will – could henceforward be understood on a popular level as a product of social Darwinism, by 'racial selection'. To one educated in the humanities – as Richard Strauss was – this primitive interpretation was utterly alien. Strauss's symphonic poem even gives an impression of optimism. He had taken his inspiration from a few chapter headings of Nietzsche's word-symphony. The listener could add his own interpretation as he pleased.

Mahler proceeded differently. Mood music was as foreign to him as the traditional ways of setting words to music. What he took from Nietzsche's text was determined by the preconceived aims of his symphony. Certainly, Man is central to this musical poem – but not Superman. For Mahler, everything human is embedded in nature. The liberating power of nature – be it the winter landscape of Zehlendorf or the summer landscape of the Attersee – does not incite him to decry civilisation. He knows what he owes to the city. This is not surprising, for no Austrian would urge the provinces to revolt against the metropolis, Vienna. Such war-cries were the prerogative of the Germans, who had not yet grown into their empire and to whom the traditionless capital Berlin must seem a technical artefact.

For Mahler nature is the storehouse from which, like the giant Antaeus touching mother earth, he replenishes his energies. Yet there is more than this to Mahler's concept of nature. It embraces the idea of universality, of the world's oneness that was the message of the Second Symphony. This unity of all things pervades the Third Symphony. Its six movements originally had programmatic titles:

1. Pan awakens. The triumphal entry of summer.
2. What the flowers of the meadow tell me.

3. What the beasts of the forest tell me.
4. What man tells me.
5. What the angels tell me.
6. What love tells me.

The first and second movements are purely instrumental. So is the third movement, though it harks back to an early *Wunderhorn* song (*Ablösung im Sommer*) which has here lost its text and acquired a richer orchestral texture in place of the meagre piano part. For the fourth movement, Mahler selects from *Zarathustra* what corresponds to his image of man:

> *O Mensch! Gib acht!*
> *Was spricht die tiefe Mitternacht?*
> *Ich schlief, ich schlief –,*
> *Aus tiefem Traum bin ich erwacht: –*
> *Die Welt ist tief,*
> *Und tiefer als der Tag gedacht.*
> *Tief ist ihr Weh –,*
> *Lust – tiefer noch als Herzeleid:*
> *Weh spricht: Vergeh!*
> *Doch alle Lust will Ewigkeit –,*
> *– will tiefe, tiefe Ewigkeit!*

> [O man, take heed!
> What does the depth of midnight say?
> I slept, I slept –
> From deep dreams I am awakened: –
> The world is deep,
> Deeper than Day knew.
> Deep is its woe –
> Desire is deeper yet:
> Woe says: Pass away!
> Desire longs for eternity –
> Deep, deep eternity.]

This song, which Mahler gives to an alto voice, is certainly taken from Nietzsche's work, but from the one part of that work which shows no trace of the superman element. All the rest is rejected, as the tone of the rest of the symphony makes clear. Any lingering

memories of *Zarathustra* are extinguished by the sound of bells and
the ding-dong of boys' voices that open the fifth movement, and
by the naive piety of the words from *Des Knaben Wunderhorn*.
Forgotten are the mysterious changes of tempo, the veiled rhythms,
the dark groundswell of divided double-bass and cello parts, the
extravagances of the solo violin. In their place we find the fresh,
rhythmically well-articulated, sprightly chant of female voices: *Es
sungen drei Engel einen süssen Gesang* (Three angels sang a sweet
song). The last movement *Was mir die Liebe erzählt* also contra-
dicts any idea that Mahler had composed a Nietzsche symphony.
Nietzsche's Zarathustra repeats seven times: 'Never yet have I
found the woman whose children I should want; then be it this
woman whom I love: for I love thee, Eternity!' Mahler would
have been incapable of echoing this sentiment. His Finale is dedicated to Love – not the hectic yearning produced by magic potions,
but all-embracing fulfilment. Certainly his philosophy of love includes earthly love. The chromatic ecstasies which form the central
section of the Finale arise naturally out of the flowing diatonic
chant. The markings at the beginning of the last movement are:
Ruhevoll (Calmly) and *Empfunden* (With feeling), and for the final
bars Mahler writes: *Nicht mit roher Kraft. Gesättigten, edlen Ton*
(Not with crude power. Muted, noble tone).

The Third Symphony is not a turning away from this world, but
affirms faith in nature, and thus also in the nature of man. In doing
this, the symphony presents a critique of Nietzsche. The Finale is
the boldest symphonic conclusion to date: tranquil security.

The ending of this symphony has been compared to the slow final
movement of Tchaikovsky's *Pathétique*. But Tchaikovsky's B minor
Symphony, written three years earlier, has an end as unfulfilled and
tormenting as that of the dreamer Lenski, fatally wounded by
Eugene Onegin, from whose aria the symphonic finale derives its
melodic character. Tchaikovsky's symphony ends with a question-
mark. The music has a meaning which must remain a mystery to
the listener, since the composer dare not betray it. Mahler, it is
true, starts out with a programme, but ultimately he wishes to avoid
any verbal explanation. The music must speak for itself. It has

cancelled its contract with any kind of metaphysics. 'In the Adagio [the last movement]', said Mahler, 'all is dissolved in Peace and Being.'

For three summers Mahler worked on his Third Symphony at Steinbach by the Attersee. In August 1896 – the same month in which Strauss completed his *Zarathustra* – he reached the last bar. We are well informed about the progress of his work by letters and the memoirs of his friends. On 2 July he was already so sure of a successful conclusion that he invited Bruno Walter to come from Hamburg. Walter arrived at Steinbach by steamer, having crossed the lake. Mahler received him at the landing-stage. As Walter looked around, taking in the attractive landscape and resting his eye on the Höllengebirge in the background, Mahler said: 'You needn't bother to look at that – I've composed it all away.'

Mahler and his sister Justi were staying at an inn. He had had a 'composing-cottage' built for his work. It stood in a meadow between the inn and the lake shore. The small room contained a table, chairs, a sofa, and a piano brought from Vienna. Early in the morning he retired to this sanctum and stayed there till lunchtime. It was forbidden 'on pain of death' to disturb him there. Natalie Bauer-Lechner, who stayed with Justi and Gustav in the summer, tells of the trouble they had to secure the necessary peace for Mahler:

To render the numerous village children harmless, we had worked out a proper system of keeping them far away and quiet. They were forbidden to set foot on Mahler's meadow and to play by or bathe in the lake, we even got them to keep quiet in the street, and in the houses, by means of pleas and promises, sweets and toys. If a hurdy-gurdy man or street musicians appeared, we would hurl ourselves upon them with a sizeable tip, silencing them instantly. The very animals – dogs, cats, chickens or geese – got no peace when we were about.

Bruno Walter, who had been hearing from Mahler about the work before he came to hear the work itself, supplements this account. Mahler, according to Walter, did not stay all the time in his composing cottage. He wandered about the meadow, or he would run up the hill or go for longer walks, returning each time to 'bring in the harvest'. In high good humour he would then join the others for lunch, at which a lively conversation would be kept up.

It was not simply physical isolation which the composer needed and found for his work. Bruno Walter says bluntly that inspiration and creative activity were irreconcilable with Mahler's career as a conductor. In order to compose, Mahler not only had to withdraw temporarily from his immediate surroundings, but had to put some distance between himself and people and things that were normally close to him, Even his relationship with Anna von Mildenburg was affected by this. During that summer in Steinbach devoted to the Third Symphony, Mahler wrote numerous letters to his fiancée. Fragments of nine letters have been preserved. One may safely assume that the total number was much greater, since certain passages and dates suggest that Mahler wrote almost daily. In the middle of July, however, Anna seems to have complained about a falling-off in his correspondence. Mahler's reply is instructive. It reveals not only his creative psychology, but also the demands he makes of anyone who is to 'live with him'.

But I have written to you that I am engaged on a great work. Don't you see how that claims one completely, and how one is often so engrossed in it that one is virtually dead to anything else? Now think of a very great work in which the whole world is reflected – oneself is, so to speak, merely an instrument on which the universe plays. I have explained this to you so often – and if you have any understanding of me, you must accept it. You see, everyone who was going to live with me has had to learn this. At such moments I do not belong to myself. . . . There are terrible birth pangs the creator of such a work has to suffer, before it all arranges itself and constructs itself and flares up in his head, there has to be a good deal of absent-mindedness and self-absorption and deadness to the outside world. . . . My symphony will be something such as the world has never yet heard! The whole of Nature finds a voice in it, and tells of such secret things as one may perhaps divine in a dream. I tell you, I myself get an uncanny sensation at certain points, I feel as though I hadn't written this myself.

This anticipates what Alma, Mahler's future wife, was to call his 'sense of mission', which she blamed for his 'ignoring her for years on end'. Anna von Mildenburg, knowing herself to be truly loved, still found it difficult to grasp the significance of Mahler's 'incapsulation', even though he 'had written' and 'had explained so often'. The intensity of Mahler's bond with his sister Justi becomes clear; their life together was 'almost a kind of marriage'. She had long realised what he demanded and understood the basic dichotomy of his life: on the one hand, the conductor who hated theatre routine and yet gave himself over to it with all his strength and without reserve; and on the other, the composer, moody and taciturn at times, at others irrepressible and exuberant, when he had succeeded in carrying out a plan or when, as he put it, the universe had played on him. For Mahler did not himself compose – something composed in him.

Every afternoon of his stay at Steinbach, Bruno Walter sensed the after-effects of the 'morning ecstasies'. Then at last the work was completed; Mahler played the symphony to him on the piano.

The force and novelty of the idiom literally struck me dumb – I was also overwhelmed by the sense his playing conveyed of the creative fire and rapture in which the work had been conceived. Only now, through this music, did I really understand him; his whole being seemed to breathe a mysterious rapport with nature; I had barely sensed the elemental intensity of this before, while now I experienced it directly through the sound language of his symphonic world dream.

The words chosen by Bruno Walter – symphonic world dream – perfectly epitomise Mahler's conception of the social role of the symphonic composer and the social function of the symphony. For him it was not enough to make a contribution to the concert repertoire. The world he built in a symphony must take over the listener completely. To achieve this aim Mahler needed the better part of the two hours allotted to an orchestral concert. Mozart's *Jupiter* Symphony takes a scant half-hour, Beethoven's First no more. But as early as the *Eroica* – which Beethoven expressly wished to be given pre-eminent place in any concert programme – the composer of 'universal philosophy' symphonies stakes his claim to total domination. Though it does not take an hour like the Ninth, the *Eroica* does last over fifty minutes. Brahms in his four symphonies reached a modest average length of forty-two minutes. Bruckner's maximum is the Eighth, with a duration of eighty minutes. Mahler's Third Symphony claims the public's attention for about an hour and a half. It hardly permits the presence of other music. The idea is to lure the listener into the seclusion of a symphonic world dream.

[7]

Mahler's Reign in Vienna

To this day, the appointment of a new opera director and the departure of the reigning one is a favourite sport with the Viennese, arousing fierce local passions much as the bullfight does in Spain. Anyone can take part, even those who never set foot in the opera house, and each plays the game according to his social status. There is the murmuring crowd in the background, voicing public opinion; there are the cognoscenti, who are allowed to vent their views in solo scenes; a few high-powered personalities who are in charge of the production, and others who at any rate behave as if they had some influence, since they would lose face were they to admit their powerlessness. The Court Theatre management – which nowadays goes by another name, but remains essentially the same – has the pleasure of arranging successive scenes into acts; and the journalists present their instant news, cleverly disguising the bias of their inside information.

However, in 1897 the journalists were not on the ball. With one single exception – Ludwig Karpath, and Mahler had sworn him to silence – no one in Vienna's editorial offices had any ideas that the chief conductor at Hamburg was preparing his *coup d'état* against the Vienna Opera. Rational speculation might settle on Felix Mottl at Munich, or Ernst von Schuch at Dresden, or any other man of Court Theatre standing. It simply did not make sense to consider a mere Stadttheater conductor, let alone a Jew. However, the signal for the start of the Viennese comedy had already been given. The director, Wilhelm Jahn, was a sick man. It was no secret that he was to have the support of an able second conductor. What people did not know was that the director of the Hoftheater, Josef von Beseczny, planned to promote the new conductor, once he was found, to the post of director in a very short time. For von Beseczny, the dismissal of Jahn was as good as carried out. The smooth execution of this plan was entrusted to the head of the Chancellery, Eduard Wlassack. He – as the well-informed Karpath expressed it – was to conduct this comedy. The stage management was undertaken by Anna von Mildenburg's teacher, the court singer Rosa Papier.

Mahler's dream of 'being summoned by the god of the southern regions' was at least as old as his differences with Pollini, and gained intensity from the increasing tension between the two men. Mahler had long resolved to leave Hamburg at the first opportunity. This is clearly shown in an undated letter he addressed to Ödön von Mihalovich in Budapest, which is not among the *Collected Letters* edited by Alma Mahler. His decision was primarily on artistic grounds. 'As far as I know,' he wrote from Hamburg long before applying for the Vienna post, 'negotiations are afoot with Strauss in Weimar, who, as he told me, is keen to become my successor here. Even now I feel sorry for the poor chap. Knowing this splendid character, I can tell he isn't the man to make concessions either.' Meanwhile, casting around for a better position, he also told his Hungarian friends that he might return to Budapest. He did not spend the entire summer holidays locked in his composing-cottage on the Attersee, but tried to renew contact with Count Apponyi, who was spending his leave at Aussee. Occasionally, too, he cycled over to Ischl, then the fashionable summer residence of the Emperor. Here he was received by Brahms who, although horrified by the score of the Second Symphony, had retained his esteem for Mahler the conductor. Again, here he could usefully sound the opinions of the all-powerful critic Eduard Hanslick, and various less influential Viennese colleagues.

How Mahler eventually realised his bold plan has been described by many writers. Looking through all the records and reminiscences, one cannot avoid the impression that dozens of helpful sponsors competed to smooth the way for him. The true story can only be disentangled by realising that, the moment he saw the faintest hope of a position in Vienna, Mahler set everything and everyone in motion to achieve his goal. He canvassed artists and politicians, natives and foreigners, plain citizens and aristocrats, friends and strangers. Everyone who had been thus energetically pressed into service could not but believe that in the end he, and he alone, had done the decisive deed for Mahler. Ultimately, however, all who acted in this comedy were manipulated by Mahler himself. Wlassack, the director of the Chancellery, hoped that by appointing a thirty-six-year-old conductor he would get a docile young man who could be easily governed, both now and in his subsequent directorship. Mahler did not disabuse him of this delusion until he himself was firmly in the saddle. Jahn honestly believed that he was being given an assistant and supported Mahler's engagement in this belief.

Even Anna von Mildenburg was at this point a pawn in the game. This is not to suggest that Mahler's love for her was self-seeking or superficial. Without calling on the hitherto unpublished letters Mahler addressed to his fiancée, published documents prove that he wrote to her almost every day on his journeys to the Attersee and to Vienna, Berlin and Moscow (where he was conducting concerts). That he subsequently broke with her is a different matter, to be discussed later. She was certainly a loyal ally in his struggle for the Vienna appointment, and she mobilised her teacher Rosa Papier, who was a friend of Wlassack's, on his behalf.

On 21 December 1896 Mahler made his formal written application for the post of conductor at the Vienna Court Opera. The Vienna Court and State Archives have preserved this application, addressed to the director, von Beseczny, together with another one dated 23 December which mentions no addressee, though one may assume it went to the head of the Chancellery, Wlassack. Mahler begs him to throw 'his powerful influence' into the balance, and in a postscript informs him that one obstacle to his engagement in Vienna has gone: 'As things stand at present in Vienna, perhaps I should tell you that quite a while ago, in pursuance of a long-standing resolution, I entered the Catholic faith.'

In attempting to win the favour of the Vienna authorities, Mahler had to allow for the difficulties arising from his reputation as a self-willed and relentless orchestral leader and man of the theatre. In Budapest and Prague, Leipzig and Hamburg, countless artists had experienced his severity at rehearsals. He knew that he was charged with 'irritability and eccentricity'. Enquiries on this point, which Wlassack was sure to make, must be countered. Mahler sent his friend Lipiner to see Wlassack. Lipiner followed up the discussion with an official-looking letter, on the headed notepaper of the chamber of deputies, in which he wrote:

I have been informed that Mahler's temperament, his manner of dealing with opposition, have drawn adverse criticism. Nothing could be more unjust. Mahler is a man of genius, of a passionate nature, that is true; but his passion is far removed from the impatience of superficial characters. To achieve as much as possible and to see that others do likewise: that is his aim.

The Court Theatre management was likely to be impressed by Hungarian testimonials, so Mahler procured recommendations from Budapest. Ödön von Mihalovich's letter disposed of two objections levelled against Mahler by his opponents: that he was a Jew – which no longer applied – and that he was mad and preposterous – a malicious calumny invented by enemies at a loss for just reproaches.

The former Budapest director, Franz von Beniczky, expressed himself more guardedly in a letter that reached Vienna in January 1897:

I must confess that I consider Mahler a very excitable person in some ways, no doubt owing to his profession; but I would nevertheless recommend him most warmly to Your Excellency, knowing him for a man who, apart from his great gifts as a musician, conductor and director, also has a healthy regard for the commercial side of an artistic institution. Above all, he is a thoroughly honourable character, and I am convinced that his merits far surpass the weaknesses.

But the most impressive testimonial, to be found in file No. 1610, is a letter of 10 January 1897 from Count Albert Apponyi. He speaks with the authority of a distinguished politician, yet his statement has the character of an all-round artistic appreciation. I think I am right in stating that this letter, obviously addressed to the Director, has never yet been reproduced in the Mahler literature.

File 1610/1897

Your Excellency,

I am informed by a reliable source that the Imperial and Royal Vienna Court Opera is on the verge of a crisis concerning its conductor or director, and that among others Herr Gustav Mahler is considering the post. Since the work of this outstanding artist at the Budapest Opera is vivid in my memory and since in my fairly comprehensive acquaintance with distinguished conductors I have not found his like, I take the liberty of saying a few words by way of recommending him.

Through the incompetence and misplaced ambition of Count Geza von Zichy during the latter's unhappy directorship of our opera house . . . this institution has to its detriment lost a leader who within two years succeeded in training a completely discredited company to achieve considerable artistic results; built up a rich and varied repertoire; and, while preserving the highest artistic ideals, ended his second season with a not inconsiderable financial surplus. Mahler is not merely – like some famous conductors I could name – an orchestral musician, but with all the works he produces he dominates the stage, the action, the expressions and movements of actors and chorus, with supreme control, so that a performance prepared and conducted by him attains artistic perfection in every dimension. His eye ranges over the entire production, the decor, the machinery, the lighting. I have never met such a well-balanced all-round artistic personality. I would beg Your Excellency by way of confirming this opinion to ask Brahms what he thought of the *Don Giovanni* performance conducted by Mahler which he watched in Budapest; please to ask Goldmark how *Lohengrin* under Mahler's direction struck him. Both will remember their impressions, for they were of the kind one remembers for a lifetime.

When I add that Mahler as a person, too, is a highly estimable, eminently respectable character, I shall have completed a portrait which, I trust, suggests that the Opera would be fortunate indeed to gain his services.

Albert Apponyi

By February 1897 negotiations had progressed to the point where Mahler was assured not only of the imminent signing of his contract as conductor of the Vienna Court Opera, but also that the Vienna management would honour its promise, given orally and *sub rosa*, to make him director soon after. Pollini's business assistant, Max Bachur, has described in his memoirs of the theatre how vigorously Mahler worked from the beginning of the year for an early termination of his Hamburg obligations. 'If I can get away by the first of June, I can take up the Vienna post,' he is said to have told Bachur. To Bachur's question whether his Jewish origins did not stand in the way of such an appointment, Mahler replied: 'That doesn't matter, that's a detail – just see to it that I have an answer by to-morrow.' Bachur obtained the consent of Pollini, who wanted to get rid of Mahler anyway. On 15 April 1897 Jahn in Vienna signed the contract engaging Mahler as conductor for a year from 1 June. The ratification of the contract by the imperial general management – a procedure that usually took some time – went through on the same day. The director cannot have known that by signing this document he was opening the door to his successor. Mahler, however, was aware of it. Five days later he wrote to Max Marschalk: '. . . what I feared most was to be burdened with a director's job; and now *that* has happened. However: verederemo!' He was a little frightened by this tactical success. He knew that he 'was going to be led a dance', but he was resolved to 'call the tune' himself. At times he had moods of despondency, where he longed for a 'remote, peaceful life in some quiet corner of this earth', and dreaded 'the terrible treadmill of the theatre'.

On 11 May 1897 Mahler conducted his first performance at the Vienna Opera. It was *Lohengrin*, and he had been granted only a single rehearsal. All the same, it was a success, which Mahler ascribed not solely to his own efforts: 'The principal credit must go to Austrian musicianship, to the elan and warmth and the great natural talent everyone brought to bear.'

At last Mahler was 'home'. That alone would have made him happy. But on top of that there were favourable reviews and the ovations of young musical enthusiasts who waited for him after performances at the stage door. In his delight and excitement, Mahler neglected to send his daily bulletins to Anna von Mildenburg in Hamburg. On 17 May he apologised:

Yesterday and the day before I couldn't even get down to writing to you. It was one huge turmoil of visitors, messages of congratulation, etc. Thank God, it's all over now. The whole of Vienna has greeted me with real enthusiasm. Next week there will be *Walküre*, *Siegfried*, *Figaro* and *Zauberflöte*. There can be little doubt I shall be director soon.

As early as July 1897 Mahler took over the schedule of the ailing Wilhelm Jahn. On 12 October Mahler's appointment as 'artistic director' was announced: the carefully planned conquest of the Court Opera was completed. Rosa Papier, whose tactical advice had contributed materially to Mahler's victory, also tried to effect an engagement in Vienna for the woman Mahler loved – Anna von Mildenburg, waiting hopefully in Hamburg. When Mahler's sister Justine heard of this scheme, she did everything in her power to prevent Mahler's reunion with Anna. Apparently Mahler himself began to waver in his support for Anna, as convincing arguments were advanced about complications that might arise from the director's intimate friendship with a member of the opera ensemble – the more as a Vienna newspaper had already reported that Mahler's first action as director would be to bring his 'girl friend' to Vienna. The files of the general management, to be sure, do not mention support for, or opposition to, von Mildenburg's engagement on the part of Mahler. He let things take their course.

Eventually in February 1898 the singer, having done some guest performances, joined the Vienna ensemble. Ludwig Karpath's account suggests that when Anna first visited Mahler at his office, he 'erected an impenetrable wall between himself and her'. Many years later, the great singer firmly denied this. Nor is Karpath's assertion that they had broken off their engagement even before Mahler's departure from Hamburg borne out by the published letters. What actually happened when those two met again in the director's room of the Court Opera is unknown. However, the personal bond between them definitely grew less close, until in the end only a profound understanding on artistic matters remained. In December 1907, when he left the Court Opera, Mahler still addressed a letter to his 'dear old friend', in which he assures her of 'his longstanding attachment and affection'. 'In any case, you know that wherever I am I shall always be a friend on whom you can count.'

In her memoirs, published in 1921, Anna von Mildenburg paid full tribute to her friend and mentor, describing enthusiastically how much she owed to his instruction, and tactfully avoiding any allusion to a relationship which, both in her own and in Mahler's life, was obviously much more than a passing episode.

The separation, which was not sudden but gradual, is understandable in view of Mahler's fixation on his sisters Justine and Emma. He rationalised this unconscious motivation by laying great stress on his duties and responsibilities towards his unmarried sisters. Add to this a thoroughly egocentric motive. Justine, in his own words, had learnt what all those who were to live with him had to learn; she was willing to adapt herself to the demands that resulted from his varying 'sense of mission' – now as conductor and director, now as composer. She gave him the advantage of feminine care without the emotional counterclaims a wife would have made. It is not easy to decide whether she was really such a bad housekeeper as Mahler's future wife asserted. Anyway, she knew how to look after her brother's mental comfort, and that was obviously what counted with him.

In February 1898 Mahler moved into a flat at No. 2, Auenbrugger-strasse, in the third district of Vienna. A service telephone was installed, enabling him to get in touch with the opera house at any time. The general management also put a motor car at his disposal. Mahler, that keen cyclist who had spent his holidays pedalling all over the Salzkammergut, quickly developed a great love for the motor car which he kept to the end. One roared along, at an average speed of twenty kilometres an hour, either in an electric car or in the petrol-engined vehicle that finally conquered all. There was an international automobile race in Vienna in 1899. Ten years later over 3000 car licences were issued, and the number of fatal accidents on the roads rose to sixty-one.

A new era had begun. Its beginning was marked by the preparations for the jubilee celebrating the fiftieth year of the Emperor Francis Joseph's reign (1898). In this flourishing capital where peace seemed assured forever, Mahler now held a dominating position. In 1898 the Vienna Philharmonic Society elected the opera director as their conductor. Although there were some vicious attacks on Mahler – he had to ask the general management to start a disciplinary investigation against an anonymous writer who supplied the press with 'adversely critical and damaging articles' – there was no lack of recognition and power, fame or money. In 1899 he was able to buy a plot of land at Maiernigg on the Wörthersee where he later had a villa built.

It is only recently that the cultural significance of the epoch beginning with Mahler's entry into Viennese operatic history has been fully appreciated. We are at last at a sufficient distance from those last years of peace under the Austro-Hungarian Empire to make a just assessment. The antidynastic emotions of the democratic Left under the First Austrian Republic after 1918 prevented a fruitful exploration of the past, as did the pan-German fantasies that survived in nearly all political camps. It is understandable that the national aspirations of the new states which were detached from the Austrian core after 1918 had to start by denying the historic role of Vienna, simply to justify their own ideologies. It was rare to find a balanced political wisdom that could appreciate, even in monarchist guise, the beauty of the cultural landscape in the Danube region: a character like Thomas G. Masaryk, who served his nation without bowing to national prejudices, remained a praiseworthy exception. Among Austrian politicians and historians there were very few who could rank with the great Czech statesman in this respect. Austrian history seems to have passed over the international lawyer Heinrich Lammasch (1853–1920), pacifist president of the last cabinet under the monarchy, as over the scholar Josef Redlich (1869–1936), a member of Lammasch's cabinet, who dreamed of the rebirth of Austria in the spirit of English parliamentarianism and English local government.

It was only in the *Second* Austrian Republic, emerging from the Second World War, that it became possible to remember dispassionately the cultural and artistic achievements of 1900 and the following years: the inspiration emanating from the 'Secession' (1897); Gustav Klimt's magnificent sensuality, which overcame Makart's debased style of painting; the architecture of Otto Wagner, trying to do justice to a century brimming with intellectual ideas; the anti-ornament functionalism of Adolf Loos; and the close relationship between Sigmund Freud's *The Interpretation of Dreams* (1900) and the clinical study of *Leutnant Gustl* which Arthur Schnitzler, himself a doctor, produced in the same year.

The list of achievements could well lead to a renewed idealisation of that epoch. Such a glorification would, however, throw a false light on the figure of Mahler. Certainly he too was spurred on by the upsurge of the arts. He adopted the motto of the 'Secession' ('To the age, its art – to art, its freedom') for his own, and showed complete sympathy with the aims of the group of artists around Klimt, particularly the painter Alfred Roller (1864–1935), whom he later made his stage designer at the opera house. Yet it would be wrong to dwell only on the artistic splendours of the epoch without mentioning its dark side.

It needs no special effort to understand the pressures under which the intelligentsia of that era lived. The loathsome alliance of vulgar antisemitism with the criminal technique of the political show trial is familiar to us from recent examples. The famous *affaire Dreyfus* was very similar. It began in 1894 with the trial rigged by a military clique, at which a French army captain of Jewish descent was convicted of allegedly betraying military secrets. The struggle for the rehabilitation of Captain Dreyfus, who was stripped of his rank and imprisoned on Devil's Island, lasted for years. When, in January 1898 the journal *L'Aurore*, edited by Georges Clemenceau, published Emile Zola's open letter to the president of the French Republic under the title of *J'accuse*, the intellectuals of France, and indeed of all Europe, split into 'Dreyfusards' and 'Antidreyfusards'. Georges Picquart, the staff colonel who had dared to stand up for the truth and thus for Dreyfus, and who paid for his courage with a term of imprisonment, became the hero of all who clamoured for justice.

The Dreyfus controversy left its mark not only on the journals and pamphlets of its time, but on later literary works. Echoes of it haunt Marcel Proust's great novel. Schnitzler's *Der Weg ins Freie* (The Way to Freedom), though it does not rank with his best work, throws light on the intellectual atmosphere of Vienna in 1898 in a way that helps us to a truer understanding of Mahler's environment. The core of the ideological disputations that fill this novel, making it a questionable work of art though a most valuable historical document, is the argument between those Jews following the European path of assimilation and those who wanted to found a state in Palestine which 'will one day shelter the Jewish nation'. This formula, used by the First Zionist Congress held in August 1897 at Basle, was inspired by an essay of Theodor Herzl's, recently published in Vienna. Herzl, who had witnessed the Dreyfus trial as correspondent of the Vienna *Neue Freie Presse*, put forward his alternative to the assimilation of European Jewry. His book on the Jewish state intended to present 'a modern solution of the Jewish question'.

Schnitzler's novel summed up both the case for and the case against Zionism put by members of the Austro-Jewish intelligentsia. Thus an Austrian poet of Jewish origin is made to say:

My instinct tells me infallibly that my homeland is here, here alone, and not in some other country which I do not know; which, from the descriptions I hear, would not suit me in the least; and which certain people now want to persuade me is my homeland just because my distant forebears some thousands of years ago were scattered over the world from that particular place.

To this statement the spokesman of Zionism retorts that the personal instinct of the artist is irrelevant. The point at issue was the fate of the masses of eastern Jewry, about which the artist of Jewish descent assimilated in Vienna could have no idea. 'You are always thinking of yourself and of the unimportant fact that you are a poet who, born in a German-speaking country, happens to write in German, and, living in Austria, happens to write about Austrian people and affairs.'

The discussion in which Schnitzler involves the characters of his novel underlines the historical dilemma of the Austrian artist of

Jewish descent. His sense of belonging is entirely conditioned by the tradition he inherits and by the place in which he works. Consciousness of being an outsider, or forcible expulsion from the milieu, will change him only in exceptional cases. Mahler felt the rebuffs he often suffered. But even the feeling of political and social rootlessness which he sometimes expressed could not undermine his sense of belonging, as an artist, to Austria. His music grew out of the native tradition, a native land which, however, comprised not only Vienna and Austria within its present-day political boundaries, but also other regions of the Habsburg Empire which helped to shape his work.

Max Brod – much to the astonishment of many Mahler enthusiasts – discovered Jewish tunes and rhythms in Mahler's music. I cannot share this astonishment, as Brod's suggestion by no means conflicts with the universal character of the old Austrian culture. Would it not, conversely, be surprising – indeed, wellnigh inexplicable – if Mahler's art showed no trace of the Jewish musical tradition? The arguments against Max Brod's view (first stated in 1915) overlook the manifold national sources that had fed Austrian music since the days of the classical Viennese composers. Brod himself, though he speaks of a 'basic Jewish component' in Mahler's work, does not underestimate the Austrian character of his music. For instance he counts Schubert's music among 'Mahler's foundations', refers to Bruckner as 'a major influence on Mahler', and is reminded of Smetana by the 'Bohemian element'; he also recognises the pervading influence of the Viennese classics, Haydn, Mozart and Beethoven, in Mahler's symphonic output.

To classify Mahler's work simply as Jewish music would be wrong – not only because it recalls the crass musical racism of the Hitler regime, but because it would not explain the profoundly Austrian traits in Mahler's mental make-up and creativity. His relation to Judaism was so complex that it cannot be summed up in a simple formula. He did not follow the religion of his ancestors. He felt drawn to Christianity, though he never denied his Jewish origin. He did, however, dislike certain Jewish-Viennese habits, such as the telling of Jewish jokes, which were an abomination to

him. His Christianity was deeply felt, but it never attained to the
state of dogmatic manifestation which would have allowed him to
compose a mass. In his mind Christian thought was amalgamated
with the pantheism revealed in his commentary on the Third
Symphony. The religious impulse was for him part of a general
acceptance of European culture, of 'assimilation' to the artist's
predetermined homeland.

Mahler's decision, then, is understandable not only for the sake
of his career, but from the creative point of view. His conversion to
Catholicism took place some months before he started work in
Vienna. With this step he did not cut himself off from feeling for
the wronged and downtrodden of this earth, such as the masses of
poor eastern Jews. As a Dostoevsky enthusiast, Mahler was at the
very least sympathetic to the struggles of the Fourth Estate; and he
was impressed by the rise of the Austrian labour movement, the
campaign for a universal franchise and the democratisation of public
life. Progressive developments in Austria continued, in spite of the
virulent antisemitic forces at work; doubtless confirming Mahler's
belief that he belonged to an enlightened, tolerant Christian society.
The very men who had championed the cause of truth in the
affaire Dreyfus were soon to be among his closest friends. Among
the Mahler fans in Paris were Paul Clemenceau (the brother of
Georges), Colonel Picquart, Captain L'Allemand and Paul Painlevé
(the famous mathematician and future prime minister). Mahler felt
drawn to these 'Dreyfusards', and they for their part appreciated
him not only as the director of the Vienna Opera, but as a composer.
From 1900 on, according to Paul Clémenceau's Viennese sister-in-
law Berta Zuckerkandl, Mahler's French friends attended almost
every concert he conducted abroad. They followed him everywhere.
Picquart and L'Allemand used to play his symphonies on the piano.

Mahler lived to see the triumph of his French friends. Georges
Clemenceau became prime minister in 1906; that July Dreyfus was
finally rehabilitated and Picquart reinstated with the rank of
brigadier-general. Picquart and his friends announced their forthcoming visit to Vienna in the autumn. Mahler decided to put on a
'secret festival' for his friends, and arranged a special programme

with top-ranking singers. To fulfil Picquart's dearest wish, there was to be a performance of *Tristan und Isolde* with Anna von Milden-burg and Erik Schmedes in the title roles. But Picquart, now minister of war, was fated not to enjoy this treat. A telegram from Clémenceau reached him in the director's box at the Court Opera: the guest from Paris had to leave without hearing Mahler's inter-pretation of *Tristan*.

Mahler's work as director and conductor of the Vienna Court Opera has been variously criticised and vindicated in a number of accounts, most of which clearly betray the bias of their authors. Any attempt to bring some order into the ample material and collate it with the evidence of the official files will show that it is quite impossible to arrive at a fair overall verdict on the ten years of Mahler's tenure. It is generally acknowledged today that his reign was a 'golden age' of the Vienna Opera. But that in itself tells one nothing about the particular quality of individual performances. Even the overworked concept of 'ensemble theatre' – as opposed to the singers' theatre, with soloists pre-eminent – is not very en-lightening. Certainly Mahler attached great importance to ensemble studies and ensemble effects. He replaced the star system that had prevailed under the former director Jahn by a method designed to do justice to every individual work of art.

The energy shown by Mahler in building up his ensemble was almost universally admired. But he had such a hatred of routine that he could never rest content with what had already been achieved. 'Better, more beautiful, more perfect' was his motto, even when he had accomplished something that seemed splendid enough to everyone else. A retrospective review in the annual *Deutsche Thalia* for 1902 calls him 'a man of sensations and explo-sions. What he cannot bear is rest.' The author, a young critic named Max Graf, enlarges on Mahler's restlessness:

When, during the first few years, the cast was changed at every per-formance, one welcomed Mahler's untiring efforts to improve the en-semble. Of course one believed that all this experimenting and exploring would lead to a definite goal; but now we see to our astonishment that for this artist constant fiddling with performances is an end in itself. Thus we have at present four Wotans, three Evas, innumerable Second and Third Ladies for the *Magic Flute* – but, on the other hand, very few productions that might be considered 'played in'. With this unremitting reshuffling of casts, the character of the performances changes all the time. And having watched Mahler ploughing and reploughing his furrow, one could wish at last to see the harvest sprouting from the ground undisturbed.

The factual information contained in this criticism, viewed from another angle, reflects credit on Mahler. How magnificent, after all, for an opera house to have four singers equal to the part of Wotan, and three sopranos that could hold the stage as Eva. Indeed, there were many in Mahler's own time who reversed the judgment in this way, which should teach us not to trust summary verdicts. This makes individual testimony all the more important. Again, the image that emerges is of the constantly experimenting director and conductor – who would never 'stand by his word' for long, according to his opponents; who was always 'striving for perfection', as his partisans had it.

The continual changes which marked Mahler's work as an executive artist repudiated the whole concept of opera as a museum-piece. It was not his intention to bring a production to the static point of 'having played itself in'. Musical drama, to function as a total work of art, must derive its effect on the public from ever-changing impulses: hence the need for not only remodelling the productions, but also experimenting with new singers. More and more did the critics, as the years went by, hold the innumerable guest performances against the director. Mahler was not looking for 'beautiful voices' as such, but for distinctive yet malleable dramatic singers who could fit in with his idea of an ensemble.

The Viennese public which, today as in the days of Jahn, clings to its ideal of a feast of bel canto, did not always find Mahler's offerings to its taste. The general character of the performances was, of course, appreciated, and during the early years praised, but there was already an occasional grumble about 'ensembles of disagreeable voices'. This was essentially a criticism of Mahler's long-term policy, his attempt to change a stage of singing stars into a sacred place for transmitting the message of the composer. Mahler considered himself the composer's representative, the zealous servant of the work of art who must not shrink from dictatorial measures to ensure its victory. The singer must 'retract' his voice if the context demanded it; he must forgo applause-raising top notes when these were not written in the score; he must say goodbye to his favourite coloraturas if Mahler asked him to. For the orchestra, he insisted on well-shielded desk-lights, so as not to interfere with the stage lighting. He even bullied the public. Like Toscanini, who was carrying out reforms at the Scala in Milan in 1898, he demanded unconditional surrender to the work itself: latecomers were not admitted; lights in the auditorium were reduced; untimely applause was drowned by music.

All these measures define Mahler's basic attitude as director of the Opera – to preserve the integrity of the work of art, the opera itself. However, during the ten years of his rule he did not always proceed to this end in the same way, or with the same intensity. We can distinguish three phases. The first, roughly from 1897 to 1902, was characterised by the striving for musical integrity. In this period Wagner's stage works were at last presented without cuts. The second phase saw the beginning of all the new décors designed by Alfred Roller. This period started with a new production of *Tristan und Isolde* (première on 21 February 1903), and reached its peak with the première of *Fidelio* on 7 October 1904. The third phase covered the years 1906 and 1907, a time when the energy of the opera director was somewhat curtailed by the demands the monumental Eighth Symphony made on the composer. The fact that Mahler in those two years conducted numerous concerts abroad also detracted from his concentration on the affairs of the Opera. Even so, this last stage, which included the Mozart Jubilee of 1906, bestowed on the opera-going public all the splendour of Mozart's operas, especially *Don Giovanni* with Roller's sets.

This chronological division of Mahler's time at the Vienna Opera will make it easier to analyse Mahler's achievements, and also to

Gustav Mahler. Engraving after an etching by Emil Orlik

Gustav Mahler at the age of
six, 1865

Gustav Mahler's mother

Above left Gustav Mahler on leaving school (1878)
Above right Kapellmeister at Olmütz (1883)
Below left Music Director at Kassel (1884)
Below right Opera Director in Budapest (1888)

First Kapellmeister in Hamburg (1892)

Above Alma and Gustav Mahler
Left Anna von Mildenburg
Right The Court Opera Director on
his way to the Opera (1904)

Alma Maria Mahler

In the loggia of the Vienna
Court Opera (1907)

Above Gustav Mahler's summer home on the Attersee
Below The composer's study on the shore of the lake

The last photograph (New York, 1910)

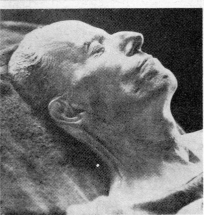

Gustav Mahler's deathmask, taken by Carl Moll

distinguish, in all the criticism levelled at him, the dogmatic emotionally motivated from the more realistic objections.

In the autumn of 1897 Mahler added some new works to the repertoire of the Court Opera. Smetana's *Dalibor*, first performed on 4 October, strictly falls within the period of Mahler's deputising for the director; the actual directorship became his a few days after the première. A survey of the new introductions up to 1902 gives some insight into Mahler's intentions:

1897	Tchaikovsky: *Eugène Onegin*
1898	Bizet: *Djamileh*
	Leoncavallo: *Bohème*
	Reznicek: *Donna Diana*
1899	Haydn: *Der Apotheker*
	Lortzing: *Die Opernprobe*
	Siegfried Wagner: *Der Bärenhäuter*
	Anton Rubinstein: *The Demon*
1900	Zemlinsky: *Es war einmal*
	Tchaikovsky: *Iolanta*
	Giordano: *Fedora*
	Josef Reiter: *Der Bundschuh*
1901	Thuille: *Lobetanz*
	Offenbach: *Tales of Hoffmann*
1902	Richard Strauss: *Feuersnot*
	Josef Förster: *Der Dot Mon*
	Mozart: *Zaide*
	Tchaikovsky: *The Queen of Spades*

However, many notable new works had entered the repertoire under Mahler's predecessor Wilhelm Jahn, too: *Manon* and *Werther* by Massenet, *Cavalleria Rusticana* and *L'Amigo Fritz* by Mascagni, *The Barber of Baghdad* by Cornelius, *Hansel and Gretel* by Humperdinck, and (after 1894) even *Die Fledermaus*. It was not the new works alone, important though they were, that formed Mahler's crucial contribution to the Viennese operatic life of his time, but the discriminating care he expended on the existing repertoire, and above all on the works of Wagner. His efforts to reconstruct the original form of Wagner's operas concentrated in the first place on the scores. Of the four scores that constitute *Der Ring des Nibelungen*, only *Das Rheingold* had been performed uncut before Mahler's arrival in Vienna. In February 1898 Mahler's work of restoration began with the first uncut performance of *Siegfried*. In the autumn he boldly staged an unabridged version of the entire *Ring* tetralogy. *Das Rheingold* was presented on 20 September; the next day, *Die Walküre* with Anna von Mildenburg as Brünnhilde. After a day of rest, *Siegfried* followed on 23 September with Erik Schmedes in the title role, and on the 25th *Die Götterdämmerung*, with the hitherto omitted scene of the Norns restored.

The reviews reflect the risk Mahler was taking. 'Much can be said for, and much against, such unabridged Nibelung-cycles,' wrote Theodor Helm.

The practical consideration will always be whether it is possible for an ordinary opera house to draw a sufficiently large audience equal to the great physical and mental strain involved. In this respect, at any rate, success has justified Mahler: night after night the house is completely sold out, the audience in a mood of reverence and festive excitement; there is ecstatic applause after each act, culminating at the lofty conclu- sion of the whole with the final chords of *Götterdämmerung*. Obviously the performances, every one of them led by the director in person, had been thoroughly rethought and worked over. Ten days later, Mahler repeated the whole Nibelung cycle, with substantially the same artistic, and even financial, success.

The unabridged *Ring* tetralogy was followed at the end of October by the first uncut performance of *Tristan*. This, too, had been 'thoroughly rethought and worked over'. The same process of restoration was extended to other works in the repertoire. Detailed rehearsals were lavished on *Der Freischütz*, the overture of which Mahler went on polishing for a long time, to the annoyance of some members of the orchestra. The musical result met with general approval; not so his attempt to spring-clean and stylise the scene in the wolf's glen. Mahler yielded to the demand for the restitution of the zoological and other decorative trimmings specified in the libretto: repeat performances of *Freischütz* reinstated the eerie paraphernalia so dear to the unsophisticated.

Extensive rehearsal time was not reserved for himself alone. He ensured favourable conditions for the operatic début of Ferdinand Löwe, a pupil of Bruckner's who was at the time conductor of the Kaim Orchestra in Munich and head of the Vienna Singakademie. To the great surprise of the old hands, Löwe was allowed two full rehearsals for the preparation of *Hansel and Gretel*, a standard item of the repertoire. This shows how intent Mahler was on raising the standard even of those performances that were not under his immediate control. He turned his own attention chiefly to Mozart and Wagner. His interpretations of Wagner's music must have appeared strange and novel to the Viennese, who were used to Hans Richter's style. Richter, who had worked at the Vienna Court Opera for over twenty years and who kept his position as chief conductor for a time under Mahler, was considered the authentic interpreter of Wagner: after all, the master himself had made Richter the first conductor of the *Ring* at the original Bayreuth Festival of 1876. It was natural that Mahler's version should be compared with Richter's familiar style.

After the complete *Ring* performances of autumn 1898 a Viennese critic of undeniable competence attempted a detailed comparison. Gustav Schönaich, who had been present at Wagner's Vienna concerts of 1872 and 1875 and at the Bayreuth rehearsals of 1875 and 1876, and who was fully conversant with Hans Richter's methods as demonstrated in Vienna over the years, stated in the *Wiener Allgemeine Zeitung* that Mahler took a good many passages at different tempi from those of 'the master himself and Richter, who always had Wagner's unqualified approval'. More instructive than this general statement is the closer examination that follows:

It is not a preference for slow or fast tempi, but rather his predilection for the effect of excessively dramatic contrasts which on occasion makes Mahler drag or hurry the tempo unduly. He often succeeds to a surprising degree in bringing out these contrasts – rarely, however, without in some way damaging the effect on the listener of what comes before and after. Allied to this is his close attention to detail and tendency to invest certain hidden features of the score with a significance that is perhaps not wholly their due. Not all themes are equally congenial to him. His rendering of the Valhalla-motiv lacks – not breadth – but calm; on the other hand, when it comes to the oppressive mysteries of the Tarnhelm-theme, he gives us an insight rising to a sense of terrifying menace. The general trend of Mahler's tempi is certainly in the direction of hurry rather than slowness. His treatment of the gods' exchanges in the second scene of *Das Rheingold* is undoubtedly not in the spirit of Wagner. Here, by being driven too hard, Wagner's melodically conceived recitative comes dangerously close to secco recitative. Though often splendid, spirited and well thought out, Mahler's conducting at times lacks the beautiful balance, and continuity of argument, and the majestic calm which is the strength of Richter's approach.

This critical evaluation, the significance of which is enhanced by the writer's basic goodwill towards his subject, gains added import by its agreement with what we know of Mahler's interpretations of Wagner at Leipzig, his modifications of tempo so unlike Richter's relaxed rendering. To the temperate style of the bearded, fifty-five-year-old Richter, the thirty-eight-year-old Mahler opposed a 'highly-strung art' whose splendour and spirit even an understanding friend of Richter would not deny. We are dealing here not with a mere difference in individual style, more with a change in the style of a whole period.

Not all reviewers or music lovers judged the transition from the Richter era to that of Mahler as fairly and thoughtfully as the critic quoted above. Nor did Mahler for his part always appreciate Richter's services to Wagner's cause. When it was pointed out that Richter had learnt his tempi from Wagner himself, Mahler responded mockingly: 'Perhaps he knew them then – he's forgotten them now.'

The relationship between the two men was a source of interest to the Viennese public right from the start of Mahler's appointment. At first Mahler showed all due respect for Richter, whom he doubtless admired, and apparently had hopes of keeping this most popular musician on at the Opera even after he had become its director. Richter held a dominating position in the musical life of Vienna. As a conductor, he had nominally been Jahn's subordinate, but Jahn had restricted his own conducting to French and Italian *verismo* opera. He had left the Mozart opera, Beethoven's *Fidelio* and the Wagner repertoire to Richter, who, moreover, from 1875 led the concerts of the Vienna Philharmonic, and for a few years those of the Gesellschaft der Musikfreunde as well. The change of director at the Court Opera was bound to result in a narrowing of Richter's field of activity. He knew that Mahler would not hand over to him the great masterpieces of the repertoire in the casual way of Jahn. What had come to him without effort, he would now have to struggle for. The young and vigorous newcomer had the advantage of social position, too, as opera director. Add to this that Richter was not satisfied with his salary as Court Conductor. When in 1897 an offer reached him from Manchester, he began to toy with the idea of leaving his Vienna post. In the autumn of 1898 he gave up the direction of the Philharmonic concerts. An ailment of the arm, real or pretended, served as an excuse for his gradual withdrawal from Vienna. Although Mahler made another attempt to tie Richter to the Opera by getting him a new contract at a higher salary, Richter, in a letter from Manchester early in 1900, asked for 'unconditional release from the service of the Imperial Court Opera', and this was granted. Mahler could now look for younger conductors to assist him. In 1900 Bruckner's disciple and friend Franz Schalk was engaged as conductor, and a year later Mahler at last succeeded in bringing to Vienna a young friend of his Hamburg days: Bruno Walter, who had meanwhile been working at Breslau, Pressburg, Riga and Berlin, was engaged for the Vienna Court Opera in July 1901.

When, shortly before the start of the 1898–99 season, Hans Richter retired from the direction of the Philharmonic concerts, the orchestra offered these to the director of the Court Opera. On 6 November 1898, in the great hall of the Gesellschaft der Musikfreunde, Mahler for the first time faced the Vienna Philharmonic – though he had, in fact, been conducting the same musicians for the last year. This statement requires an explanation for readers unfamiliar with the facts of Viennese musical life. The instrumentalists who constitute the Philharmonic Orchestra are members of the Vienna Opera. At the opera house they stand under the director's orders; a few streets away, in the building of the Gesellschaft der Musikfreunde they form a musical republic that makes its own laws. This was so even in the days of the Empire. The Vienna Philharmonic could perfectly well have asked for another conductor in 1898, but they actually preferred to give the master they obeyed at the Court Opera a trial run on their own republican ground. The collaboration of Mahler and the Philharmonic lasted barely three years. In retrospect, one feels it could not have gone on any longer. Mahler's autocratic fanaticism over rehearsals accorded ill with the traditional spontaneity of the famous orchestra. Mahler, as Max Graf pointed out in a thoughtful retrospective essay of 1921, was:

a tyrannical character, a man whose will-power was concentrated in his nerves. He simply would not see that this orchestra could only give of its best if left to its own enthusiasm. He wanted to impose his own will on it: the orchestra was to renounce its personality and its independence. In this way he failed to recognise the true worth of the orchestra, but the orchestra also failed to see the true worth of Mahler.

The conflict began with the very first concert. Anonymous letters to the editors of several Vienna newspapers alleged that Mahler had tampered with the orchestration of Beethoven's *Coriolanus* overture and the *Eroica* symphony. At rehearsals for the concert, which included Mozart's G minor symphony as well as the two works by Beethoven, were not held in public, this information could only have come from the players themselves. Mahler certainly did retouch the orchestration of some great works, but what he did was never unscrupulous or arbitrary, it was always most carefully considered. However, the fact that he was already applying these methods in his first Philharmonic concert must have added to the difficulties he encountered. Very gradually, movement by movement (in those days there was applause after every movement of a symphony), Mahler won the audience over. A contemporary report by Theodor Helm shows what a fight he had of it:

Mahler's great success had to be literally wrested from an audience consisting mainly of sceptics, many of them influenced by hostile propaganda. There was icy silence at the entrance of the new conductor, and even after the towering *Coriolanus* overture, a breathtakingly dramatic performance, only sparse applause. Mahler's conception of the first movement of Mozart's G minor Symphony – basically the traditional one, familiarised by Richter – found the audience more responsive. Then came the charming, floating andante with its delicate ebb and flow: even the most hardened sceptics were conquered, and for the first time there was heartfelt general applause. This was repeated for the next movement, the minuet and trio, the former played with proudly contained power, the latter with enchanting discretion, but both taken more slowly than usual. The Finale, truth to tell, seemed a little too slow to me, a veiw the majority of listeners appeared to share. The climax of the concert, for sheer overt success, was the first movement of the *Eroica* (although it was Mahler's conception of this which most sharply divided opinion *after* the concert). The immediate effect of Mahler's brilliant direction and of the magnificent playing of the Philharmonic was overwhelming, expressing itself in frenetic bursts of applause which in the end – as had often happened under Richter – forced those fine musicians to rise as a body from their places by way of acknowledgement.

This report faithfully reflects the reservations of a public determined to keep faith with what Mahler seemed to be attacking. There was loyalty to Hans Richter, which must not be betrayed by premature approval of the young opera director; there was also loyalty to Beethoven, with whose work Mahler dared to meddle. In the end, as reports and reviews show, no one could resist Mahler's impact. But the reservations, fostered by a gradually growing anti-Mahler faction, remained. The greater part of the orchestra was still on his side; but his mania for experimenting roused constant opposition. His first Philharmonic season was certainly controversial. Thus he had a Beethoven string quartet played by the entire string section of the orchestra. It did not help that he was able to point to von Bülow's precedent. Opposition was even more violent when the perfectionist composer-conductor requested that for the performance of his own Second Symphony (April 1899) the number of double basses should be increased from ten to fourteen. This was considered an 'extravagant use of resources' which people were unwilling to concede to either composer or interpreter. Orchestral retouching of Beethoven's

Fifth Symphony (included in a concert of November 1899) gave further provocation, and the attack finally came when Mahler ventured to subject Beethoven's Ninth to a revision.

The performance of Beethoven's Ninth under Mahler's direction took place in February 1900. Several critics complained bitterly about alterations to the score. Thus, the composer Richard Heuberger wrote in the *Neue Freie Presse* after the concert:

In contemporary music there is a tendency to adopt the thoroughly reprehensible system of 'overpainting' the works of our great classical composers. What was proffered yesterday as 'Beethoven's Ninth Symphony' is a deplorable example of this aberration, this barbarism. A vast number of passages were completely re-orchestrated, altered in sound and therefore in sense, against the clearly expressed intention of Beethoven, whose genius rose to unprecedented heights in this very Symphony.

Similar objections are still raised against Mahler's methods at the present time. We live in an age of musical archaeology, which makes laudable efforts to furnish us with the 'original scores' of classical masterpieces. But the striving for 'guaranteed authenticity' has unfortunately led to a rather more dubious vogue for original scores which seems derived, however inconsciously, from a consumer society's faith in brand names. The fact that Mozart did not scorn to set the most successful 'numbers' from *Die Entführung* for wind orchestra, in order to increase their popularity and 'make a profit out of them', must seem as strange to the original-score enthusiasts as Beethoven's endeavour to bring his symphonies in chamber music arrangements to the homes of music-lovers. Nor is it generally realised that fidelity to the original score does not necessarily guarantee the original sound. Even if we use the old instruments, even if we perform in halls with the acoustic properties familiar to the old composers, can we, as Wilhelm Furtwängler put it, count on people listening today as people listened a hundred and fifty years ago? In his retouching of scores Mahler by no means started out from his own ideas of what the sound should be. He based his corrections (which he kept to a minimum) on the intentions of the composer as revealed by the score. In the process he made allowances not only for the changed construction and technique of certain instruments, but also for the historical growth of the orchestra. As the researches of H. Becker and A. Carse have shown, the concert orchestra at the time of the classical Viennese composers contained about twenty-five string players – sometimes considerably fewer. In the course of the nineteenth century, the string section might be inflated to as much as sixty intruments. Obviously the relation between strings and wind intended by the classical composers was radically altered by this. Mahler's 'corrections' aim, amongst other things, at righting this imbalance. Even among Mahler's many admirers today there are some who, when the subject of his retouching of other composers' scores comes up, retreat into embarrassed silence, as if this were a regrettable lapse on the part of a genius. Though one can fault individual instances of Mahler's orchestral corrections, taken as a whole they show a novel and much-needed notion of the tasks of the interpretative artist. Strict adherence to the original scores when almost all the factors that determine the sound effect and its perception by the audience have changed, does not really make sense. The large concert halls that were built in the nineteenth century, among them the Grosse Musikvereinssaal in which the Vienna Philharmonic played from 1870 onwards, have altered the sound pattern of the classical symphony. They have modified the balance of sound, and reduced the distinctness of the single voice demanded by Beethoven's scores in favour of a late-Romantic, reverberating mixture of sounds. By increasing the number of violins, violas and cellos, they have caused an indefensible suppression of the woodwind passages, and thus prompted occasional 'doubling' of the woodwind instruments.

None but musical philologists, staring fixedly at manuscript since they lack the capacity for listening to actual sound, can be satisfied with the mere preservation of the original score. Mahler was no copy-clerk. He was a musician, and he could hear that in the course of the years Beethoven had been distorted, unintentionally and unknowingly, in the new concert halls. He simply set out to redress the balance, as deduced from Beethoven's scores. The results were bound to shock his contemporaries. They insisted on a tradition which they believed to be authentic, whereas Mahler had discovered the disfiguring effect of this tradition. They demanded the right to experience Beethoven's symphonies in romanticised, echoing waves of sound: Mahler fought against this 'confused noise' in which the classical clarity of Beethoven's part-writing became totally blurred.

Mahler left us no manual on his technique for obtaining a correct sound. We must divine his intentions from the extant scores – an undertaking of great topical interest in these days of electronically recorded and transmitted music. Only once did he see fit to justify his method theoretically. After his first attempt with Beethoven's Ninth, which met with opposition and incomprehension, he drew up a text with the help of his friend Lipiner, which he had printed and distributed when the concert was repeated. The leaflet read as follows:

As a result of certain public utterances, a part of the audience might form the opinion that in tonight's performance the conductor has arbitrarily changed details of Beethoven's symphonies, especially of the Ninth. Therefore it seems necessary to issue a statement clarifying this matter.

As his ear complaint grew into actual deafness, Beethoven lost that indispensable inner contact with reality, with the world of physical sound, just at a time when his conceptions were developing most powerfully and moving him to find new means of expression, to use the orchestra in such a drastic manner as had been unimaginable before. It is also well known that the quality of brass instruments in his time completely precluded certain tone sequences necessary to the melody. This very shortcoming ultimately led to the perfecting of these instruments, and it would seem outrageous not to use them now to achieve as perfect a performance of Beethoven's works as possible.

Throughout his life Richard Wagner sought to rescue Beethoven's works from intolerably negligent performance. In his essay 'On the performance of Beethoven's Ninth Symphony' (*Collected Works*, vol. 9) he has shown how to present this symphony so as to get closest to the composer's intention. All modern conductors have followed his lead. Fully convinced of the rightness of this by his personal experience of the work, tonight's conductor has taken the same course, without materially overstepping the limits of interpretation indicated by Wagner.

There can be absolutely no question of re-orchestration, alteration, let alone 'improvement' of Beethoven's work. The long established augmentation of the string instruments resulted, also long ago, in a corresponding augmentation of wind instruments, purely with the object of strengthening their volume *and without assigning to them a new orchestral role.* In this as in every other point concerning the interpretation of the work, as a whole or in detail, it can readily be shown by reference to the score (and more convincingly the closer the study) that the conductor, neither indulging in arbitrary wilfulness nor blinded by regard for so-called tradition, has made it his sole aim to pursue Beethoven's will down to its minutest manifestations, not to sacrifice one iota of the master's intentions in the execution, nor let them be submerged in a confusion of sounds.

Vienna, February 1900
Gustav Mahler

In this leaflet Mahler meant to defend his intentions, but the significance of the document goes much further. The allusion to 'the world of physical sound' forms the basis of a new way of musical thinking. The science of musicology, sprung from musical philology, did not attain to a consideration of the reality of sound until the twentieth century, but Mahler anticipated this development. The pamphlet of February 1900 is the first manifesto of an approach that seeks to analyse actual sound, in contrast to mere textual scholarship. Experienced conductors had long known that a mezzoforte required from the full orchestra does not mean the same for all instruments: in practice to get the right effect one would curb a naturally strong, and boost a naturally weak instrument. Wagner and Verdi actually prescribed such dynamic differentiation in their scores. Composers of earlier days did not yet do this, perhaps because they did not want to set down such precise instructions, or because they knew they could depend on a style of performance familiar to all. The modern interpreter does not leave anything to chance that can, by fixing the details of performance, help to ensure the desired total effect. In retrospect he will discover passages in more than one work of the past that require closer definition. For instance, nearly all the great conductors of our time have found the interpretation of Schumann's symphonies a recurring problem. Mahler, too, was much involved with retouching Schumann's scores. Mosco Carner, who has investigated the (unprinted) Schumann arrangements by Mahler, summarises his work thus:

1. Loosening up of the dense instrumental texture
2. Clarification of thematic lines and rhythmic patterns
3. Change of dynamics and re-orchestration of certain dynamic effects
4. Improvement of phrasing
5. Changes in execution
6. Thematic alterations
7. Suggested cuts

With the exception of the last two headings, these retouchings are in every case attempts to bring out the composer's intentions more clearly. For Mahler, clarity was a basic requirement of musical communication. Where an idea of the composer's, detectable in the score, did not reach the listener's ear by means of a 'faithful' rendering, he considered it his duty to modify the sound in such a manner that the original purpose stood out unmistakably.

To apply this carefully thought out method to the works of Beethoven in the Vienna of 1900 was not without risk. He was accused of pursuing originality for originality's sake. Many critics, including those who had paid tribute to him as composer and opera director, turned against him. The Philharmonic Orchestra itself, burdened with the extra work of the revised orchestral parts, felt less kindly towards him. It could be foreseen that they would soon look out for a less exacting conductor. In February 1901 Mahler conducted his last Philharmonic concert. In April he informed the orchestra that, in view of his great burden of work and his impaired health, he 'no longer felt able to conduct the Philharmonic concerts'.

During his relatively short association with the Philharmonic Orchestra, Mahler did extremely well by that institution, and the musicians appreciated this. In June 1900 the orchestra was to go to Paris for the World Fair. Since according to the statutes then in force the Philharmonic gave concerts only under the leadership of their permanent conductor, they invited Mahler to join them on their trip, which was financed by wealthy Viennese patrons. Mahler was not keen on the idea. The concert tour fell into his holiday period (the Court Opera then being closed every June and July); moreover, he feared that at this time of year the music-loving public would be away from Paris. He eventually agreed to go, but his fears were partly realised. The money supplied from a 'guarantee-fund' was quickly used up in Paris, and there was a danger that the costs of the return journey could not be met. Mahler managed to obtain the necessary sum for the Philharmonic from the Rothschild family. The orchestra on that occasion gave him a bigger ovation than the Paris public ever bothered to do. The concerts were ill-starred from the first. The very misprint on the advance posters by which the director of the Vienna Court Opera was called Gustav *Malheur* did not augur well. The press failed to give advance publicity. The visit threatened to go unnoticed amid the welter of other events. Three of the concerts took place at the Théâtre Châtelet, two at the cavernous Palais du Trocadéro, which damped down every orchestral fortissimo to a feeble mezzoforte.

We have a review of the first of these two concerts by an illustrious Frenchman: Catulle Mendès, companion of Verlaine, Mallarmé and Debussy and one of the leading-Wagner enthusiasts of his country, sent a report to the *Neue Wiener Tagblatt* which appeared, translated into German, in the issue of 22 June 1900. The terse essay of this poet, who was equally conversant with the German and French orchestral traditions, is illuminating.

Herr Mahler's orchestra captivated us at once by its display of perfect discipline and by its rare richness of sound, now powerful, now tender. The strings vibrate in a wonderful ensemble. As regards the ideas underlying the conductor's interpretation, many have shown sincere enthusiasm for them. Others felt disturbed – particularly in the case of Mozart's G minor Symphony – by certain rallentandi, by an excess of refined nuances, and by too stark a contrast between pianissimo and fortissimo. Certain it is that for some time now a number of conductors, among them extremely able and famous men, have been trying out 'personal' interpretations even of works of genius, in a laudable effort to excel their colleagues. Should one blame them for this? I think it is fair to say that the originality to which they force themselves is not cultivated for eccentric distinction, but in the nobler hope of gaining a deeper understanding of the masterpieces; and they act like worshippers who in their fervent piety observe the religious rites down to the minutiae of superstition. But there is no one to touch Mahler, with his simple stance, the straightforward gesture, that will suddenly flare up to marvellous impetuosity – a man whose whole appearance bespeaks his powerful and nervous will – with his special insight and manner of conducting: his performance of the *Meistersinger* Overture, solemn and popular at the same time, showing such a fine awareness of the prominence and interrelation of the principal themes – Richter himself could not improve on it; his *Freischütz* Overture so poetic, the *Oberon* Overture so light and delicate, fairylike as it were. Herr Mahler has brought off a success that amounted to a triumph.

Four days later Pierre Lalo, son of the composer Edouard Lalo, had an article in *Le Temps* about the concerts given by the Viennese visitors. He too noted the original, personal quality of Mahler's interpretations:

We as a people do not give enough thought to the scores of the masters; our neighbours, on the other hand, think about them a little too much. A purpose is discovered in every note; everything is made explicit; the structure is invested with so much complexity that the basic design is destroyed.

Apart from any definitive value judgment, Mendès and Lalo alike pick out the characteristic traits of Mahler's conducting. And there is one particularly interesting sentence in Lalo's review: 'We should like to express our regret that Herr Mahler, one of the most remarkable symphonic composers of the German school, has not seen his way to performing one of his own works.'

Evidently people in Paris were already aware of Mahler the composer, and were possibly wondering whether the composer would now be eclipsed by the hard-working opera director and conductor. But this was far from being the case. Mahler hurried away from Paris straight to Carinthia to find the solitude he needed to get his ideas down on paper. At Maiernigg in the summer of 1900 he completed the first draft of his Fourth Symphony.

*　　*　　*

'So my Fourth is finished. I'll make a fair copy in the winter.' The letter of August 1900 in which the composer announced the conclusion of the summer's work was written to Lipiner, and is full of disquisitions on questions of form and the psychology of creation, with reference to Lipiner's dramatic work, in which Mahler was deeply interested. Mahler's comments reveal both his understanding of the dramaturgic requirements of the straight stage and his knowledge of the drama from the classics to Ibsen and 'the other moderns'. He is not sparing with his advice. If Lipiner gets stuck at any point of his epic drama cycle *Christus*, he should confidently go on to do a later part; the connecting links would then come more easily.

Mahler has just applied this method himself, and admits to often finding himself in this situation. When some movement of a symphony refuses to take shape, and he simply decides 'to get on with the rest, then often the "miscalculation" eventually shows up. Invariably I find that I took a wrong turn at that point.'

The plan of the Fourth Symphony is conceived retrospectively from the Finale, a song finale that goes back to a composition of 1892: *Das himmlische Leben* (Heavenly life), a piece for voice and orchestra on a text from *Des Knaben Wunderhorn*. In making this the final movement of his symphony, Mahler determined the character of the whole work. After the monumental Symphonies Nos. II and III, each lasting well over an hour, the new work returns to normal proportions. The orchestral apparatus, too, is much reduced in comparison with the preceding scores.

Of all Mahler's symphonies, the Fourth is the one that became popular most quickly. Its relatively modest technical requirements doubtless contributed to this, but above all its friendlier, less demanding idiom. The experimental Mahler is not discoverable at first hearing. His boldness as an orchestrator – applied more deftly than before, and hence only discernible to the alert ear – is subordinated to music which may be enjoyed quite straightforwardly. The first movement is in free sonata form. The second, scherzo–like, betrays only in certain passages for a strange-sounding solo violin Mahler's penchant for the ludicrous and the eerie. The strings of this solo instrument are tuned up by a whole tone, giving the violin a pale, and at the same time exciting, sound. 'Like a fiddle' Mahler writes in the score, thinking of Death striking up to speed the soul on its way. *Freund Hein* (Goodman Death) – this was the original title of the movement – is not frightening in effect. The uncanny mingles with the cosy. The mystical discords of the baroque-style violin are embedded in the rustic dance, the Ländler.

The third movement has a restful tempo. The adagio uses variations in more than the usual sense, for it even contains variations on themes stated at the beginning of the symphony. Anyone familiar with Mahler's music will recognise in the 'heavenly joys' of the Finale at least one melodic formula taken over from the Third Symphony: the soprano passage *Sankt Peter im Himmel sieht zu* (St Peter looks down from Heaven) is melodically related to the alto solo in the Third Symphony, *Ich hab' übertreten die zehn Gebot* (I have transgressed the Ten Commandments). When this obvious thematic link was pointed out to him, Mahler is said to have found it strange and disturbing. However, the phenomenon bears out his known creative trends. He himself related almost every work to the preceding one. In the Second Symphony he buried the hero of the First, and in the Fourth Symphony, he said, he wanted to look at the world of the Third from a humorous angle.

To us the Fourth Symphony seems a 'friendly' work. It did not get a friendly reception at the first performance, which Mahler conducted in the autumn of 1901 with the Munich Kaim Orchestra. In the first movement, according to Natalie Bauer-Lechner, the listeners were surprised by the simplicity of the themes, expecting something more *outré* from Mahler. The movement was received with hissing, though also some applause from the Mahler fans. The following movements, too, roused strong opposition, nor did the Finale earn unanimous approval. Among the most hostile was a group of French Wagnerians looking out for new developments in Germany. But one of them was to become an enthusiastic admirer of Mahler's. Wilhelm Ritter, born in French Switzerland but educated in Paris, was thirty-four, sophisticated and a lover of the arts. As he sat whistling fiercely in the Kaim Hall, his animosity was heightened by knowing that Mahler was Jewish. For Ritter was no Dreyfusard: he was proud of belonging to the opposite faction. But the excitement the Fourth Symphony roused in him really caused him to think. Later he wrote down his thoughts at that time, concluding with the following sentences: 'I protest against this music. All my thoughts and convictions condemn it. Yet I am fighting my own enjoyment. At heart I love only this music. I give in. I admire it . . .' This conflict of conscience caused Ritter to write a letter to Mahler in which he set out his dilemma. Mahler's reply was to forward the proofs of the as yet unpublished full score and the as yet unpublished piano transcription of the Fourth Symphony. The music itself, Mahler thought, would resolve the conflict in the soul of that curious devotee.

Henceforth William Ritter was one of Mahler's champions. He joined those enthusiasts who travelled around after Mahler and his symphonies. He published respectful reviews in the Paris *Courrier musical* and in the *Revue musicale de Lyon*. In 1905 he wrote an essay on Mahler under the title 'Un symphonist viennois'. No Paris editor was prepared to publish this somewhat violent declaration of love; it appeared later in his collection *Etudes d'art étranger*. In it he writes:

By force or voluntarily – but in fact under compulsion rather than by free decision – from this day on I acknowledge the genius of Mahler in its totality. These lines are the document by which I, a traditionalist and antisemite, lay down my arms before the work of this Jewish-Nietzschean magician. One wonders whether he may not even inscribe his suspect name on the opening page of the golden book of the music of all time, the page which has precedence even over that with the single name of Wagner on it: the page which hitherto has borne only the thrice-holy names of Bach, Beethoven and Bruckner.

The effusions of this convert to Mahler occupy a unique place in the non-German literature of the time. Ritter shows insights into the essence of Mahler which were normally granted only to the composer's closest friends. He soon grasped the autobiographical character of Mahler's creative work. Once, when he commented on this to the composer, Mahler seemed utterly surprised, but had to agree with him. Ritter's wide experience in artistic and aesthetic matters enabled him to determine the historical place of Mahler's art with more precision than could most German or Austrian commentators of that era. Ritter, who had studied the art of Czech and Romanian painters, the music of the Russian Rimsky-Korsakov and the Czech Karel Kovařovič, the work of Arnold Böcklin and Edvard Munch, and who, moreover, knew the cultural scene of Vienna from personal experience, realised at the very beginning of this century that Mahler was no 'late-Romantic', no rearguard of the troupe led by Berlioz, Liszt and Wagner, but something altogether new, a figure about to conquer the twentieth century. Mahler's music was in step with the century, a true reflection of it. 'Play this music in the architectural creations of Otto Wagner, as decorated by Klimt and Kolo Moser, and it will be seen to symbolise modern Vienna.' Ritter understood the affinity of Mahler with the Vienna Secession.

In 1875, when Mahler first came from Iglau to Vienna to study at the Conservatoire, the population of the capital was still below the million mark. A quarter of a century later there were 1,675,000 inhabitants. The buildings of the Ringstrasse were completed. The actors at the Burgtheater had a grand new building since 1888. The electrification of the tramways had been started and their lines extended to the suburbs. The urban scene had changed. The route from the Conservatoire of the Gesellschaft der Musikfreunde to the Karlskirche no longer traversed a bridge over the River Wien: the water-course was covered over and beside it, below street level, there ran the (still active) Wien Valley line of the metropolitan railway, in those days still driven by steam. The plan of this urban transport system was closely linked with the architectural projects of Otto Wagner, the most important Viennese architect at that time. The stations of the metropolitan railway at the Karlsplatz, whose demolition is being considered at the time of writing, were also designed by Wagner. They reveal an artistic drive inspired mainly by function and material. This is also shown by two other buildings of Wagner's, the Vienna Post Office Savings Bank and the church at the Steinhof Mental Hospital.

Walking from the Karlsplatz to the Wienzeile, one comes to a building designed by a pupil of Otto Wagner's, the architect Josef Olbrich. The 'Secession', opened in 1898, was the temple of those painters, sculptors and architects who wanted to free themselves from traditional schooling and routine. 'Down with borrowed styles' was their slogan; they were far from advocating one uniform new style for all, but wanted every artist to 'speak his own language'. The later concept of a Secessionist style – an Austrian variant of the movement that elsewhere was called *Jugendstil* or *Art Nouveau* – does not therefore entirely correspond to the ideas held by the protagonists of the movement in Vienna. Their aspirations are summed up in the motto which since 1898 has graced the front of the Secession building: 'To the age, its art – to art, its freedom.' (Only in the years of Hitler's rule was this motto obliterated.) The ruling principle of the Secession was to encourage the full development of diversified individual styles. A free, creative attitude was also desirable towards the art of other nations: 'We want an art without xenophobia. The art of other nations should stimulate us and shows us what we ourselves are; we shall appreciate it, and admire it if it is worth admiring; but imitate it we shall not.'

The programme of the Secession, as laid down in the periodical *Ver sacrum* (Sacred spring), sounded self-assured, but it was not meant to be narrow-minded or parochial. Cézanne, Rodin, Munch, Hodler and Segantini were represented in the exhibitions of the Secession. Among the most distinguished members of the association were Gustav Klimt (1862–1918), Carl Moll (1861–1945), Kolo Moser (1868–1918), Alfred Roller (1864–1935) and Emil Orlik (1870–1932).

From 1902 on Mahler was connected with this group of artists. In April 1902 he even appeared as musical arranger and conductor at the Secession's Max Klinger exhibition, when Klinger's Beethoven sculpture was shown for the first time. Manifesting their particular aesthetic ideal, the artists of the Secession provided a decorative setting for their guest. Their manner of mounting an exhibition, combining sculpture, painting and music, may be traced back to Wagner's idea of the 'total work of art'. But it could equally be maintained that this experiment of the Vienna Secession was anticipating a Bauhaus idea of the 1920s, as frescoes by Klimt and others were united with Beethoven's music to create a fitting stage for Klinger's Beethoven monument.

Gustav Klimt's Beethoven frieze, which is thematically connected with the Ninth Symphony, has been preserved, but the music Mahler conducted is lost. True, it was basically Beethoven's music, but Mahler had considerably remodelled it. He chose a section from the Finale of the Ninth, the choral passage with the text:

> *Ihr stürzt nieder, Millionen?*
> *Ahnest du den Schöpfer, Welt?*
> *Such ihn überm Sternenzelt!*
> *Über Sternen muss er wohnen.*

> [Do you fall down, you millions?
> Do you sense your creator O World?
> Seek him above the star banner!
> He must reside above the stars.]

The mighty passage from the Choral Symphony did not sound forth in the familiar vocal setting, but was intoned by wind instruments: certainly reminiscent of Beethoven, yet no closer to him than Klinger's statue or Klimt's frescoes.

Emil Orlik painted a portrait of Mahler that year. The artists of the Secession became his friends. Mahler, who a few years ago had still declared that 'musicians have little interest in the plastic arts', began to use his eyes. He had conversations with Alfred Roller, who as president of the Secession had given the address at the Klinger celebrations, and it did not take him long to realise that the new art had much to give to the musical theatre. Roller translated the functional ideas of Otto Wagner's architecture into scenic principles. The stage, he asserted, dealt not with 'pictures' but with 'space'. In discussing the production of *Tristan und Isolde*, Mahler and Roller discovered a creative harmony. The director of the Court Opera offered Roller the task of designing a new production of *Tristan* which was to have its première in February 1903. It inaugurated a new period – the most brilliant of all – in the work of the opera director. But how had Mahler strayed into this circle in the first place? What had led the 'aural type' to the plastic arts? Who had persuaded him to look at things?

At the beginning of 1901 Mahler was troubled by a chronic, painful ailment that caused him to lose a lot of blood. An operation was indicated, after which he had to take sick leave, which he spent at Abbazia. Although for some months he had to walk with the support of two sticks, the complaint seems to have been a trivial one by present-day medical standards, and Mahler soon got over it. At Maiernigg in the summer he began work on a new symphony, his Fifth, and also set some poems by Rückert. The opera season, beginning in August, found him fully recovered.

Since early in 1898 Mahler had lived in the Auenbruggerstrasse, in the third district of Vienna, with Justine keeping house for him. She cosseted her brother and protected him fiercely against intrusion. The two of them must have had some unspoken agreement to 'keep faith' with one another, which is probably why Justine kept her feelings for Arnold Rosé, the leader of the Vienna Philharmonic, hidden from her brother for so long.

After the trip to Paris in 1900 Mahler's circle of friends expanded a little. At the Austrian Embassy in Paris he had made the acquaintance of Sophie Clemenceau, the sister-in-law of Georges Clemenceau, and of her sister Berta Zuckerkandl, wife of the distinguished anatomist Emil Zuckerkandl, and a Viennese society lady trained in music and interested in the visual arts. Through Clemenceau, the companion of Manet's youth and subsequent friend of Rodin, she was well informed about artistic developments in France. In Vienna she felt drawn to the Secessionists Kolo Moser and Gustav Klimt. Indeed, she wrote an essay about the latter – who would take his sketchbook to her husband's dissecting class – one of several she published on artistic subjects between 1901 and 1907.

The acquaintance begun in Paris continued in Vienna. That November at the home of the Zuckerkandls Mahler met a girl who attracted his interest from the first moment: Alma Maria Schindler. She lived in the house of her stepfather, the Secessionist artist Carl

Moll. There the first meetings were held that eventually led to the exodus of the avant-garde from the Künstlerhaus and the founding of the Secession; there, too, Alma had met Klimt, who fell in love with the sixteen-year-old girl, but their friendship was not approved of by her stepfather. In her memoirs, Mahler's future wife, who after his death married the Bauhaus architect Walter Gropius and in 1929 the poet Franz Werfel, speaks frankly of the many distinguished men that paid homage to her beauty. Though a brief mention of some will be sufficient here, it is important to stress the fascination she evidently exerted on them all, for it would help to explain Mahler's swiftly kindled love. It seems that for a time Alma was courted simultaneously by the acting director of the Opera and the ex-director of the Burgtheater, Max Burckhard, who had laid down his office in 1898. Burckhard, who during his eight years as director had enlarged the repertoire of the Burgtheater by the works of Gerhart Hauptmann, Ibsen, Anzengruber and Schnitzler, must have had a formative influence on Alma's mind; he introduced her to Nietzsche and Schopenhauer and she regarded him as her mentor.

It is readily understandable that such serious reading in a girl of twenty greatly impressed Mahler. His feelings were aroused even more by the musical education Alma had enjoyed. She had been thoroughly instructed in counterpoint by the blind composer and organist Josef Labor. When she first met Mahler her teacher of composition was Alexander von Zemlinsky, a composer Mahler thought highly of and whose opera *Es war einmal* he had given its first performance in 1900. Zemlinsky seems to have been even more notable as a teacher, for Arnold Schönberg, who for a short time had been his student, later declared that he owed to Zemlinsky nearly all his knowledge of the technique and problems of composition.

The compositions of the twenty-year-old Alma Schindler are by no means negligible. Nine songs, subsequently published, reveal at the very least taste and technical skill. The texts Alma chose are by Heine, Rilke, Dehmel, Otto Julius Bierbaum, Otto Erich Hartleben and Gustav Falke. In a study devoted to these songs in 1950, W. S. Smith emphasizes the characteristic difference between Mahler's diatonic melodies and the Wagnerian chromatic melodic line of Alma's *lieder*, and he justly relates it to the whole phenomenon of women composers. These *lieder*, in Smith's opinion, do not deserve their almost total neglect, though he admits that 'they make great demands on singer, pianist and listener'.

A few weeks after their first meeting, Mahler's marriage to Alma was a settled conclusion. On 28 December 1901 the general management was informed of their engagement. Shortly before there had been a confrontation which gave great pain to Alma: Mahler had 'forbidden' her to compose. She wept as she agreed to conform to his wishes. Many years after Mahler's death she wrote: 'I buried my dream then. Perhaps it was for the best. But it left a nagging wound which never completely healed.'

On 9 February 1902 the wedding took place at the Karlskirche, and on the following day Justine was married to Arnold Rosé. In May Mahler conducted his Beethoven arrangement at the Klinger exhibition of the Secession. An opportunity arose at last of performing his Third Symphony, never hitherto given in full. In June, accompanied by his young wife, Mahler went to Krefeld at the invitation of the *Allgemeine Deutsche Musikverein*, in order to conduct this performance. The work had an enthusiastic reception, and was performed in four other cities that same year. The young couple spent the summer at Maiernigg where Mahler was working on his Fifth Symphony. As on the Attersee, here too he had a little forest hut to which he retreated in order to compose. Alma, who was expecting a child, copied out the music. On 3 November 1902 a girl was born whom the parents named Maria Anna.

The appendix of the catalogue (edited by Franz Hadamovsky) of the exhibition 'Gustav Mahler and his times', which was held in 1960 at the Secession building, lists the new works produced at the Court Opera. For the years under discussion, they are:

1903   Charpentier: *Louise*
       Puccini: *La Bohème*
1904   Hugo Wolf: *Der Corregidor*
1905   d'Albert: *Die Abreise*

Leo Blech: *Das war ich*
Wolf-Ferrari: *Le donne curiose*
Pfitzner: *Die Rose vom Liebesgarten*

More remarkable than the additions to the repertoire were the
experiments in staging carried out in conjunction with Alfred
Roller, whose artistic potential for the stage Mahler discovered and
who soon afterwards was employed by Max Reinhardt as well.
Even to our generation Roller's work is a living reality – at least in
the settings created for the Vienna *Rosenkavalier* of 1911, basically
unchanged for over half a century.

Mahler's collaboration with Roller began with a new production
of *Tristan und Isolde* in February 1903. Oscar Bie attempted to
depict the scene in a review. He concluded: 'The localities can be
described but not the light. When the tent is opened, when morning
dawns, when Isolde sinks into the light – these are strokes of genius.
Here is something of the music of light.'

Nor do reproductions of the settings convey more than a superficial
idea of what this new *Tristan* had to offer. 'Light and air make music
with the Wagner orchestra', wrote one reviewer in March 1903.
All accounts agree that the naturalism of traditional stage décor had
been thrown overboard. This was in line with the principles of the
Secession. 'For two generations Nature has been the model – it is
worn out now. A general desire for stylisation is abroad.' These
words written by the eminent art critic Ludwig Hevesi on the
occasion of the Klimt exhibition of 1903, have an obvious relevance
to Roller's stage designs. Mahler and Roller wanted everything
shown on stage not merely to 'be something' but to 'mean something'. A wide range of artistic experience, including commercial
art, had predisposed Roller, a native of Brno the Moravian capital,
to understand and sympathise with Mahler's aesthetics. He was
Mahler's junior by four years. As a teacher at the School of Commercial Art (from 1899) and a leading member of the Secession –
which he left in 1905 together with its most active artists under the
leadership of Klimt – he developed the functional concept of art
which corresponded to Mahler's view of the musical theatre.

Mahler, according to Roller writing many years after the former's death, 'had the utmost contempt for mere outward show on the stage, for any purely decorative detail, however brilliant and dazzling that did not arise inevitably from the total conception'.

The functional stage design, then, complemented Mahler's shaping of the music. Fifty years after that memorable *Tristan* performance, Erwin Stein recalled what he had experienced at the age of eighteen. According to Stein, the dramatic climaxes served Mahler as structural pivots:

> To him they were not only a means of expression, but also a means of architecture. There was in every piece he performed, in every act of every opera, a point at which the music's dynamics or tension culminated, with lesser climaxes in between; one main centre of gravity, as it were, and other subsidiary ones. In *Tristan* the first act culminated in Isolde's drinking of the potion; the second, not in Tristan's arrival, but with the last *crescendo* of the duet before the anticlimax of Marke's entry; in the third act it was the fortissimo during Isolde's appearance which towered above the earlier climaxes of Tristan's monologues.

Integration of setting and music also prompted Mahler to reconsider the illumination of the entire theatre area. Aware of the benefit to the stage of the low-lying, roofed-over orchestra pit at the Bayreuth Festspielhaus, Mahler in the first year of his collaboration with Roller asked for the pit at the Court Opera to be lowered. Musical considerations, to be discussed later, certainly played a part in this experiment, which sharply divided critical opinion in the Viennese press. However, the optical effect seemed equally important to Mahler. In an interview he pointed out the advantages of lowering the orchestra:

> I am thinking, for instance, of *Tristan und Isolde*, and how unavoidably the electric lamps on top of the orchestra stands interfered with the illumination of the stage. Try as we might to achieve harmonious lighting in accordance with the mood, the unromantic glare from those orchestra lights threatened to spoil it all. This irritating defect would of course disappear if the orchestra were invisible.

The orchestra pit was actually lowered in the summer holidays of 1903. Such innovations caused some agitation among the tradition-minded Viennese. They began to think Mahler wanted change at any price. Mahler for his part took no notice of the conventional who clung to tradition. His famous dictum against tradition, of which several versions are quoted, must have been known by 1902, as Hans Richter in an interview with the *Neue Wiener Tagblatt* thought fit to declare his formal opposition to Mahler's view. Mahler carried on undeterred, as is clear from his work on Beethoven's *Fidelio*, as presented to the public on 7 October 1904. Incidentally, it is not quite accurate to say that Mahler had simply equated tradition with slackness. The way Roller recorded the pronouncement was: 'What you theatre people call tradition is really just complacency and slackness.'

What Roller wrote down was said at a *Fidelio* rehearsal of 1904. In the old production, what had happened for the prisoners' scene in the first act was that the whole chorus stepped into the prison yard from their cells to left and right, formed a semicircle on the brightly lit stage, and away they went: '*O welche Lust, in freier Luft den Atem leicht zu heben* . . .' Roller considered this primitive arrangement inadequate to the deeply moving nature of the music. He showed Mahler his sketches and told him how he envisaged the scene: the prisoners should come up from the depths in groups of twos and threes, staggering into the light, unused to walking, dazzled by the daylight, dizzy with fresh air, groping along the walls, clay-coloured, sick men. Mahler agreed. He only asked, for musical reasons, that a double quartet should emerge sufficiently early on. At rehearsals the choir-master protested against the new procedure. The so-called producer, who in the director's presence saw himself reduced to the role of stage-manager, also tried to make Mahler change his mind: the 'number' was a showpiece for the chorus, and one should not cheat them of their success. It was in this context that 'tradition' was flung at Mahler, and that he replied with the saying as handed on by Roller.

Mahler's *Fidelio*, like his *Tristan*, was conceived with one principal climax in mind: the heroism of the loving wife was what he wanted to emphasise. The partly submissive, partly honourable figure of Rocco would not fit into this conception. Mahler eliminated the simple decent side of his character by omitting his aria *Hat man nicht auch Gold beineben*. Even more incisive was his treatment of the overture. Before Mahler began his reforms, it had for many years been the custom in Vienna to play, not the 'little' Overture in E major finally intended by Beethoven to open the work, but the *Leonora* No. 3 Overture in C major. This great dramatic piece was ill-suited to begin what is, after all, more or less a comic opera up to the entrance of Pizarro. Mahler decided to restore the short E major overture at the beginning. But this would have meant the loss of an attraction the Viennese music-lovers had become attached to. When Roller pointed out that he needed time for the scene change before the finale, which was to show the parade ground of the castle, and therefore he needed a pause at that point, Mahler hit on the idea of playing the *Leonora* No. 3 Overture during the scene change. Knowing the Viennese, however, he breathed not a word about the technical motives behind this. He realised that a public whose interests were predominantly musical, and a critical fraternity little conversant with theatre technique, were not to be convinced by such arguments. Instead he spread the word that the great C major overture had found its proper place just before the finale as it contained 'a recapitulation of the whole drama'. The Viennese gladly believed him, and many an opera enthusiast would still resent it if the familiar legend were replaced by a sober statement of the facts. Mahler's placing of the *Leonora* No. 3 Overture has, at any rate, not only maintained itself in Vienna but been accepted by other opera houses.

It was problems of scene-shifting again that provided the impetus for innovations in the new production of Mozart's *Don Giovanni* of December 1905. Ludwig Hevesi, art critic and sympathetic chronicler of the Secession, also followed the progress of Roller's work for the stage. He wrote about *Don Giovanni* the day after the performance:

For Mahler and Alfred Roller, the musico-dramatic creation is the one and vital whole to which all interpretative labours are directed. I can only wonder at the view held by a large section of the public about previous Mahler-Roller productions, that the work itself is swamped by scenic additions. When people talked about 'lavish spectacle' in connection with these earlier productions, they merely displayed their lack of training in the visual arts. Roller's conception does not, of course, spring complete and immutable from his mind. It develops gradually, it formulates itself, and the form it assumes in *Don Giovanni* is not even the final one. Here we see a markedly stylised stage picture. There are some architectural focal points in the shape of wooden towers or pylons which define the stage space, while at the back the stage is cut off by a coloured back-drop. For simple scenes, two pairs of towers right and left on the proscenium are sufficient. In more complex scenes, more are employed as required, as for example in the ballroom scene, with its three orchestras and its comings and goings. The towers are quite simple, practicable constructions, with openings on the first floor level serving as windows of houses, oriels or balconies; these are sometimes hung with tapestries, or curtained off when not in use. It is an idealistic architecture, a kind of structural passe-partout creating an ideal space. This space is made just as deep and broad as the purpose of a scene demands. So it cannot happen that the stage turns into a vast wilderness on which a single person makes enormous gestures because he instinctively wants to take up as much room as possible. This caricature of operatic acting is, quite incidentally, done away with.

Hevesi's comments not only define the character of the historic Mahler-Roller stage, but still have – unfortunately, it must be said – a topical relevance, since the intimate connection between the design of the stage setting and the actions of the performer is even now imperfectly understood. It happens frequently nowadays that designers send their 'little sketches' to the place where a new production is planned, and leave it to others to translate their impressive but unfunctional drawings into actual settings. Mahler and Roller furnished examples of responsible stage interpretations that deserve more than purely historical appreciation. They always, in the truest sense of the words, 'kept in view' communication to the public; they strove for an audiovisual effect not only from the best seats in the stalls and boxes, but, if possible, over the whole auditorium. With *Tristan und Isolde* Roller had not been completely successful. He, too, had approached his first attempt at stage work from a preconceived image. Later on he would experiment in his workshop with a scale model of the theatre showing the distances of all the seats from the stage, in order to study the likely effect on various groups of spectators. During rehearsals Roller continued to try out effects. 'Untiringly', says Emil Lucka, 'he carried out his tests, moving from the stage to the stalls, from the stalls to the gallery, experimenting with screens, coloured discs, light-intensities, altering, improving, dealing in nuances.'

This *Don Giovanni* production, which glowed with black and coloured velvet in place of painted backdrops, and in which every scene was given the amount of space suitable for its action, was also a triumph of stage technique: the numerous scene changes took place without a break in the action. No transformation required more than thirty seconds. Thus the unified effect Mahler wanted was achieved. His endeavour to integrate action and space, colour and light, words and music, went even further – he ordered a new German translation, which was done by Max Kalbeck. Again, he was not out to make changes at any cost. Passages of the text which by their popularity had become an integral part of the work were allowed to remain unmodified, but where musical logic or dramatic consistency was violated, the changes came in. He was against calling the opera *Don Juan*, as it had always appeared on the play-bills; why translate the Italian title into Spanish if the singing was in German? What was the point of substituting the ugly three-syllable 'Don Ju-an' in the Commendatore's call, where Mozart had carefully allowed for the four syllables of 'Don Gio-van-ni'?

Mahler's version of Mozart presents one feature which even his admirers have not always appreciated, let alone approved; his treatment of the appoggiaturas, acciaccaturas and grace notes which are not usually written out in the music yet must be observed by the faithful interpreter. Mahler seems to have largely eliminated the appoggiaturas. Erwin Stein in his above-mentioned account put it very tactfully: 'Mahler, it is true, expunged the additional top notes and cadenzas which the singers used to insert, but he kept those appoggiaturas which he considered compatible with the character of the music.' This statement indicates that Mahler did not make the technique of Mozart's time his criterion, but followed his own subjective feelings. I think the importance of Mahler as an interpreter of Mozart will be in no way diminished if we openly admit the discrepancy between the historically correct, and the Mahlerian Mozart style. We may even conclude that at a certain point in operatic history Mahler's procedure was unavoidable if the dramaturgic significance of Mozart's music was to be re-established. In the minds of Mahler's contemporaries, any element of bel canto singing was indissolubly associated with the idea of rococo style. They did not distinguish between the coloraturas that fractured a style and those demanded by the style. Mahler, wishing to prise the works of Mozart away from the disfiguring rococo mould, had to take his stand against musical ornamentation *per se*. He removed what he and his public regarded as 'extraneous trimmings' and 'decorative detail', in order to bring out the essence of the music, its expression, its dramatic function and its spiritual power. Here Mahler's aesthetics approached the artistic beliefs of Adolf Loos, who wrote in 1908: 'Lack of ornament is a sign of spiritual strength.'

It may seem farfetched to bracket together Mahler and Loos, the Austrian pioneer of unadorned architectural space, the ornament-hating critic of society. Adolf Loos, born in 1870, belonged for a short time to the Secession, but he soon turned fiercely against the Secessionists' continued liking for non-functional though 'modernistic' embellishments. Mahler, by virtue of his collaboration with Roller, might seem a loyal ally of the Secessionists, but this is deceptive. He fell in with the Secessionists, and at the same time outgrew them. Informed critics agree that his musical theatre was not committed to any single artistic movement, but had evolved by his ranging freely over the technical resources opened up by the new art. In the existing literature on Mahler, this aspect has hardly been mentioned. It seems to have escaped the notice of researchers that he expressed himself very precisely on this point. In a statement to the *Illustriertes Extrablatt* (9 September 1903) he said: 'All modern art must serve the stage. I did say modern art, not Secession. What matters is the collaboration of all the arts. There is no future in the old standard clichés; modern art must extend to costumes, props, everything that can revitalise a work of art.'

[174]

That was the guiding principle of Mahler as a stage producer: he had come a long way from the type of opera conductor who thinks only of the music. He was, indeed, the first modern operatic producer. Certainly he owed much to Wagner's concept of the 'total work of art', but whereas other Wagnerians of that epoch were content to preserve a few aspects of the Bayreuth formula, Mahler pursued Wagner's ideas of the musical theatre beyond their own confines. Twenty years after Wagner's death mere conservation was not enough. New achievements of stage technique, like the resources of modern art, had to be put in the service of the creative music-drama. Mahler went on to apply the idea of unity between music and stage not only to the works of Wagner but, as a fundamental law, to the entire musical theatre, thus founding the art of opera production in the modern sense.

In acknowledgement of that fact, playbills of his opera performances should certainly have named Mahler as the producer: but the programmes of those days mentioned neither producer nor conductor. The whole idea of the 'singers' opera' – the star system, as we would call it today – masked the revolution that Mahler instigated in the musical theatre. Only in retrospect can one see that it was Mahler – and apart from him only Toscanini – who elevated the conductor to his present-day supremacy. His own age, as the story of his life shows, was not ready for this change: but Mahler was the contemporary of the future.

To attempt to interpret opera as a total work of art was inevitably, in Vienna, to provoke the opposition of those who judged the quality of a performance or, indeed, of an opera house, solely by the lustre of famous voices. Comparatively few operagoers were excited by the employment of new artistic means. A unified performance meant little to the habitués whose applause was reserved for bel canto. The balletomane aristocracy of Vienna thought it unforgivable that Mahler gave no new impetus to ballet and seemed rather uninterested in their favourite art form. On the other hand, an article by Ludwig Karpath published in March 1904 shows that Mahler did give some thought to a renovation of the ballet. Fantasy ballet and genre ballet had, in his view, had their day. He longed for:

a new man, with new ideas. But as this impatiently awaited Messiah was not forthcoming, in the end he fell back on the old things. He realised at long last that in a great opera house with an audience of international character there is a place even for lesser art. Mahler the artist came to realise that he must compromise with Mahler the director. . . . Only the few who understand the real springs of his actions will recognise that he tolerated the commonplace merely because he could not attain to his highest aim.

Another reason why Mahler did not reorganise the ballet along lines similar to his opera reforms may have been his lack of experience with the medium. Doubtless, too, there was a tactical consideration: he was surely not prepared to wage war for the modernisation of the theatre on several fronts at once. On the ballet front he stabilised his position with conventional productions. When Oscar Nedbal's first ballet, a spectacular pantomime called *Pohádka o Honzovi*, scored a great success at the Prague National Theatre in 1902, Mahler took the work into the Vienna repertoire, and it reached the stage of the Court Opera under the title *Der faule Hans* in April 1903, produced by Josef Hassreiter, mentor of the Vienna ballet school since 1869. The public was well satisfied with productions of this kind, as is shown by the box-office receipts; the work was performed thirty-five times during Mahler's tenure.

So Mahler let the dancers get on with it. Work on the operatic repertoire claimed all his energies. He paid little heed to the attacks by conservative operagoers who were, of course, trying to restrict his authority. There was no lack of interference from would-be influential personalities in Vienna who thought themselves competent to pronounce on the not uncomplicated work of an opera director. There is evidence of these intrigues even in the files of the Court Theatre Management. Under the registration number 3587/1904 we find a letter addressed to the General Director by twenty patrons of the Court Opera. They complained of the lack of a suitable 'cast for the main roles', and on the other hand regretted that first-class singers were most inadequately employed, 'in minor roles or not at all'. The petition was quite right in pointing out that Mahler had departed from the established principles of casting, but the conclusions drawn were wrong. The petitioners could not see that for Mahler a beautiful voice was not the only criterion of casting, that he demanded more than vocal accomplishment, namely musicianship, variation of vocal colour and the ability to fit into the ensemble. Though unable to accept Mahler's operatic aesthetics, they acknowledged his outstanding ability as a musician and conductor, but accused him of 'being swayed perhaps rather by his subjective preferences than by his artistic convictions' in questions of casting. The signatories revealed that they were broaching these questions not simply as operagoers but also on behalf of certain singers who felt themselves slighted by Mahler. The petition continues:

One constantly hears the artist complain that the director in his personal dealings with them frequently disregards the most elementary rules of courtesy. This naturally gives rise to conflicts which have already cost the Court Opera many valuable and well-nigh irreplaceable members of its staff. . . .

and culminates in a request designed to limit the director's power:

Let there be a competent and unprejudiced man at his side who, equipped with the necessary powers, would be in a position to restrain him from harmful errors and blunders, and to redress the all too predictable consequences of his sympathies and antipathies.

The note attached to this letter by the correspondence clerk of the General Management adds that 'Herr Direktor Mahler should be informed of these not wholly unjustified comments'. The expert dealing with this matter was evidently not averse from following it up. However, the General Director seems to have given it no further thought. He rarely concerned himself with running the affairs of the Opera, for Mahler had long since gained direct access to the man who was lord over all Court Theatre matters, the General Director's superior, who was the Grand Chamberlain.

The Grand Chamberlain for his part made it absolutely clear that he had not the slightest intention of curbing Mahler's powers, let alone depriving him of his office. All attempts made in 1904 to oust Mahler from the Court Opera foundered against the Grand Chamberlain's resolution. Mahler knew well what a powerful supporter he had in the person of the Grand Chamberlain, particularly as the Emperor himself refrained from any interference in official business. Although the Opera was financed from the privy purse, Franz Josef did not issue any direct orders. On one occasion when the Emperor expressed some wish concerning the Court Opera, and Mahler, though unwilling to meet it, declared himself ready to obey an express command, Franz Josef is supposed to have said: 'I may wish, but I do not command.'

The confidence the Grand Chamberlain reposed in the opera director was founded not least on Mahler's financial success. It was the director's duty to carry out his tasks within the limits of a set budget and without making any additional demands on the Emperor's privy purse. The budget also made allowance for the takings expected from the sale of tickets, and the anticipated receipts were entered in the form of estimates. Over the years Mahler succeeded in achieving a sizeable surplus of actual takings above the estimated. Receipts for the year 1903, for instance – the first year of the collaboration with Roller – were assessed in advance at 1,485,000 kronen. In the event, the Opera had a surplus of 58,765 kronen. In March 1904 this aspect of Mahler's work was discussed in an article in a Munich paper. According to this account, it was the surplus balance achieved by the Vienna Opera director that weighed in his favour in the highest circles, and against this fact

nothing can be done, either by members of the Court or by high-ranking noblemen, many of whom are not exactly well disposed towards the director of the Court Opera. It may be counted one of Mahler's merits to have incurred their displeasure; for it proves that his pride yields to no man, that he will not curry favour with the aristocracy. Never before has a director dared to affront the wealthy as Gustav Mahler has done again and again. He will not defer to anyone's wishes in the choice of a new opera, and has even disdained to oblige a nobleman by engaging some young lady with an inferior voice. To be sure, he is supported in this attitude by the constitutionalism of the monarch, who will never act without consulting his advisers.

Good financial progress was maintained throughout 1904. In the spring the General Director was able to inform the public in a press interview that the Opera had made a surplus of 48,909 kronen in the first four and a half months of the year. Mahler's regard for his financial responsibilities proves once again what a clever tactician he was. He knew he could not realise his ambitious plans unless he made some compromises. Certain critics were already accusing him of opportunism, of not paying enough attention to contemporary trends in Austrian and German opera, though such a reproach is not substantiated by the record of operatic events and Mahler's exertions. In the summer of 1905 he tried to secure for Vienna the recently completed score of *Salome*, in spite of having had no success with Strauss's earlier opera *Feuersnot* in 1902, for he was an early believer in the outstanding musico-dramatic talent of Richard Strauss. When the expected friendly reception did not materialise, Mahler wrote to the composer: 'I am so sick and tired of the attitude of the Vienna press, and above all of the gullibility of the public.'

His experiences with *Feuersnot* and other contemporary productions warned Mahler to be careful. He resolved to sponsor only works he himself considered stageworthy and likely to repay the trouble taken with them. This principle determined his attitude to *Der Corregidor*, the opera by his old friend Hugo Wolf which the latter tried to press Mahler to perform in September 1897 when he had only just taken up his appointment. It was the occasion of Wolf's first fit of insanity. He told his friends that he was the new opera director and was about to oust Mahler from his post. This mental illness was a consequence of the infection he had contracted in his youth. Wolf's friends began to understand why its first manifestation was connected with Mahler when they heard about the immediate events leading up to the tragedy. Wolf had looked up Mahler at the Opera. On Mahler's desk – so Frank Walker tells us in his biography of Wolf (1968) – lay the score of Rubinstein's opera *The Demon*. Wolf

had made some derogatory remarks about this work, and a dispute had ensued, in the course of which Mahler had said some uncomplimentary things about *Der Corregidor*, and in spite of the fact that he had promised to produce it, had expressed doubts as to whether, after all, the opera would be performed in Vienna. With rage and bitterness in his heart, Wolf had left Mahler's office vowing revenge for this severe disappointment, and his mental distress as a result of this interview, coming at a time when he was already in the fever of creation, had unhappily provided the spark that had kindled a conflagration in his brain and brought on the long threatened insanity. Brooding upon revenge, he had conceived the idea of himself becoming director of the Opera and so getting rid of Mahler and removing the last obstacle in the way of *Der Corregidor*'s success in Vienna. This idea obsessed him until he believed it was true.

The fate of this companion of his Conservatoire days must have moved Mahler deeply. The press gave more attention to the madness of the mortally ill composer than it had ever given to his works. The episode of the last encounter between Mahler and Wolf gave rise to rumours which not only reached the papers at the time but still recur to some extent in Alma Mahler's memoirs of her husband. It was held against Mahler that for a long time he refused to perform *Der Corregidor*. He felt there was little chance of success for a work which had been submitted under the aegis of his predecessor Jahn, and which had aroused no response either at its first performance at Mannheim (1896) or in a revised version at Strasbourg (1898). When in February 1903 Wolf was at last released from his suffering, Mahler decided to put *Der Corregidor* on the programme. The première on 18 February 1904 was purely an act of homage to the friend of his youth, and he was unable to secure a lasting place in the repertoire for the opera (which Frank Walker described as 'a song-book with orchestral accompaniment'). Mahler was by no means entirely uncritical of Wolf even as a composer of songs, perhaps because the aims they pursued were so different, even in their *lieder*. In any case, unlike Wolf, Mahler had long devoted his creative energies to the development of a new orchestral language. The dream of composing an opera, which in their youth he had shared with Hugo Wolf, was forgotten.

Mahler was now developing a revolutionary orchestral idiom, presenting a familiar vocabulary of fanfares and marches, rustic dances and waltzes, song tunes and endless melodies, in a new melodic syntax, in an unusual polyphonic grammar, and with an exciting orchestral style. Between 1901 and 1905 – during the time of his most concentrated and successful work at the Opera – Mahler created three symphonic scores which took a long time to be fully appreciated even by the musical public and have only recently found acceptance in wider circles.

It is easy to understand the prolonged resistance to Mahler's new symphonic idiom. What he effected with his innovations can be compared only approximately with the breakthrough of the Secession in the visual arts. Mahler's symphonic Secession goes much further. It includes elements of Expressionism, without renouncing the Austrian heritage of sonata structure. We are only now beginning to appreciate the Expressionism of Egon Schiele as much as the specialised *Jugendstil* of Gustav Klimt. Clearly Mahler's symphonic inauguration of the twentieth century could not be comprehended more quickly than its counterparts in the realm of painting and graphic art. The timelag is explained by the inertia differential between optical and acoustical habits of perception and acceptance. Novelties in music have a tougher job of it than those in the visual arts: the ear is lazier than the eye.

What is immediately apparent about symphonies Five to Seven is their Romantic or late-Romantic attitude. This façade is part of the character of these works. All the same, we shall misunderstand them unless we penetrate to what is hidden behind this façade, with its often monstrously aggrandised orchestral architecture.

Mahler constructed his symphonic edifices in a new way, with the finale dominating the whole plan. As early as 1921, Paul Bekker wrote about the Sixth Symphony: 'All the essentials of the symphonic action are entrusted to the finale more decisively than ever.' The sheer expansiveness of this unusual finale – it lasts about half an hour – makes it more difficult to understand. No wonder, then, that the Sixth has repelled popularity longest of all, and that the mysteries of its structure provoked analysis. No one who sees a composer's inspired idea in terms of an easily grasped tune can hope to understand the meaning of this final movement. The main theme, agreeably haunting the memory after the concert, does not represent the composer's overall conception, for Mahler's inspiration for this Finale was the idea of its form, as Theodor Adorno pointed out in his essay *Mahler* (Frankfurt, 1960). Erwin Ratz, too, significantly chose the Finale of the Sixth to show in an extensive analysis – available in the symposium *Gustav Mahler* (Tübingen, 1966) – how the new type of symphonic structure arose from Mahler's masterly handling of the technique of variations.

Closely linked with the special formal character of these three works that usher in the symphonic development of this century, two notable features emerge: the evolution of an unusual polyphony, and the irrevocable emancipation of orchestral sound from the pianoforte. These features must be considered in detail, as they prove the so-called late-Romantic Mahler to have been, in fact, a Secessionist – and, above all, the pioneer of an epoch-making musical reorientation.

Most composers of the nineteenth century, and many of the twentieth, have conceived their orchestral works 'at the keyboard'. Mahler certainly did. For him a work was complete in its essentials when he had written a draft that could be roughly reproduced on the piano. The actual work of creation, which he did during the holidays, was then orchestrated during the theatre season. This is not to suggest that Mahler's drafts were not worked out with a view to orchestral instruments and timbres – of course they were. All the same, during the first period of his symphonic output Mahler considered the 'piano score' an adequate source for getting to know the essentials of a work. He played his Third Symphony to Bruno Walter on the piano, in his cottage by the Attersee. And in 1905 he agreed to play the Finale of the Fourth Symphony on a grand piano made by the firm of Welte; their special process enabled Mahler's performance to be preserved on punched rolls of paper which could be reproduced as often as desired, so that we can still listen to this interpretation of Mahler's on records today. Obviously with the Finale of the Fourth a piano version was still practicable. From the Fifth onwards, such an attempt would have been quite hopeless. Henceforth Mahler's orchestral compositions were entirely geared to the orchestra's spirit and technique. He had long been working towards it. In April 1896 he alluded to it in a letter to a composer who had asked his advice and help: 'You must rid yourself of the pianist! All this has no orchestral texture, it is conceived for the keyboard.'

Mahler's struggle to shake off the domination of the piano is, of course, noticeable well before the Fifth. It shows in his increasing renunciation of so-called 'filling-in parts', in his striving to give each instrumental line its own significance. Long sections of the Third demonstrate this many-stranded, 'unpianistic' concept, most beautifully in the polyphony of the last movement, where it is the exception for individual groups of instruments to be relegated to a choral, melodically subordinate function. In this respect the Fourth represents a retreat to older positions (a fact that doubtless contributed to its early popularity); but from the Fifth on, almost all harmonic configurations are liberated from the grip, and from the idiom and mannerisms, of the pianist. 'The individual parts', Mahler said during his work on the Fifth, 'are so difficult to play that they all really need soloists. Some pretty bold passages and figures escaped me here, just because I do know the orchestra and its instruments so well.'

Thus the basic concept of the composition is joined by an element of colour which assumes an integrating function. The list of instruments used by Mahler in the Sixth emphasises the emancipation from the piano. Besides the usual, numerically augmented orchestral body it includes a glockenspiel, cow-bells, tubular bells, two harps, a celeste, a whip, and a hammer whose task is described by the composer as 'short, strong, but dully reverberating stroke of a non-metallic character (like an axe-stroke)'.

The expressionist features of this music are too prominent to need further elucidation. Less familiar to the listener is an element which, if roughly classified, would have to be referred to as impressionism. To listen for the first time to the beginning of the Finale of the Sixth with an open mind is to be reminded of Debussy. The distribution of the chord (C – E flat – F sharp – A flat – B flat – D), which lacks any tonal reference, over celestas, harps, horns, woodwind, double-basses and pizzicato cellos, and the obscuring of this

Band III. — Nr. 68   Wien–Leipzig, 19. Jänner 1907   Preis 32 Heller.

DIE MUSKETE

Alle Rechte vorbehalten
Nachdruck verboten

Humoristische Wochenschrift

Preis im Abonnement
vierteljährlich K 4.— 6

(Zeichnung von Fritz Schönpflug.)

„Tragische Sinfonie."

«Herrgott, daß ich die Hupps vergessen habe! Jetzt kann ich noch eine Sinfonie schreiben.»

A satire on the instruments employed in Mahler's Sixth Symphony

splash of colour by the big drum and a cymbal struck with a sponge-headed baton, does not, in itself, prepare the hearer for the contrapuntal and formal strictness that characterises the planning of the mighty final edifice.

The total emancipation from the keyboard is, historically speaking, the outcome of a development that was started in Austrian music by the classical Viennese composers. In the old days musical thinking was founded on the basso continuo. The 'filling in' of the texture according to the rules of figured-bass playing, which determined almost mathematically which fingers should be placed on what keys, gave way to the so-called 'filigree texture' of the classics. In this, the middle parts also acquired an individual profile, independent of keyboard figuration. Vertical sound, obeying the laws of harmony, was skilfully combined with horizontal polyphony obeying the laws of counterpoint. Around 1900 some composers worked out a new approach to polyphony and harmony. It is instructive in this connection to compare Mahler with Claude Debussy, two years his junior. The Frenchman rebelled against traditional harmony, the laws that were meant to establish the succession of different chords. At the age of twenty-one, Debussy showed his fellow-students at the Conservatoire a few chord combinations that one report calls 'crazy escapades'. To his shocked colleagues, Debussy exclaimed: 'Can't you listen to chords without knowing their provenance and destination? Where do they come from? Where do they go to? Do you really *have* to know that? Listen to them: that's enough. But if you don't *want* to understand, run along to the Head and tell him I'm ruining your ear.'

Mahler proceeded differently. Though he did freely employ impressionist sound combinations, he could never wholly renounce the logic of harmony, however loosely defined. Symphonic form needed that logic. Debussy, while working on the score of *Pelléas et Mélisande*, publicly declared war on the symphony: 'Since Beethoven, the futility of the symphony seems to me an established fact.' In 1901, when this sentence appeared in the Paris *Revue Blanche*, Mahler was vehemently affirming his faith in the 'futile' genre by writing his Fifth Symphony. His retreat to the purely instrumental

symphony without text or voices was, however, by no means a
conservative gesture. Even the external, formal plan of the symphonies discussed here shows novel elements.

Symphony No. 5 in C sharp minor
Five movements. Movements 1 and 2 form the 'first section' not
only in name, but intrinsically. The second movement is a large-
scale development of the first. The third movement (scherzo) is
succeeded by a romanza-like adagietto, using only strings and harp.
The last movement is a rondo finale.

Symphony No. 6 in A minor
Four movements
1. Allegro energico, ma non troppo
2. Scherzo (*Wuchtig*) (Vigorous)
3. Andante
4. Finale (Allegro moderato)

Symphony No. 7 in E minor
Five movements
1. Langsam – Allegro
2. Nachtmusik I
3. Scherzo
4. Nachtmusik II
5. Rondo–Finale

However, Mahler's revolutionary re-creation of polyphony goes
far beyond his formal rearrangement of symphonic structure. He is
not satisfied with a multiplicity of voices, but progresses to a complex
differentiation. To describe these instrumental lines pressing against
each other, tearing at each other, coalescing with each other and
constantly fanning out again, we could do with a scientifically precise
yet vivid terminology. We must fall back on visual comparisons:
Mahler's differentiation of voices has something of the character of
collage. In this acoustic collage, then, lines of variegated hues are
mounted to make a symphonic whole. Such awkward metaphors
merely hint at what discloses itself to the ear. The listener who stops
at the façade of orchestral architecture will, to be sure, not perceive

the essential newness of these symphonies, and may be inclined to reject the interpretation attempted here: but Mahler himself spoke so vividly to the same effect that we advance it without hesitation. On a walk through the woods in the summer of 1900 Mahler and some friends came upon a country fair, with barrel organs blaring from all the roundabouts, swings, shooting booths and Punch-and-Judy shows, mixed with the strains of a military band and a male choir, all of which, on that clearing, 'regardless of one another produced an incredible noise'. According to this reliable report, Mahler exclaimed:

Do you hear that? That's polyphony – and that's where I got it from. When I was a small child, in the woods of Iglau, this used to excite me strangely and impressed itself on my mind. It does not really matter whether you hear it in this sort of row, or in the song of a thousand birds, in the howling gale, the splashing waves or the crackling fire. But that is how – from a lot of different sources – the themes must come, and like this they must be entirely different from each other in rhythm and melody – anything else is only part-writing and disguised homophony. What the artist has to do is organise them into an intelligible whole.

Though the representatives of the school of *Musique concrete*, established in the Paris of the 1950s under the leadership of Pierre Schaeffer, have neglected to call on Mahler for support, their 'concrete music' based on electronic sounds and the noises of the surrounding world could have had Mahler for its spiritual patron, especially since Mahler too sounds employs of the actual world, like cow-bells and hammers. With him, however, these are exceptional, for on the whole his orchestration rests firmly on the foundation of the traditional orchestra.

He did, on the other hand, radically change the uses to which orchestral instruments are put. Gabriel Engel, one of the foremost champions of Mahler's music in America, has shown this, using the Fifth Symphony as an example. The solo flute, formerly the carrier of honeyed melodies, with Mahler sounds ethereal, free from pathos, and as though coming from an infinite distance; the pungent small E-flat clarinet, not used in symphonies before Mahler, emerges rogish, grotesque, sometimes even ludicrous; the oboe is not restricted to the melancholy of its upper range, but sounds forth untrammelled in its natural middle range; the comical bassoon suddenly produces the voice of suppressed pain in its highest register; the contra-bassoon is allowed coarsely bizarre solo interjections; the horn seems never before to have played such an important role.

He uses other instruments, too, in an unusual way – the aim throughout being maximum differentiation of sounds and timbres. Where the traditional instruments are insufficient, he does not hesitate to call in reserves – thus he employs the tenor horn in the first movement of the Seventh Symphony, and emphasises the nocturnal character of the fourth movement by using a guitar and a mandoline as well as the harp.

The second nocturne of the Seventh Symphony shows that Mahler was not always concerned with making the orchestra larger and more imposing. As in some sections of the Sixth and the adagietto of the Fifth, in this nocturne he anticipates the symphonic chamber style which Arnold Schönberg, with due respect for Mahler, established with his Chamber Symphony for fifteen instruments in 1906. Even the method of building up chords from the interval of a fourth, characteristic of Schönberg's Chamber Symphony, is anticipated in Mahler's Seventh.

The multiplicity of individualised voices and the alternation of the monumental and the subtle within one symphony have had a very considerable and at times a deleterious influence on the interpretation of these works. The concert halls erected during the second half of the nineteenth century favoured the late-Romantic mixed sound. Mahler's music in contrast tends to demand the utmost emphasising of the single voice. To achieve this the composer marks very detailed directions in his score. Practically every page bears witness to his well-nigh desperate desire for 'distinctness'. Here, he prescribes *Schalltrichter auf* (with bell raised) for a wind group that is meant to stand out in a powerful passage; there he opposes, within a single bar, the mezzopiano of the strings to the fortissimo of the high woodwind and the piano of the low woodwind; he gives instructions like *hervortreten* (prominent), *rufend* (calling), *antwortend* (answering), *verklingend* (dying away). Again and again we find the word *deutlich* (distinct): sometimes in the guise of concrete instructions concerning the bowing and phrasing of the strings, or indicating the 'pauses for breath' which should markedly separate one chord from another, one note from the next. Tempo indications are frequent. They must not be taken literally, but always in relation to Mahler's purpose, which he defined thus:

A tempo is right if everything still comes across. If a figure can no longer be grasped by the ear because the sounds merge into one another, then the tempo is too fast. In the case of a presto, the upper limit of distinctness is the right tempo – beyond this, it loses effectiveness.

This limit that must not be overstepped if symphonic polyphony is to remain clear varies with the acoustics of the hall. In a late-Romantic concert hall (such as the hall of the Vienna Grosse Musikverein) the acoustics work against everything Mahler intended (from 1901 on, anyhow): the many-layered sound collages of Symphonies Five to Seven lose clarity, and therefore effectiveness. The resistance of the public to these works – a prolonged and obstinate resistance – should therefore be seen as not purely a question of taste. It is due also to the disparity between the functional sound structure of symphonies which belong to the twentieth century and their acoustic fate in the concert halls of the nineteenth century. It is only the modern concert halls, and even more the recordings on disc and tape, relatively independent of surrounding space, that have won general appreciation for these particular symphonies. Mahler's saying, 'My time will come', is often quoted. One thinks of the obligatory interval that must elapse before genius is recognised. I would give that saying a secondary meaning. The ideal of distinctness for music the themes of which arise from 'a lot of different sources' and are so vastly differentiated 'in rhythm and melody' is better served today by a stereophonic recording, integrated through the mixer, than by most live performances in the concert hall. The gramophone record has been the saving of Symphonies Five, Six and Seven. Not that Mahler conceived them with an imaginary, manipulated space in mind: he did dream of such a variable space, but even he could not have foreseen the possibilities of electro-acoustic sound manipulation and preservation. In this respect, too, Mahler was the contemporary of the future.

'Above all, I believe that Mahler suffers acutely from the hypnosis of power . . .' This sentence occurs in an essay published by the *Revue de Paris* on 1 July 1905. The author was Romain Rolland. He had recently seen Mahler conducting at the Alsace Music Festival in Strasbourg, and also heard a performance of his Fifth Symphony. Rolland calls the Fifth 'a mixture of strictness and incoherence'. All the same, he meant no disrespect, for he believed in Mahler's message. One could expect good work from Mahler the composer, if only he would divest himself of his offices. Art, Rolland argued, demands complete dedication; Mahler should sever himself from the musical scores of others, as well as from the administrative burdens weighing on him: 'Caught up in feverish activity and weighed down by heavy tasks, he works incessantly and has no time to dream.'

This is exactly how Mahler must have struck the impartial observer at the time. That in a period of exhausting activity in the opera house and on the concert platform he should still have had enough time and energy to realise his dreams of composition staggers the imagination. Friends continually warned him against overwork. They did not understand that the variety of Mahler's work had on him the reviving effect of a sauna bath. If he was advised to rest after some taxing job, or if his own state of exhaustion was pointed out to him, he would say that this was 'perfectly ordinary physical fatigue'. His spirit never faltered. On the contrary, his experiences in opera house and concert hall, at performances and rehearsals, seemed to give such stimulus to his creativity as a composer that one wonders whether he would have done any composing at all without this stimulation. As he himself put it, he positively needed practical activity 'as a counterweight to the momentous internal upheavals of creation'.

Romain Rolland's diagnosis, that Mahler was suffering from the hypnotic effect of power, was therefore incorrect. He needed the exercise of this power – even as a composer. Given this particular psychological mechanism, it will be readily understood that the year 1905, which found him at the summit of power, was the happiest year of his life. His position as Court Opera director was secure, despite endless attacks and intrigues. As a conductor he was famous in Austria and Germany, in Russia (where he had given several concerts) and in France. Six of his symphonies were in print, and the score of the Seventh was completed. In Holland a sizeable group of Mahler fans had grown up since 1903, led by the conductor Willem Mengelberg and his Concertgebouw Orchestra. Mahler was the father of two healthy girls, Maria Anna, born in 1902, and Anna Justine, born in 1904. He enjoyed the friendship of distinguished artists, not only in Vienna. Though the press was still divided in its attitude to Mahler's music, there were experts, journalists and writers in more than one country who stood up for him. In Vienna the university professors Guido Adler and Richard Wallaschek appreciated his work. From Königsberg, Ernst Otto Nodnagel raved about Mahler in the *Ostpreussische Zeitung*, publicised him in the Berlin *Kunstwart* and published analyses of his Second, Third and Fifth Symphonies. Ludwig Schiedermair, who became a notable musicologist, had published a study of him in Leipzig as early as 1900. The Viennese Richard Specht's first essay on Mahler appeared in Berlin in 1905.

In Vienna itself, acclaim for him was never greater than in that triumphant year. The Fifth Symphony was performed there on 5 December 1905 under his own direction. None of Mahler's later works was played in Vienna during his lifetime; the Sixth was not performed until 1933 under Clemens Krauss; the Seventh had its Vienna première in 1916 under Felix von Weingartner, and the Eighth in 1918 under Franz Schalk. Bruno Walter introduced the Ninth to Vienna in 1912, the *Song of the Earth* in 1915.

Changes on the political scene also helped to make 1905 a memorable year. The conflict of nationalities and the antisemitism particularly rampant in the German-speaking parts of the empire receded into the background before the struggle of the working class for universal franchise. The emergence of an organised social democratic movement, the campaign of the Hungarian opposition against the rule of the aristocracy, and not least the revolutionary rising in Russia caused the Emperor to reconsider his position. His prime minister, Freiherr von Gautsch, declared in parliament that 'there could be no objection in principle to drawing new strata of the population into formulating the nation's policy'. The democratisation of Austria seemed to be going ahead. Soon afterwards the new laws of suffrage enabled the Social Democrats to enter parliament as the second strongest party.

Mahler's sympathy with this movement is shown by an entry in his wife's diary. The dating of this entry is dubious, since mention on the one hand of 'May 1st' hardly agrees with mention on the other hand of a rehearsal of Pfitzner's opera *Die Rose vom Liebesgarten*, the first performance of which was at the beginning of April 1905. However, the note itself is of interest. Alma Mahler writes that Pfitzner, who came to visit her, had encountered a workers' demonstration on the Ringstrasse and remarked irritably on their 'proletarian faces'. Soon after, Mahler got home and told her of his experience on the Ringstrasse: 'He had met the workers' procession on the Ring and had marched along with them for a while . . . they had looked at him like brothers. They *were* his brothers. These people were the future!'

There is no other evidence of any direct political commitment on Mahler's part. The episode on the Ringstrasse does not by itself make him a social democrat, but it tallies with the picture of a man who felt great social compassion. He loved to quote Dostoevsky, especially the saying that no man could be happy so long as a single person on earth still had to suffer. But this expresses his ethical principles rather than any conviction as to the necessity of practical political action. His music is that of a man of deep human feeling. Though he may not have believed in any particular method for alleviating social injustice, there is no doubt that it grieved him.

Within his personal circle, however, he was ready to take action. He encouraged others, and gave financial help to friends. The published letters give many hints of this, in various discreetly edited passages. One important piece of rescue work must be mentioned in detail, for it is part of musical history.

In 1903 Mahler met Arnold Schönberg. Mahler's brother-in-law Arnold Rosé, leader of the Philharmonic and first violinist of the quartet called by his name, had taken up the young composer (he was still under thirty) and was holding rehearsals for the first performance of Schönberg's string sextet *Verklärte Nacht* in the Court Opera building. On this occasion Schönberg was introduced to the director, who henceforth took a lively interest in him. At that time Schönberg was by no means a wholehearted admirer of Mahler's work. In a memorial speech after Mahler's death, Schönberg himself pointed out that his first reaction to the Second Symphony had been a mixture of rapture and scepticism, and that he tended to think Mahler's themes 'banal'. 'I think I ought to confess' – this is Schönberg in 1912 – 'that I was Saul before I turned into Paul.'

Mahler recognised Schönberg's talent. When Schönberg and his friend Zemlinsky decided to establish a forum for contemporary music in Vienna they could count on Mahler's help. He agreed to become honorary president of the Vereinschaffender Tonkünstler, founded in March 1904. The Society's aim was 'to provide for contemporary music a permanent centre of cultivation in Vienna, and to keep the public informed about the current state of creative music'. Mahler himself conducted some of the Society's concerts. In November 1904 he performed the new *Sinfonia domestica* of Richard Strauss, a work Strauss himself had premièred in New York during his American tour in March of that year. Largely through Mahler's influence Schönberg was able to conduct the first performance of his symphonic poem *Pelléas und Mélisande* in January 1905.

In spite of Mahler's help, the Vereinschaffender Tonkünstler only functioned for one season. But Mahler's interest in Schönberg persisted, although he confessed that he could not completely accept everything the younger man did. When in 1907 the Rosé Quartet first performed Schönberg's First String Quartet in D minor, and some listeners registered their disapproval by hissing, Mahler leapt to Schönberg's defence. 'You mustn't hiss!' he shouted at one malcontent, who retorted: 'I hiss your symphonies too!'

Incidents like this must have made for a feeling of solidarity between the two composers. Yet as far as Schönberg's music is concerned, Mahler did not go much beyond showing fundamental goodwill, as is shown by a letter of 1901 in which he wrote: 'Schönberg is one of those firebrands who will inevitably excite opposition, but surely also appreciation and admiration, and who have always exerted a fruitful and beneficial influence on people's minds.'

He was also strong in support of Richard Strauss. The worldly poise and great business acumen of Strauss were unlikely to endear him to Mahler as a person, but Mahler was unstinting in his admiration for the sheer ability of this artist, who was prepared to conduct at an American department store and who instigated active measures for the protection of musical copyright. For Mahler music retained a certain sanctity in the midst of all routine. Once during a concert when he caught himself thinking that he was only conducting for the money, he had such a shock that he made this 'sin' the subject of an epistolary confession. Strauss's attitude was very different: doubts hardly touched him, his self-confidence seemed boundless. 'I don't see why I shouldn't write a symphony about myself. I find myself quite as interesting as Napoleon or Alexander.' The symphony he wrote about himself is the *Sinfonia domestica*, a musical home movie complete with 'children's games', 'parents' bliss', the striking of the clock, interjections from uncles and aunts. One cannot imagine a starker contrast to the symphonies of Mahler, which are autobiographical in quite another sense. No conductor or programme arranger today would dream of putting on Mahler's Fifth Symphony in the same concert as the *Domestica*. Beside Mahler's orchestral saga, the homely happiness of the *Domestica* would appear philistine; the funeral march that opens Mahler's Fifth, the brass-armoured scherzo, the romanza-like adagietto and the tremendous rondo finale would be like the eruption of a musical volcano next door to the well-ordered landscape of the *Domestica*.

Yet this juxtaposition was attempted at the concert on 21 May 1905 that formed the highlight of the Alsace Music Festival at Strasbourg. Mahler opened the concert with his Fifth, Strauss concluded it with his *Domestica*. In between – programmes were

longer in those days! – came the Alto Rhapsody by Brahms and a
Mozart Violin Concerto. Even though Brahms and Mozart stood
appeasingly between the two antipodes of the new music, their
contrast must have been felt in all its force. Romain Rolland called
the *Domestica* perfect, while he carped at Mahler's work. In our day
the judgment appears to have been reversed. The *Domestica* has
faded, while the appeal of the Fifth to the public is growing.

It is strangely moving that Mahler, whose musical make-up was
so different from that of his worldly contemporary, was yet able
to recognise the realm in which Strauss might make significant and
enduring contributions. Strauss had completed the draft of his
opera *Salome* in the autumn of 1904. At the time of the meeting in
Strasbourg work on the full score was nearly finished. Mahler had
known about this new work for some time. He had even tried to
dissuade Strauss from setting this libretto, not only on ethical
grounds, but because it was to be feared that such an opera would
prove unperformable in Catholic countries. All the same, Mahler
was eager to get to know the work. In Strasbourg Strauss played and
sang some passages to him. Alma Mahler writes in her memoirs:
Mahler was enthralled. We got to the dance. It was missing. "Ain't
got down to it yet," said Strauss, and, leaving a large gap, played on
to the end. Mahler said: "Isn't it risky just to omit the dance, and
come back to it later when you might not be in the mood?" But
Strauss laughed in his light-hearted way: "Never you fear, it'll come
to me all right."

Mahler resolved to fight for permission to give the first performance of this work in Vienna. He realised that it would be a
tough struggle to wrest agreement from the censorship. But when
should he risk such a fight if not now, at the height of his power?
'This is sheer madness!' Cosima Wagner had exclaimed after
Strauss had played her some passages of the score. Mahler, who
had been so against the libretto, grew enthusiastic about the music.
In September 1905 he reported to Strauss the state of his battle with
the Court Theatre censorship: 'Even though I have not been able
to get an agreement yet, I can already sense a promising "waver-
ing".' A few weeks later the decision came: it was negative. On 11

October Mahler wrote to Strauss: 'I cannot refrain from telling you what an overwhelming impression your work made on me at renewed reading. This is your best so far! I would even say that nothing you have written up to now can be compared to it. As I have known for a long time, you are the perfect dramatist!'

Two years later when Mahler left the Vienna Opera, a critic remarked that he had missed his moment for glorious resignation. After the rejection of *Salome* he should have asked the Grand Chamberlain for his dismissal. Such a purely artistically motivated step would have secured him a martyr's halo.

Mahler was no saint, as his disciples made him out to be, and he did not aspire to the role of martyr, although he did not mind if circumstances made him appear one. In 1905 he was not yet thinking seriously of turning his back on the Vienna Court Opera. Nor was he reluctant to use his Vienna position as a secure base from which to sally forth hither and thither in defence of his works. He knew that the fate of his symphonies was not assured by their committal to paper.

We musicians are worse off than the poets. Everyone can read. But a printed musical score is a sealed book. Even the conductors, who can decipher it, present it to the public imbued with their varying conceptions. The important thing is to create a tradition, and I'm the only one who can do it.

In the files of the Vienna General Management can be found Mahler's requests for leave. For the year 1905 the following concert tours are entered: seven days for Hamburg, ten days for Strasbourg, Berlin, Trieste and Breslau. Mahler was creating his tradition. At times he toyed with the idea that performance of his works might be useful financially. And to a group of friends he confessed: 'To be frank, I'm beginning to neglect my theatrical duties.' We may assume that his standard in such matters was very high, for neither in this nor the following year was there any sign of neglect. He was still in command.

The politically turbulent year of 1905 ended in Vienna, as was fitting, with a new operetta. On 30 December the first performance took place at the Theater an der Wien of Lehár's *Merry Widow*.

Mahler knew the music. He liked to dance with his wife to the waltz 'Lips are silent' – but only in secret and without witnesses: had Alma not said so in her memoirs, we should never have known.

In the happy year of 1905 Mahler published two collections of songs which were in striking contrast to the powerfully orchestrated symphonies. *Sieben Lieder aus letzter Zeit* (Seven songs of recent times) is the title of one series, which contains two settings of *Wunderhorn* texts and five *lieder* on poems by Friedrich Rückert (1788–1866). The Rückert texts contrast with the image of the practical opera director, commander of vast orchestral forces. They all show the desire to withdraw from the noisy world. *Ich bin der Welt abhanden gekommen* is the title of one composition in which renunciation of the world by Love and Song – an idea that had been characteristic of the young Mahler – is taken up again.

> *Ich bin gestorben dem Weltgetümmel*
> *und ruh in einem stillen Gebiet'.*
> *Ich leb allein in meinem Himmel,*
> *in meinem Lieben, in meinem Lied.*
>
> [Dead to the turmoil of the world,
> I dwell in a realm of peace.
> I live alone in my own heaven,
> in my love, in my song.]

The adagietto of the Fifth Symphony in its melodic line harks back to this song. Here too, then, Mahler continued his method of deriving the melodic outline of a symphonic movement from the expressive character of a song. At the same time, the Rückert *lieder* show entirely new features that cannot be traced in his earlier songs. They may be briefly summarised thus: the new songs are fully emancipated from the piano, scaled down to give a more intimate sound, the instrumental parts are individualised, and the vocal line becomes drawn into the all-pervading yet transparent contrapuntal texture.

Kindertotenlieder is the name of the second cycle published in 1905. The prophetic newness of these moving orchestral songs on poems by Rückert is unmistakable. Their musical diction, as H. F.

Redlich recognised, anticipates the language Mahler found later in the *Song of the Earth*. The orchestra for the *Kindertotenlieder* is much reduced in comparison with the symphonies being written at the same time. The beginning of the first song ('*Nun will die Sonn' so hell aufgeh'n*') is unusually ascetic in its means: a plaintive oboe above a solo horn; the softly entering vocal line is surrounded by the tormented accents of bassoon and horn, its timbre modified by the muted violincelli playing in a higher register.

Mahler's choice of texts – laments on the death of one's own children – has posed a psychological puzzle. People could not understand how a father of two children could publish and perform such songs. It seemed to be tempting fate; and duly – as it must have appeared to the superstitious – the blow fell a year later when Mahler's elder daughter died. But speculations of this sort, however persuasive, are misleading, for Mahler had begun the composition of these songs in 1901, before his marriage. If there is a psychological motive for the choice of Rückert's poems, it stems from Mahler's own childhood: from memories of the death of his beloved brother Ernst, and four younger brothers who died in infancy; from the early deaths, too, of his married sister Leopoldine and the gifted Otto whom he had tried to protect and who had ended his life by suicide. Mahler had reason enough to be moved by these romantic elegies, which had only been published after Rückert's own death. The last two songs, to be sure, were written in the summer of 1904, when his children had been born. It is understandable that the mother of those children was frightened by the composition, and saw the subsequent death of one daughter as a punishment.

These biographical details are carefully mentioned in the programme of every performance of the *Kindertotenlieder*, and on the sleeve-notes of every recording. The compassion they evoke in the listener seems – strange as this may sound – actually to detract from the immediate effect of the songs. The association with Mahler's personal tragedy blunts our perceptions to the historical significance of the music. The *Kindertotenlieder* usher in a new era of composition. Mahler's music, freed as it here is from all the hallmarks of his earlier song style (folklore simplicity, marching rhythms, military signals and popular dance associations), reaches a height from which Schönberg's *Herzgewächse* (1911) and *Pierrot Lunaire* (1912), Anton Webern's *Rilke-Lieder* (1910) and Alban Berg's *Altenberg-Lieder* (1912) can be discerned.

The first performance of the *Kindertotenlieder* took place on 29 January 1905 at a concert of the *Vereinschaffender Tonkünstler*, among whose members was Bruno Walter, the subsequent owner of the composer's manuscript score. Walter has vividly recalled the atmosphere of this concert, which was conducted by Mahler:

Mahler responded with true warmth to the veneration of the young composers, headed by Schönberg and Zemlinsky. Thus the evening, on which only orchestral songs were performed, turned into a veritable Mahler festival. That evening Mahler felt really happy – in the boundless devotion of the young musicians around him, a devotion more welcome and satisfying to him than the acclamations of a mass audience, he sensed the answer coming back from other hearts to the cry from the heart of his own songs. All these aspiring, talented young men took away from their occasional meetings with Mahler an invariable impression of sympathy, interest and generous kindness.

There seems to be some contradiction between monumental symphonies designed to communicate, and a lyrical soliloquy removed from this turbulent world. Mahler was a man of contradictions, of lightning changes. This goes not only for Mahler the creative artist, but for the man of the theatre and the conductor. At the conductor's desk, as even his enemies admitted, he was a god, at the director's desk, a devil. The opposition claimed that he made impossible demands on the artists he worked with, though they would add that he drove himself even harder. His friends were amazed by the supreme efficiency with which he planned his rehearsals, and then again disconcerted by his absentmindedness, his whims and inconsistencies. It was said that he had no sense of humour; instances were given of his irrepressible high spirits. The diversity of individual observations is not solely due to the observer's subjectivity. It shows rather the genuinely varying aspects of Mahler's behaviour towards the people he met. It is snapshots, 'stills' perhaps, which these observers give us – as do the various caricatures of Mahler – for they never saw the film of his life in its entirety, with its montages of different moods and facets, its sudden cuts to new scenes and superimpositions of seemingly disparate new material.

Certain habits were misinterpreted, as for instance the twitching and stamping of the right leg, about which complaints are found in an early file of the Kassel Theatre Management. Alfred Roller's description of Mahler's outward appearance mentions this twitching leg, and Leo Slezak, the famous tenor, speaks of Mahler's 'syncopated quickstep'. We have no certain explanation of this involuntary movement. There are some indications that it had a psychological cause, a strange link in memory with his lame mother, to whom he was so attached. An organic origin seems unlikely, for Mahler could stop the twitching by an effort of will. But it returned when his concentration slackened. Nor did it make any difference whether the slackening of self-control was caused by anger or joy. Roller, who knew Mahler well and observed him with a professional eye, refuted the view that Mahler stamped his foot in anger and impatience. This widely held view was, according to Roller, merely proof that 'Mahler had to speak much more often to people who annoyed or bored him than to those he could enjoy himself with'.

This spontaneous movement of the right leg was especially pronounced in his youth. Later on Mahler was better able to control his body. His conducting movements are even said to have attained a restrained economy. Schiedermair, who watched Mahler conduct before 1901, stresses this:

Mahler's manner of wielding the baton is very different from that of most of his colleagues, even at first sight. He is singularly free from the usual ruling passion, the striving for effect. On the rostrum Mahler does not go in for nervous gesticulation, there is no extravagant bobbing up and down, no movement of the body that degenerates to the level of a stagy pose, such as unfortunately delights a section of the public.

All sources agree on the well-nigh magical power of command Mahler had over the orchestra. The gradual growth of this silent authority enabled him – so Bruno Walter tells us – to change to a less emphatic style of conducting.

The external pattern of Mahler's conducting became infinitely simplified in the course of the years. The excellent silhouettes by Boehler show the vigour and vividness of his gestures during his first years in Vienna. Although he always conducted opera sitting down, his mobility at that time, as in Hamburg, was astonishing. Yet it never seemed excessive – intensely persuasive, rather. Gradually his stance and gestures became quieter; his conducting technique became so intellectualised that he achieved musicianly freedom combined with unfailing precision quite effortlessly by a simple-looking beat, while keeping almost still. His enormous influence on singers and instrumentalists was conveyed by a look, or the sparsest of gestures, where before he had exerted himself with impassioned movements. Towards the end his conducting presented the image of an almost eerie calm. I well remember a performance of Strauss's *Sinfonia domestica* under Mahler's direction, where the contrast between the frenzy of the orchestra and the immobility of the man who released it created an almost ghostly atmosphere.

To arrive at a true picture of Mahler's appearance as a conductor, such evidence must be set against the wildly gesticulating caricatures. Speculations about his physical constitution run into similar complexities. For many years he worked intensively as a conductor, undertook the administrative chores of an opera director, was in charge of new productions, and filled his holidays with the no less strenuous work of composition. Yet one is inclined to think of the little man (Mahler was no taller than five foot four) with his irregular plodding gait as physically underdeveloped. Anyone watching Mahler when he felt unobserved and sat biting his nails (a habit he is said to have given up only under Alma's influence) must have thought him a completely indoor person, a stranger to nature or any kind of sport. When during a rehearsal Mahler leapt from the orchestra pit on to the stage and bodily lifted up a singer standing in the wrong spot and carried him to the right one, people marvelled at this sudden show of strength. Only his close friends knew that he had the trained body of an athlete. He had always been fond of hiking, and the habit of going for long hard walks across country remained with him. The

A caricature of Mahler in *Fliegende Blätter*, March 1901

holidays he spent in the Salzkammergut when he was chief conductor at Hamburg were filled with excursions on foot and by bicycle.
On the Attersee, and later on the Wörthersee, he liked to go rowing,
which he did so energetically and at such a speed that few could
keep up with him. His way of starting a fine summer day was to dive
head first into the lake. Then he would go on swimming under
water for a while, surfacing a long way out, 'wallowing in the water
like a seal'. He enjoyed sunbathing, too, and Roller, seeing him
naked, remarked in surprise on his well-developed muscles. 'Mahler
laughed good-humouredly,' writes Roller, 'when he saw that I had
been influenced by the general gossip about his poor physique.'
Mahler gave the impression of someone in perfect health.

He slept very well, he loved his cigar and in the evening a glass of beer.
Spirits he avoided completely. Wine he drank only on special occasions,
preferably Moselle, Chianti or Asti. One or two glasses were sufficient to
put him in a good humour, and he would then start making puns which,
in Alma Mahler's words, he himself found terribly funny. But with all
his sensuous enjoyment of eating and drinking, he was very temperate:
he never did anything to excess. Drunkenness was an abomination to him,
as were filthy language or indecency. The strict cleanliness he observed
with regard to his body he maintained also, without prudishness, in his
conversation, and doubtless in his thoughts.

Mahler's love of nature was not that of the townsman who never
saw it. The mountain world was familiar to him. The cow-bells in
the Sixth and Seventh Symphonies recall the liberating experience
of the Austrian landscape of high mountain pastures. I am not sure
whether lovers of Mahler's music who are unfamiliar with this experience can grasp the full symbolic significance of these symphonic
passages: the loneliness, the freedom, the peace, the relaxed breath-
ing under a blissful sky. Such listeners, while they may appreciate
the refinements of the mixture of trilling flutes, horn calls, harps and
celestas, triangle and cow-bells, in the E flat major adagio of the
Sixth Symphony, will miss the natural associations and the element
of religious feeling. Mahler, however, would not have shared my
regret for the loss of such flashes of association. He was of the opinion that his music was intelligible without any overt programme,

although, on the other hand, he emphatically held the view that every significant piece of 'absolute music' contained a secret programme.

This unresolved contradiction is typical of Mahler. He must not be taken too literally. Alma Mahler tells of a peculiar agreement between the two of them: what Mahler thought right one day he did not necessarily have to uphold on the next. This made it impossible for Alma to counter any surprising assertion of her husband's with the words, 'But Gustav, yesterday you said the opposite.' He claimed the right 'to be inconsistent'. Naturally such complete turnabouts disconcerted all who had to deal with him. Singers on the operatic stage, too, had to count on sudden changes in his directives. Even those singers who most admired him and wanted to comply with his wishes were often at a loss. Whenever they thought they had discovered Mahler's 'method' or his 'formula', the chances were that he would change the seemingly established theatrical or musical routine. Marie Gutheil-Schoder, who sang for nearly seven years under Mahler's direction in Vienna, said that the most tractable singers were the most puzzled, since they could not discover the law governing his instructions.

Mahler's work at the threatre did not follow any hard and fast rule. He regarded the inculcation of definitive conceptions to which musical interpretations had to conform as injurious to any musician. It was all part of his fight against tradition and routine. Ludwig Schiedermair wrote in 1900:

As a conductor, Mahler belongs to no school, no fashion. This can be seen from his renderings of the works of Mozart, Beethoven and Wagner. If Mahler were committed to any one school one would expect his interpretations of Mozart or of Wagner to have certain points in common. But this is not the case. There are very few personalities so powerful that, though moulded by their own age and by history, they arrive at this independent attitude. The secret of style is contained in this.

It is amazing that Mahler's biographer should have recognised this essential feature of Mahler's interpretative art so clearly at the early age of twenty-four. Mahler belonged to no school, and he did not form a school, regrettable though this may be. If my reading of the accounts and reviews, letters and pictorial representations, is correct, there is no such thing as a Mahlerian style of interpretation. Mahler went in search of the particular style of each work he was going to perform. As an interpreter he had a 'feminine' nature. This term coined by Wyzewa and St Foix for Mozart as a composer applies very much to Mahler's work as an interpretative artist (though not as a composer). When he devoted himself to a work of the musical theatre, he lost himself in it so entirely that he forgot not only his own self and his status as a composer, but all his standards of comparison. On one occasion the most convinced and convincing interpreter of *Tristan* and the *Ring* surprised his collaborators by exclaiming enthusiastically: '*Rienzi* is ultimately Wagner's greatest work!' No one could understand this enthusiasm for Wagner's youthful opera, until it was discovered that Mahler had just begun to study the score of *Rienzi* with a view to producing it (*Rienzi* was performed twenty-seven times in all during Mahler's tenure).

Mahler's intellectual approach was determined by his willingness and capacity to involve himself completely in every work he performed. He had to become a 'holiday composer', for it was only away from his opera and concert activities that he felt free 'to be himself'. He was masculine, not to say domineering, when composing and conducting his own works. As an interpreter of other men's scores he may sometimes have appeared a tyrant, yet he always felt that he was merely executing another's bidding: 'deputising for the composer', as he used to put it.

Many of the reported value judgments – some of them most peculiar – which Mahler delivered on composers and their works must be understood in connection with his emotional commitment to a given task. Perhaps he really did say that 'Schubert's skill fell far short of his sensibility and invention', as Natalie Bauer-Lechner reports; perhaps he did largely disparage Hugo Wolf's songs; perhaps he did refer to Wagner's *Parsifal* jokingly as the work of a Wagnerian. It would be wrong to assign too much importance to these spontaneous utterances. They do no more than provide a negative reflection of the positive concentration Mahler brought to bear on some other small area of music: his recognition of values outside its confines was then temporarily in abeyance.

His emotional and intellectual make-up is by no means fully de-lineated by referring to the feminine character of his interpretations and the masculine character of his creativity. Writings about Mahler have largely neglected his other intellectual interests, although his published letters and the reminiscences of his friends provide suf-ficient evidence of these. We have already mentioned that Mahler was well-read, conversant with classical poetry and with the novel and drama of his day, as well as with the works of Schopenhauer, Nietzsche and Dostoevsky. Bruno Walter refers to Mahler's exten-sive interest in philosophy. Nor did his interests stop short at humanistic problems, or intellectual fashions of the time; he was also fascinated by the natural sciences. A key figure to the understanding of Mahler as an intellectual is the distinguished physicist Arnold Berliner, two years younger than Mahler, whom he first met in Hamburg. Berliner began by working in the laboratories of A.E.G., spent some time with the General Electric Company of America at Schenectady, and later became director of the electric light bulb factory of the German A.E.G. In Hamburg when Mahler was pre-paring for his guest appearance in London, Berliner taught him a little English. In a financial sense, too, Mahler was indebted to this music-loving friend, for a loan that enabled him to hold concerts in Hamburg and Berlin. We can only guess at the intensity of the spirit-ual bond between the two men. In his letters Mahler expressed in-terest in Berliner's *Manual of Physics*. Even when he was Court Opera director in Vienna, Mahler still found time to keep in touch with the physicist. However, Berliner seems to have complained about the infrequency and shortness of his letters, for Mahler writes: 'I hope to come to Berlin in the course of the coming winter. I shall make sure to visit you then, and I am convinced that we shall find our old intimacy from the first moment.' What comes next reveals the special character of the friendship: 'The genesis of our re-lationship seems to vouch for that: seeing that it was our outlook and common interests that brought us together, and not, as so often happens with very young people, a fortuitous sentiment or mood.'

Thus Mahler distinguishes his friendship with Berliner from the emotional friendships of youth on the one hand, and from artistic alliances, as with Lipiner, Roller and Bruno Walter, on the other. His conversations with Berliner must have been chiefly on scientific subjects. This is suggested, for instance, by a present of books Berliner sent to Mahler's holiday home. Mahler acknowledged receipt of a veritable 'library', and thanked Berliner for spreading enlightenment among his friends. He adds that Alma, seeing the books, feared there would be nothing at all for her – but she was mollified by finding a miniature edition of Goethe among them. Evidently all the other books in that parcel presupposed specialised knowledge and interests which Alma did not share.

Mahler's exchanges of ideas with Berliner – who in 1942, at the age of eighty, committed suicide in Berlin because the Nazis were going to turn him out of his apartment – have unfortunately not been investigated, although suitable sources must presumably exist. An undated letter of Mahler's, however, possibly written in 1907 and addressed to a recipient whose profession is not indicated, gives some hint of Mahler's intense preoccupation with the problems of the new physics. In this letter, which refers to a newspaper article on matter, ether and electricity, mention is made of a previous discussion between Mahler and the recipient, in the course of which Mahler had arrived at the conclusion that the laws of nature remain constant, but that man's understanding of them would change. By way of amendment, he now adds that even this no longer seems quite certain.

It is conceivable that in the course of aeons (perhaps in consequence of some law of natural evolution) even the laws of nature might change; that, for instance, gravity might cease to function – just as Helmholtz posits even now that the law of gravity loses its validity for infinitesimally small distances. Perhaps also (I would add) over immeasurably great distances – as between vastly separated star systems. Consider all this down to its ultimate consequences.

This passage betrays an unusual familiarity with a problem of physics that was highly topical at the time. In his *History of Physics* (1947), written at the instigation and in memory of Arnold Berliner, the German physicist Max von Laue points out that at the beginning of this century the concept of 'gravitational force at a distance' was falling out of favour; a process much accelerated by the appearance of Einstein's *Special Theory of Relativity* (1905). In this respect, too, then, Mahler was abreast of contemporary thought. I can think of no other significant composer of the time who could compare with him in that.

Mahler did not show off with his knowledge. He never talked of these things to musicians, who rarely have much interest in such problems. It is thus not surprising that the reminiscences of Mahler's musician friends hardly mention his thoughts on philosophy and the natural sciences. Yet his intellectual development, including his progress as a musical thinker, can only be understood in the light of his constant struggle to master ideas. His changing moods; the highly subjective partiality of the interpreter engrossed in a particular work; the elevation of some detailed aesthetic instruction to the status of a definitive principle, to be as uncompromisingly overthrown the very next moment: all these were the contradictory elements of a mind that must have seemed restless and changeable even to his best friends. The true stability of this intellect reveals itself only on careful analysis and from a distance in time. The constant factor is his endeavour to find out the truth about everything. From this arises another notable trait – Mahler's modesty, his aesthetic tolerance, his reluctance to take sides in the musical arena.

This tolerance emerges clearly when we think of various controversies and feuds of the time from which Mahler conspicuously stood apart. He was, like Hugo Wolf, a Bruckner enthusiast, but unlike Wolf in that this never made him speak ill of Brahms. He understood the greatness of both Brahms and Bruckner, and conducted works by both composers in Europe and later in America. Mahler was aware of the essential difference between his own music and that of Strauss, but he disliked the facile way in which certain critics would plump for one or the other. He did not wholly approve of everything performed by the young group around Schönberg and Zemlinsky at the Vereinschaffender Tonkünstler, but he did not grudge them his support. For more than one reason, Mahler did not care for Pfitzner as a man, yet he performed his works. Mahler, as a composer of pronounced 'symphonic mentality', cannot have been entirely in sympathy with Debussy's music, but this did not stop him as a conductor from giving the first American performances of Debussy's *Iberia* and *Rondes de Printemps*.

Last but not least, a critical tolerance governed his relation to Richard Wagner. He had started out as a complete Wagnerian. His emotional and spiritual acceptance of Wagner had gone to the lengths of obeying the master's most superficial and irrelevant precepts, as though a vegetarian regime were the precondition not only for a correct rendering of the *Ring* music, but for the salvation of humanity. However, to a thinking person who had familiarised himself with the concepts of philosophy and the new theories of physics, many of Wagner's doctrines must inevitably appear suspect. In the end Mahler rejected Wagner's writings in so far as they dealt with matters outside music: 'One really has to forget their existence, to give Wagner's genius its due.'

Mahler's obsessional advocacy of every work he re-created, and the passion with which he defended his own creations, blinded his contemporaries to the coolly critical side of Mahler's mind. He was far cleverer than appears from descriptions of him by well-meaning Mahler fans during the last years of his life and shortly after his death. He even knew his own weaknesses and realised his mistakes.

This representation of Mahler's life up to the present chapter has made use of a temporal framework while tending to concentrate on separate aspects such as his psychological make-up, or his composing, conducting or stage-producing. But there is one part of his life where this method proves inadequate. If, in dealing with the years 1906 and 1907, we were to attempt tidy segregation of the various personal and professional areas, we should lose the very essence of the period. No sedately judicious account could convey the vertiginous, breathtaking rush of it. A mere sober recital of Mahler's achievements during those years strikes us like a quick motion sequence from a biographical film. The very chronology – which normally tends to bore the reader – gives the alarming impression of an artist working at a feverish pace.

The year 1906 saw the hundred-and-fiftieth anniversary of

Mozart's birth. Mahler continued the Mozart cycle he had begun in December 1905 with *Don Giovanni*. On 29 January he presented *Die Entführung aus dem Serail* with Roller's sets. *Lohengrin*, the opera with which Mahler had begun his work in Vienna, was also given a new production. On 27 February the curtain rose to reveal Roller's new designs. On 1 March Mahler left Vienna to conduct in Antwerp and Amsterdam. Returning ten days later, he took charge of the rehearsals for the new *Figaro*, in a revised translation by Max Kalbeck, which the Viennese were to hear for the first time on 30 March 1906. Richard Mayr, hitherto employed chiefly in Wagnerian roles, sang his first Figaro. In May Mahler went to Graz to witness a first performance he had failed to put on in Vienna: Richard Strauss conducting his *Salome*. After this he travelled to Essen where he conducted the first performance of his Sixth Symphony at the Music Festival of the Allgemeine Deutsche Musikverein. A few days after his return, on June 1, the Mozart cycle was resumed with Rollers' *Zauberflöte*, Selma Kurz appearing as Queen of the Night, Georg Maikl as Tamino, Marie Gutheil-Schoder as Pamina, and Anton Moser as Papageno.

After such a busy season – it also included a new *Cosi fan tutte*, making five Mozart productions in all – Mahler surely deserved a good summer holiday. But even at Maiernigg by the Wörthersee he would not rest. Plans for a new work absorbed him. On his desk lay the text of a Latin hymn of the ninth century: *Veni creator spiritus*. Before setting it, Mahler wanted to make sure that he had understood its meaning. He sent express letters to his friend Löhr in Vienna, asking about the stresses on certain Latin words and the strange syntax of one sentence. Löhr, knowing that his friend was hard pressed for time, cabled his replies to Maiernigg. Alma tells us: 'Mahler made a superhuman effort that summer. He would often play me passages from the new work, and he felt incredibly happy and elated. Unfortunately he had to interrupt his work to conduct *The Marriage of Figaro* in Salzburg, for a music festival.'

The Emperor had ordered a Mozart celebration to be given by the ensemble of the Court Opera under Mahler's leadership. 'By gracious command of His Majesty' Mahler conducted a gala performance of *Figaro* in the town of Mozart's birth. Bernhard Paumgartner, the son of Rosa Papier who had helped Mahler to get his post in Vienna, dwells on the quality of this performance: '. . . marvellously worked out to the last detail, the first truly distinguished ensemble effort of the Salzburg Festival weeks, perhaps even of modern operatic history.' Julius Korngold, the critic of the *Neue Freie Presse*, writing twenty years after the event, asserted: '*Figaro* in Salzburg was the ideal *Figaro*: in its enchanting grace, in its light, supple mezza-voce recitative, in the incomparable harmony of its ensembles. No one who experienced this performance will ever forget it.' This chronicler mentions one significant detail: Mahler had been very happy, and a little dog-eared book had peeped out of his coat pocket – Goethe's *Faust*.

The short stay in Salzburg had not disrupted the progress of the composition begun at Maiernigg. The Latin hymn formed the first part of the new symphony; passages from *Faust* were to form its second part. Back at his holiday resort, Mahler resumed work. On 18 August he was able to announce final victory in a letter to his Dutch friend Willem Mengelberg: 'I have just completed my Eighth – it is my greatest work to date. And so unusual in content and form that one cannot describe it in a letter. Imagine the whole universe beginning to sing and resound. These are no longer human voices, but coursing planets and suns. – More when we meet.'

There was no chance in the foreseeable future of mounting a performance of this gigantic work of ninety minutes' duration, requiring about a thousand participants. Mahler was quite content to have got it all down on paper. In Vienna his directorial duties claimed him. At the beginning of October he produced the opera *Der polnische Jude* (*Le Juif polonais*) by Camille Erlanger. It was a failure; the cash receipts did not reach the estimated figure. Indeed, the fabulous Mozart year – today reckoned among the all-time highlights of the Vienna Opera – had not been a great year for Vienna audiences. Mahler had to think of putting on 'special attractions' – and they must not be too expensive, either. Tactical compromises seemed advisable. He shelved the new works he had intended to take into the repertoire (among them operas by Max von Schillings and Alexander von Zemlinsky), the more willingly as that autumn he had ample opportunity of furthering his own cause in other towns. In October he was present at a concert in Berlin where Oskar Fried conducted the Sixth. Shortly after he conducted his Third in Breslau, and in November, his Sixth in Munich. For a Christmas show he put on Rossini's *Barber*, using the old scenery out of stock. It was a box-office success, largely thanks to the coloratura additions sung by Selma Kurz as Rosina.

At the beginning of 1907 the Court Opera director requested another period of leave from the management. He travelled to concerts in Berlin, Amsterdam and Frankfurt. During his absence a press campaign started up. It was occasioned by a report in a newspaper sympathetic to Mahler, which stated that he would like to give up conducting altogether in order to devote himself to composition. His enemies, swiftly closing their ranks, at once declared that it was no longer a question of Mahler wanting to go – he would have to go.

In view of the trust the Grand Chamberlain continued to place in Mahler, there could be no thought of that. Nevertheless the attacks did not cease. Even a basically well-intentioned article by Julius Korngold in the *Neue Freie Presse* of 26 January 1907 repeated the arguments of Mahler's opponents. A section of this article, which 'does not purport to be a complaints book, let alone a bill of indictment', summarises the objections brought against Mahler, mitigated though they are by admiration:

Mahler has achieved much in bringing new blood into the cast-list. He has rejuvenated the whole personnel: one of the foremost tasks of an opera director, in view of the constant demand for good strong voices and their unavoidable decline. First-rate artists, pillars of the ensemble, such as the ladies Kurz, Gutheil-Schoder, von Mildenburg, Hilgermann, Förster-Lauterer, Bland, Weidt and others, and among the men, Slezak, Schmedes, Demuth, Weidemann, Mayr and others, have been procured for this institution. New favourites have taken the place of the old ones, prospective candidates for honourable inclusion in the calendar of Vienna's singer-saints. By the side of these, however, sprouts a crop of Court Opera juveniles that is unpromising, if not wholly dispensable. Mahler's predilection for rising talent – soft wax that can be kneaded into the ensemble – has favoured a collection of mediocrities. There is a surplus of little people on the payroll, eager to deputise at short notice, while there seems at times a lack of those for whom they might deputise. There is half a tenor here, and half a bass there, and the two of them still don't make a whole singer!

This criticism of Mahler's policy tallies to some extent with that memorandum of the twenty opera patrons we quoted above. Other newspapers took a stronger line. Mahler, whose whole aim had always been the creation of a balanced ensemble, appears in these reviews as a 'destroyer of the ensemble'. It is true that stars who wanted to be admired as such had no place in Mahler's ensemble. Nor can the statement that he looked for 'soft wax', to knead into his ensemble, be refuted. The view that considered the ensemble to be a mere sum total of good strong voices was certainly not Mahler's.

He demonstrated his own view afresh with a production of Wagner's *Die Walküre* on 4 February 1907. Ludwig Hevesi's two essays devoted to this event deserve a thorough investigation by a theatre historian. It might well prove that Mahler and Roller developed interpretative ideas that were to reappear in the teachings of Adolphe Appia and in the more daring productions of fifty years later at Bayreuth. 'The peep-show has lost out to the total work of art' – thus ends the account Hevesi wrote the day after the first performance.

On 18 March 1907 Mahler presented Gluck's *Iphigénie en Aulide*. Here the stage was radically reduced to bare essentials. There was no feast for the conservative eye. Even the Mahler enthusiasts among the public seem to have appreciated the noble simplicity of Roller's designs rather less than Mahler's creative way with the score. Mahler himself said of *Iphigénie*: 'I believe it is the best thing Roller and I have done so far.'

Iphigénie en Aulide was in fact their last collaboration in Vienna. Mahler began to realise that he would not be able to hold out indefinitely against the attacks of his enemies, which were mounting in the press. The day after the Gluck performance he left Vienna to conduct concerts in Rome, and afterwards in Brünn (Brno) and

A gramophone record advertisement: Mahler and his Stars

St Petersburg. In connection with his request for leave – possibly even some weeks earlier – the Grand Chamberlain, Prince Montenuovo, dropped a remark that warned Mahler of an impending change in his attitude. Montenuovo declared that the quality of the performances and the amount of revenue had been adversely affected by the director's too-frequent absences. As early as April 1907 Mahler must have drawn his own conclusions. Alfred Roller writes in a letter to his wife: 'At the Opera there is really great confusion, thanks to the usual Viennese love of mischief. I admire Mahler, the way he keeps calm and carries on regardless. It seems that all forces are now uniting to bring about his downfall. If people only knew how glad he is to go!'

He must already have had some tempting offers. One of these, from New York, must have reached him in May at the latest. Heinrich Conried, manager of the Metropolitan Opera since 1903, was out to capture Mahler. Conried, a native of Bielitz, had started his career as an actor at the Burgtheater, and had emigrated to New York in 1888. He was good at getting hold of star attractions. In 1903 he had engaged Caruso at the 'Met', and in January 1907 he had mounted the first American performance of *Salome*. It did not trouble him overmuch that the protests of religious circles forced him to take *Salome* out of the repertoire after the first performance. He held half the capital of the Metropolitan Opera Company and drew an annual salary of $20,000. Mahler must have felt that negotiations with this man offered a hopeful prospect.

In June Mahler met Conried in Berlin and they reached a general agreement. At least one Viennese newspaper knew about these negotiations at the time. In the *Neue Freie Presse* of 16 June 1907 under the heading 'Unmusical comments on the Mahler case' we read:

Hardly has the Old World loosened its hold on Mahler than the New World reaches out for him. The well-known siren song, accompanied by an astute impresario on a golden lyre with golden strings, sounds from across the water, tempting, tempting, and probably not tempting in vain. And we let him go. With an easy mind we let the man go, for it is time to prove once again how carelessly we husband our cultural resources.

Such comments were bound to create the impression that there had been a possibility of keeping Mahler in Vienna, and this impression haunts the subsequent literature about him. Yet clearly he did not seriously risk his position in Vienna until he was sure of New York.

Although Prince Montenuovo was no longer as well disposed towards Mahler as before, he had his reasons for conciliating him. His efforts to procure other conductors (such as Felix Mottl) for Vienna had failed. He therefore approached Mahler to say that on reflection he had come round to his point of view and would have no further objections about granting him leave of absence. Mahler now had the satisfaction of turning the tables on Montenuovo. He himself, he claimed, had come round to Montenuovo's point of view and could see that his efforts to form an ensemble theatre of uniformly high quality were unavailing. In an interview he gave to the *Neues Wiener Tagblatt*, which appeared on 5 June 1907 he stated:

It is . . . entirely untrue that any kind of 'intrigue' has overthrown me. I have not been overthrown at all, I am leaving of my own free will as I want to achieve complete independence. Among other reasons, perhaps mainly, because I have come to realise that the operatic stage is essentially resistant to permanent control. No theatre in the world can be kept to such a standard that one performance is like any other. It is that which turns me against the theatre. For naturally I would like to see all performances maintaining the same standard – the ideal, but this ideal is unattainable. No one has ever been able to do it before me, and no one ever will.

As the legal situation stood, there could be no question of ending the contractual agreement between Mahler and the Court Opera or of a 'dismissal'. He was an established civil servant. 'I don't even have the right', he said, 'to ask for my dismissal. I can only ask to be pensioned off. And if that is refused, I shall just have to stay on.' Pronouncements of this sort were in fact a smoke-screen. By then matters had long been settled between Montenuovo and Mahler, although officially the 'Emperor's gracious decision' to release Mahler was not made until the autumn of 1907. Negotiations with Conried were concluded during the early days of July. To Arnold Berliner, who was worried about his friend's future, Mahler sent a reassuring message:

My contract has been drawn up by a lawyer; as soon as it's all finished, I shall send it to you for inspection. You may rest assured, all has been carefully considered. At worst I risk being uncomfortable for three months of the year, on the other hand I shall make 300,000 kronen net within four years. That is how matters stand.

Thus Mahler had turned his back on Vienna before the public had any certain information. The press campaign against him was still in full swing. His statements of principle on the problems of the operatic stage sounded a note of resignation. People today who hold the view that it is impossible to maintain a permanent standard in a repertory theatre can quote Mahler if they please, but they should not forget his actual achievements in the eighteen months before his resignation: five new Mozart productions that made history; an exemplary Wagner performance and a Gluck revival; and finally –

not to forget – the composition of the Eighth Symphony. Any present-day theatre director who can produce a similar artistic record may be granted the right to quote Mahler's pessimistic pronouncements on the ensemble and repertory theatre.

The excessive strain of those eighteen months now took its toll. In the letter to Berliner on 4 July Mahler, after explaining about his contract with Conried, wrote: 'We have the most terrible bad luck! More of that when we meet. Now my older girl has scarlet fever and diphtheria!' On the following day, 5 July 1907, this elder daughter, Maria Anna, died. Mahler, who had loved the child dearly, collapsed with a heart attack a few days later. The diagnosis was 'double-sided congenital, though compensated, valve defect'. The doctor advised complete rest.

Mahler took leave for ever of Maiernigg, where his daughter had died. Once Montenuovo had secured Felix von Weingartner's agreement to take over the post of Opera director from Mahler, nothing stood in the way of the latter's release. All formalities tied up, on 5 October he was relieved of his post by a decree of the Emperor which granted him an indemnity of 20,000 kronen and an annual pension of 14,000 kronen. Shortly afterwards he went on leave to conduct first in Germany and then in Russia. So much for the doctor's advice to take things easy. On 24 November Mahler said goodbye to his Vienna public at a special concert of the Gesellschaft der Musikfreunde with a performance of his Second Symphony. After every movement, as one press report has it, Mahler was 'greeted by colossal applause which at the end swelled to a veritable hurricane, and moved the composer to tears. The Court Opera Orchestra and the Choral Society took part in these tremendous ovations. The entire audience remained in their places; Mahler was called out about thirty times. Many ladies wept and waved their handkerchiefs; the shouts of bravo would not stop.'

At the beginning of December Mahler handed over the administration. The many Austrian and foreign decorations he had been awarded during his tenure he left behind in a drawer of his desk. Officially no function was arranged to mark his departure. But a committee of Mahler fans sent out notices to everyone connected with him, which read:

Dear Friend,

The admirers of Gustav Mahler will meet for a final farewell on *Monday the 9th before 8.30 a.m. on the platform of the West Station*. You are cordially invited to attend and to inform people of your acquaintance. As this is meant to be a surprise for Mahler, you are earnestly requested not to take representatives of the press into your confidence.

Dr Anton von Webern
Dr Karl Horwitz
Dr Paul Stefan
Heinrich Jalowetz

About two hundred people turned up to greet Mahler for the last time. The collection of people on that platform was surely a representative section of the Austrian intellectual establishment. As the train began to move, Gustav Klimt, who was among those present, uttered what was in everyone's mind: 'All over.' An artistic epoch had come to an end.

The day of Mahler's departure, a farewell letter from the director to the 'honoured members of the Court Opera' was pinned up at the Opera House:

The time of our working together has come to an end. I leave a working community that has become dear to me, and bid you all farewell.

Instead of a complete, rounded whole, such as I had hoped for, I leave behind the incomplete, the fragmentary, as man seems fated to do.

It is not for me to judge what my work has meant to those for whom it was intended. But at this moment I can honestly say, I have tried my best, I have set my aims high. My endeavours were not always crowned by success. No one is so exposed to the refractoriness of matter, to the malice of the object, as the interpretative artist. But I have always staked all I have, putting the aim above my person, my duty before my inclinations. I did not spare myself, and therefore felt I could ask others to exert their full powers.

In the thick of the fray, in the heat of the moment, neither you nor I could altogether escape injuries or misunderstandings. But when our work was successful, a problem solved, we forgot all our trouble and felt richly rewarded – even if the outward signs of success were lacking. We have all of us made progress, and with us the establishment we sought to serve.

Accept my heartfelt thanks, then, all who have supported me in my difficult, often thankless task, who have aided me and fought by my side. Accept my sincere good wishes for your future careers and for the prosperity of the Court Opera Theatre whose fortunes I shall continue to follow with lively interest.

Gustav Mahler

Mahler's letter aroused the wrath of some unknown person, who tore it off the notice-board. The fanaticism of Mahler's opponents can only be understood by those who have experience of the spiteful enjoyment which the Viennese traditionally derive from a *Hetz*, or *battue*. The *Hetz*, which originally signified the beating up of animals for the chase, has in Vienna (not without reason) become a synonym for a popular entertainment. The case of Mahler was by no means the last of these operatic battues in Vienna: the cultivation of an ugly tangle of intrigues and a thoroughly nasty press campaign for the amusement of the masses. If a compendium were made of all the techniques of vilification and mud-slinging that operated here, of all the various methods of combining ostensibly factual arguments with personal invective, one would arrive at a fair picture of the campaign that was waged against Mahler. Even Mahler's decision to sell the villa at Maiernigg in order not to be reminded of the painful loss of his child served one Viennese journalist as an occasion for tasteless jokes spun out over two columns of his paper.

All who were loyal to Mahler in those days were contemptuously dismissed as the 'Mahler clique'. We know the names of some of them, signatories to a declaration of allegiance that reached Mahler at the peak of the Vienna crisis: Peter Altenberg, Hermann Bahr, Hugo von Hofmannsthal, Arthur Schnitzler, Jakob Wassermann and Stefan Zweig were among them. Lilli Lehmann, who did not always see eye to eye with Mahler, and Arnold Schönberg, who owed much to him, wanted it known that the hostile utterances of the press 'with their frequently immoderate tone were not a true expression of public opinion'. Visual artists like Josef Hoffmann, Kolo Moser and Gustav Klimt, and Burgtheater actors such as Kainz and Sonnenthal joined the 'Mahler clique' as readily as the scientists Ernst Mach, Theodor Gomperz and Sigmund Freud.

Mahler must have found solace in such manifestations of sympathy. He parted from Vienna without rancour. The town and the country remained his homeland: he had no desire to forget Europe. America was still alien to him. He expected to feel 'uncomfortable' over there, but he would earn enough money to enable him afterwards to live purely for his creative work in the Old World. When he boarded his ship at Cherbourg, he found a telegram: 'Dear Friend. From all my heart good luck for your journey on this good ship on which I myself years ago returned from America. Come back safely to our beloved Europe which needs people like you more than its daily bread. Yours, Gerhart Hauptmann.'

[8]

America and Europe

When Mahler signed his contract with Conried, he had one single
aim in mind: to make money in the New World and thus gain the
time he needed to pursue his creative work in the Old World. His
friends saw his decision to go to New York in the same light. They
thought of him as 'sentenced to America'. This view has been
perpetuated in the melancholy sentimental Mahler legend. It is
wrong, for Mahler was not the man to endure passively under the
onrush of new impressions. He took an active part in the musical
culture of the country, exerting a decisive influence on it, and was
by no means content with mere material gain.

Other European composers had come to the United States –
Tchaikovsky, Dvořák and Richard Strauss had preceded Mahler
there. But Mahler, as Irving Kolodin rightly pointed out, was the
first European composer of note who 'took part in day-to-day
musical life, faced the newspaper reporters, and assimilated elements of the American way of life that would re-emerge as music'.

An artist who despised feeble understatements and loved dramatic
emphasis, exuberant energy and action on a monumental scale was
bound to find America enthralling. On seeing Niagara Falls,
Mahler exclaimed: 'Fortissimo at last!' From the apartment he
took on the eleventh floor of the Hotel Majestic on Seventy-Second
Street he planned his musical strategy. At the Metropolitan Opera
he would not have to concern himself with petty administrative
details. This is very evident from the programme of his first New
York season.

On 1 January 1908 Mahler stood for the first time at the rostrum of
the Metropolitan Opera Company. The opera was *Tristan und*

Isolde with Heinrich Knote and Olive Fremstad in the principal roles. For his first *Don Giovanni* (23 January) Mahler had one of the most famous interpreters of the role, Antonio Scotti; Leporello was sung by Fedor Chaliapin. In the next month there followed *Die Walküre* (7 February) and *Siegfried* (19 February). On 20 March the curtain rose on a *Fidelio* set re-created from the Vienna original of Alfred Roller.

The general enthusiasm about this *Fidelio* was shared by the wife of George R. Sheldon, an influential banker and Republican politician. Together with an equally wealthy woman friend, she decided to provide Mahler with an orchestra so that he could give concerts. Mrs Sheldon was one of those millionaires' wives who at that particular time were playing an increasingly important role in musical life. Her plan was to have great importance not only for Mahler, but for the musical culture of New York. Its realisation, however, had to wait awhile.

A new social phenomenon in the realm of opera emerged during Mahler's first New York season. Whereas the syndicate of the Conried Metropolitan Opera Company had set out to make a profit, the new Metropolitan Opera Company formed during the first months of 1908 had artistic prestige as its main consideration, without insisting on financial gain. The financial consortium led by the millionaire Otto F. Kahn put down a substantial sum to buy out that successful manager Heinrich Conried and enforce the new policy. On 24 March 1908 a benefit performance was arranged for Conried on the occasion of his resignation. Mahler conducted the *Leonora* No. 3 Overture, and various celebrated singers contributed arias and scenes to a programme consisting of a mixture of 'highlights' which cannot have been wholly to Mahler's taste. There were bits of *Bohème* and *Madame Butterfly* and *Il Trovatore* and *Faust* and *Die Meistersinger*. The takings – $19,119 – amounted almost to Conried's annual salary.

Mahler felt uneasy about the impending changes. To be on the safe side, he terminated his four-year contract as early as 29 February. In an undated letter, written not later than 1 April 1908 to the concert-promoter Emil Gutmann, Mahler says: 'Owing to the resignation of Conried and my refusal to take over his job, everything here is unfortunately very unsettled, and I cannot say at the moment whether, or for how long, I shall return next season.' His indecision was increased by the negotiations of the Metropolitan Opera Company with Giulio Gatti-Casazza, the successful director of the Milan Scala, who was offered the position of 'general manager'. Gatti-Casazza accepted this offer for the beginning of the next season on condition that Arturo Toscanini, the conductor and artistic director of the Scala, was engaged as well. And Toscanini was in fact engaged.

Before Mahler returned to Europe in the spring he decided to revoke the cancellation of his contract and come back to New York in the late autumn. He was persuaded by the artistic and financial chances America offered. His New York schedule of work was limited. Though he had produced seven operas during his first (1907–8) season, he had only conducted nineteen performances in all; and from May onwards he was able to devote himself entirely to his own works. In Wiesbaden he conducted his First Symphony before retiring to Toblach in South Tyrol for his holidays. Here he composed *Das Lied von der Erde*. On 19 September he conducted the first performance of his Seventh Symphony in Prague. In October he gave concerts in Munich, Berlin and Hamburg, and before embarking again for New York he took in an appearance at the rostrum in Paris.

Reports from New York that reached Mahler during his holidays did not sound too encouraging. There were indications that he would have a strong rival in the forty-one-year-old Toscanini. Gatti-Casazza had pointed out to Toscanini that he would have to work in harness with Mahler, and, according to Gatti-Casazza, Toscanini's reaction was wholly cooperative: 'With a musician like Mahler, there will always be a way of collaborating.' Nevertheless, quite without personal animosity, tensions could arise merely from the individual artistic vision of these two great musicians. Toscanini had introduced some of Wagner's works – *Siegfried*, *Götterdämmerung*, *Tristan* and *Parsifal* – to Italy. It was only to be expected that the Italian conductor would wish to do some Wagner in New York.

Toscanini, who arrived in New York before Mahler, in fact wanted to conduct *Tristan*. When Mahler was notified of this, he wrote from Europe:

I took particular pains with *Tristan* last season, and I think I may say that the form in which the work currently appears in New York is my brainchild. If Toscanini, for whom, unacquainted though we are, I have the highest respect and whom I consider it an honour to greet as a colleague, were to take over *Tristan* before my return, an entirely new stamp would inevitably be given to the work, and I would be in no position to resume its direction in the course of the season. I must therefore beg you most earnestly to reserve the direction of this work for me.

Toscanini did not conduct *Tristan* during his first (1908–9) New York season. He started on 9 November 1908 with *Aida*, Emmy Destinn and Enrico Caruso taking the principal parts. On 10 December Toscanini conducted Wagner's *Götterdämmerung*. Mahler did not resume his activities until 23 December. This time he was staying at the 'Old Savoy' on Fifth Avenue, where Caruso also had rooms. It was at this time that Caruso did his caricatures of Mahler.

Mahler's first new production was Mozart's *Figaro*. Twenty rehearsals were held: fewer than Mahler was used to in Vienna, but more than had ever been given to a Mozart opera in New York. The first performance on 13 January 1909 presented a historic cast: Emma Eames as the Countess and Marcella Sembrich as Susanna, both of whom left the Met after that season; the young Geraldine Farrar as Cherubino, Adam Didur as Figaro and Antonio Scotti as the Count.

No less spectacular was Mahler's next assignment, Smetana's opera *The Bartered Bride*, which was done in German on 19 February 1909 with Emmy Destinn, who came from Prague, as Marie. The peak of Mahler's season, however, was a performance of *Tristan* on 12 March with Karl Burrian and Olive Fremstad in the main roles. For once Mahler was completely satisfied. The critics were full of praise for his achievement. Mahler, said the *Sun*, unleashed a vital torrent of sound 'such as we have never heard before'.

Mahler's and Toscanini's respective conducting of Wagner invited comparisons, and press and public eagerly debated the relative merits of Toscanini's *Götterdämmerung* and Mahler's *Tristan*. How the two musicians actually got on with each other is impossible to say now with any certainty. Alma Mahler's report that Toscanini had shown no more than 'contemptuous indifference' for Mahler was later denounced by Toscanini as 'malicious'. But subsequent developments proved that the Met could not accommodate two domineering characters.

It was easy for Mahler to attach less importance to his role at the Met than he had done at first, when he saw the chance of appearing as a concert conductor. Before he began his second opera season he had agreed with the New York Symphony Society to undertake three of their concerts. At the first of these, on 29 November 1908, he conducted works by Schumann, Beethoven, Smetana and Wagner. His attempt to perform his own Second Symphony (8 December) suffered from the laxity of the orchestra. Of one hundred and fifteen musicians under contract, only about sixty turned up at the first rehearsal! The last concert on 13 December presented Beethoven's Fifth and two overtures. Ill-satisfied by his work with the Symphony Orchestra, Mahler broke off relations with this body. At this juncture the group of well-to-do ladies led by Mrs Sheldon made its first move. The moment was right, for the New York Philharmonic Orchestra was in difficulties. This democratically organised institution, used to choosing its own conductors, was facing a deficit. Mrs Sheldon mobilised the support of various millionaires, including J. P. Morgan and Andrew Carnegie. Soon a guarantee fund of $90,000 had been set up. This sum was promised to the Philharmonic Orchestra, provided that its members accepted the harsh terms of the well-heeled music-lovers. They were to renounce the 'partnership principle', to augment their concert activities, to place themselves under the control of a governing body, and to accept Mahler as their supreme commander, who would decide on the dismissal of inferior players or the admission of new instrumentalists.

The Orchestra capitulated. On 31 March 1909 Mahler conducted

the first concert of the New York Philharmonic Orchestra at Carnegie Hall. The programme comprised Schumann's *Manfred*
Overture and Beethoven's Seventh Symphony. This was followed
on 7 April by a performance of Beethoven's Ninth. When Mahler
returned to Europe soon afterwards, he had a contract for the coming
season which gave him absolute control over the Orchestra.

Mahler himself described this position as the fulfilment of all his
desires. In the last resort, it was not opera – however much of his
artistic energy he devoted to it – but 'absolute music' which
formed his chief interest. As he wrote some months later to his
friend Guido Adler, it was just such a chance to direct a concert
orchestra that he had longed for all his life:

I am very happy to enjoy this chance of a lifetime – quite apart from
the fact that I can learn a lot from it, for the technique of the theatre is
quite different, and I am convinced that many of my defects hitherto as
an orchestrator spring from my habitually using my ears in the vastly
different acoustic conditions of the theatre.

America at last gave Mahler what Europe had denied him: New
York became his laboratory of orchestral practice. In Europe he
composed. He completed his Ninth Symphony in the summer of
1909, and began the Tenth. In the autumn he came to New York
for the third time. The Metropolitan Opera House was no longer his
goal. Although we are not in possession of direct proof, we may
state confidently that the contract Mahler had originally concluded
with Conried for a period of four years was no longer in force. This
transpires from a letter he wrote to Bruno Walter from New York
in December 1909, in which he mentions the high fee the Met
offered him to produce a new work. Had the annual contract still
been in force, he would not have been offered a special fee for this
opera. He accepted the offer, and on 5 March 1910 conducted
Tchaikovsky's *Queen of Spades*, the part of Hermann being sung
by Leo Slezak. Mahler conducted only four performances of this
opera. Directorship of the Met passed to Toscanini.

For the rest, Mahler's third winter in New York was a concert
season.

I am beginning to realise that I am incorrigible [he wrote to Bruno Walter]. People like us cannot help but do things thoroughly. And that, as I see it, means overworking. I am and always will be the eternal beginner. And the little practical experience I have acquired only serves to increase the demands I make on myself. Just as I should like to re-issue my own scores every five years, so I need to prepare afresh every time I conduct the scores of others.

In the numerous concerts which took place not only in New York but also in the neighbouring cities it supplied with music, Mahler got through an extensive programme. Works by Beethoven, Brahms, Mendelssohn, Mozart, Schubert, Schumann, Richard Strauss, Tchaikovsky and Wagner formed the staple of it. Mahler was dissatisfied with the orchestra, which he called 'untalented and phlegmatic'. 'My only pleasure lies in rehearsing a work I have not done before.' This explains the great number of new works, among them scores by American composers, such as a symphonic fantasy for organ and orchestra by Charles M. Loeffler, and Edward MacDowell's Piano Concerto in D minor. From his own works Mahler chose for the 1909–10 season only the *Kindertotenlieder*, already performed in New York, and the First Symphony, which under his leadership was introduced to the American public for the first time. It aroused no enthusiasm. 'The audience received it with what might be described as courteous applause, much dubious shakings of the head, and no small amount of grumbling', as the *New York Tribune* put it.

We are better informed about Mahler's rehearsal technique in New York than about the details of his work in Vienna. It was the Americans, not Mahler's Austrian compatriots, who thought of interviewing surviving witnesses. These accounts, recorded on tape and transmitted by the American radio station KPFK, and later issued in the form of a gramophone record, confirm what we know about the moderation of Mahler's gestures. A bassoonist remembers that the players complained about the indistinctness of his beat. Mahler replied: 'Just play the music. The conductor is a necessary evil.' All mention the careful phrasing he insisted on. Where anything was not clear, he would sing the passage in question. To eliminate slovenly execution, he would ask the players sitting at the back desks to play their parts separately. If they did not come up to standard, and failed to improve, he dismissed them from the orchestra. Clarity and distinctness were what he valued most. What distinguished him from Toscanini, according to one musician, was that Mahler would try to recreate the composer's intention with each work, while Toscanini would always impress his own personality on a score. One player gave an instructive example: Mahler had dealt fairly with the individual movements of Beethoven's *Pastoral*, giving full value to the distinctive mood of each one; whereas Toscanini concentrated everything on dramatic effect in this symphony, and was in fact building up from the start to the unchaining of the storm in the fourth movement.

Such retrospective comparisons must be treated with reserve, for in them relatively recent impressions of Toscanini may have been erroneously juxtaposed with earlier experiences of Mahler. Still, the observations are of value in that they underline the 'feminine empathy' of the latter as an interpreter to which we have already drawn attention.

In April 1910 Mahler returned to Europe. His first stop was Paris, where he was to conduct his Second Symphony. On the day before the performance, the composer and conductor Gabriel Pierné arranged a reception in Mahler's honour. Clemenceau and his circle were present, and so were Debussy and Paul Dukas. These two composers also came to the performance of Mahler's symphony at the Théâtre Châtelet, but in the middle of the second movement they registered their disapproval by getting up and walking out. His success with the public, says Alma, 'could not recompense Mahler for the bitterness he felt at being so grossly misunderstood, not to say slighted, by the foremost French composers'. Debussy's behaviour did not, however, stop Mahler from including works by the Frenchman in the programmes of his next New York concert season.

From Paris Mahler went on to Rome to conduct concerts there. Then he returned to Vienna to conclude an agreement with Universal Editions on the publication of his works. In June 1910 he

gave concerts in Leipzig and Munich. He briefly interrupted his
holidays in Toblach to meet Sigmund Freud in Holland and to
conduct concerts in Cologne. But his entire strength and – we may
suppose – not inconsiderable resources were concentrated on the
performance of a work that had been in existence for some years.
The Eighth Symphony was to be heard for the first time in September 1910.

'Imagine the whole universe beginning to sing and resound.' That
was how Mahler in the August of 1906 had described the newly
completed Eighth Symphony to his friend Mengelberg. Four years
later, on 12 September 1910, he conducted the work at the Neue
Musikfesthalle in the Munich Exhibition grounds. The work has
been called the 'Symphony of a Thousand'. The programme,
issued under Mahler's supervision, tells us that 858 singers and 171
instrumentalists participated. The augmented orchestra of the
Munich Concert Society alone comprised 84 strings, 6 harps, 22
woodwinds and 17 brass. The score also demanded 4 trumpets and
4 trombones to be 'placed apart'. From Vienna came 250 members
of the Choral Society of the Gesellschaft der Musikfreunde; from
Leipzig, an equal number of singers from the Riedel-Verein led by
Georg Göhler. These were joined by 350 children of the Munich
Zentral-Singschule, and by eight outstanding solo singers from
Munich, Vienna, Frankfurt, Hamburg, Berlin and Wiesbaden.

An undertaking of such 'American' dimensions needed careful
preparation, which started at the beginning of the year. The choirs
worked in their home towns. Bruno Walter was responsible for the
choice of the soloists and their preparation. The letter Mahler
addressed to him from New York betrays his anxiety about all the
attendant details of such an exceptional production. He had agreed
on the performance with the Munich impresario Emil Gutmann
without considering the risks. As late as March 1910 Mahler wrote:
'My happiness would be complete had I not entrapped myself in
Herr Emil Gutmann's nets.' He feared that the performance might
turn into a sort of 'Barnum and Bailey Show'.

We are indebted to Emil Gutmann for a full account of Mahler's organising work for the performance of the Eighth. 'I have in my possession a written orchestral list for the Eighth Symphony where to nearly every instrument is adjoined an indication of the quality required. It is a model of detailed work.' The rehearsal schedule of the choirs was fixed down to the minutest particulars. The soloists were expected to come to rehearsals which were held not only in Vienna and Munich but also at Mahler's holiday resort.

In June Mahler inspected the choir of the Riedel-Verein, coached by Georg Göhler, at Leipzig, and found it 'splendidly worked up'. From Leipzig he went on to Munich to lead the first full rehearsals. Arnold Schönberg, Oskar Fried and Otto Klemperer turned up. In his *Memories of Gustav Mahler*, published fifty years later, Klemperer says: 'I confess that for the first time I understood the music of Mahler well enough to tell myself: here is a great composer.'

Mahler's organisational efforts were not confined to the realisation of the music. He also created 'an atmosphere in which the work could breathe'. Emil Gutmann says: 'The external grouping of the masses was important to him . . . and the faithful Roller was able to do justice to his intentions with an architecturally most effective arrangement.' Anyone familiar with the music of the Eighth Symphony will realise that the apparently 'external' grouping was largely conditioned by intrinsic considerations of sound. Of all Mahler's works it is the Eighth that poses the most difficult problems of balance. Massed sound effects must be integrated with quieter ensembles and the most delicate solo passages. Mahler also considered the lighting. It must help concentration. With that in mind, the enormous hall was plunged into a semi-darkness in which 'the black mass of the audience coalesced with the black-and-white mass of the executants'. In order to achieve the right atmosphere of dedication, Mahler even made sure that the tram-cars rattling past the Festival Hall would, during the performance, 'glide along slowly and not sound their bells'.

All these efforts, however 'circus-like' they may have seemed to Mahler himself at the beginning, were relevant to the music. More strictly than ever did he guard the musical autonomy of his symphony. The monumental work, whose first part used the Latin hymn *Veni creator spiritus* while its second part used the final scene of Goethe's *Faust Part II*, was meant to speak for itself, without any explanatory programme notes. Mahler would not have it that he had composed a 'Faust Symphony'. The programme gave the names of the performers and the texts that were set to music, but was free from the customary effusive interpretations.

The accounts of all who attended the concert on 12 September or the repeat on the following day testify to the overwhelming effect produced by Mahler's interpretation of his own music. Munich in those days became a rallying place for Mahler enthusiasts, now joined by younger men like Otto Klemperer who had only just come to appreciate him. It is not possible to enumerate all who came. Besides Walter and Roller, who had been involved in the preparations, there were Mahler's French friends (among them Clemenceau and Ritter), Dutch fans led by Mengelberg, the physicist Arnold Berliner, the painter Fritz Erler, and many critics and musicians, including Siegfried Wagner and Alfredo Casella. From Danzig came a twenty-six-year-old conductor armed with a letter of recommendation from Schönberg, which he presented to the impresario Gutmann with a request for a free ticket: his name was Anton Webern.

Literature was also represented at this Mahler convention. Stefan Zweig came to Munich and paid tribute to Mahler in a poem called *Der Dirigent* (*The Conductor*). It was printed in a symposium entitled *Gustav Mahler: a personal portrait in dedications* which was published at that time by the Munich firm of R. Piper & Co. The volume was edited by Paul Stefan and adorned by a reproduction of Rodin's bust of Mahler. Among contributions from other famous people, it contained a panegyric by Arthur Schnitzler starting with the words: 'Of all the creative musicians of our time – and there are many I truly value – none has given me more than Gustav Mahler.'

Another who was deeply impressed by Mahler's music was Thomas Mann. At the reception that was held after the first concert, Mann had found himself at a loss for words. He therefore wrote to Mahler a few days later:

[231]

At the hotel after the performance of 12 September I was incapable of telling you how much I am in your debt for the experience of that evening. I have a strong desire to give you at least some intimation of my feelings, and so I beg you kindly to accept the enclosed book – my latest work.

It is, to be sure, a poor exchange for what I have received from you, and must weigh light as a feather in the hand of a man who seems to me to embody the most serious and sacred artistic purpose of our age.

An epic jest. Perhaps it may help to pass a few idle hours in a tolerably acceptable manner.

Yours respectfully,
Thomas Mann

The 'Symphony of a Thousand' eventually found its way to Vienna in March 1918. It reached America two years earlier, in a veritable triumphal progress. The musician who was to help the Eighth to conquer America – the conductor Leopold Stokowski, then twenty-eight years old – had been in the audience at the Munich Festival Hall on 12 September 1910. Mahler's music, said Stokowski, was as overwhelming as 'the sight of Niagara Falls must have been to the first white man'. Stokowski was determined to perform the symphony. In the year 1916 he succeeded in obtaining $15,000 for his project from the sponsors of the Philadelphia Orchestra. Mahler's Eighth was played no less than nine times in Philadelphia, and a performance in New York followed. Quite apart from any artistic considerations, the enterprise had an immensely beneficial effect on the status of orchestral music in the American consciousness. The Orchestra, which had been a sort of Cinderella in Philadelphia, was now informed by the Chamber of Commerce that it constituted 'a financial asset of the town'. After that it was no longer so difficult to raise the necessary money for symphony concerts in Philadelphia. This was only one of the many consequences resulting from the 'Symphony of a Thousand' and the Mahler convention in Munich that proved so significant to the history of twentieth-century music.

In Munich his friends noticed signs of weakness and illness in Mahler, which, however, he was temporarily able to overcome. The medical diagnosis of the summer of 1907 had frightened him at the time, but he never would keep to his resolve to take things easy. The strain of three intensive New York seasons, first at the Opera House and then, even more intensively, giving concerts with the New York Philharmonic, severely taxed his physical resources. When he left Europe in November 1910 another great schedule of work lay ahead: a total of sixty-five concerts, to take place not only in New York, but also in Seattle, Buffalo, Springfield and Brooklyn. Mahler conducted only forty-eight of these. On 21 February 1911 his strength failed him during a rehearsal, but he insisted on conducting the concert. Among the listeners was Toscanini, who had come to hear a new work by Busoni, the *Berceuse élégique*, which was presented under the title *Lullaby at the grave of my mother*. That was the last new work Mahler performed, and indeed the last concert he conducted.

Difficulties with the management committee of the Orchestra, which did not confine itself to financial matters but interfered in questions of artistic policy, may have contributed to Mahler's illness. Busoni subsequently asserted that the lady who headed the management committee of the New York Philharmonic had made Mahler's life such a misery that 'as a result of the vexations he had suffered he lacked the strength to resist his last illness'. But this view is refuted by what we know about Mahler's state of health. His constitution had been undermined by the heart defect recognised years ago. To this was added a chronic susceptibility to attacks of angina, which plagued him constantly throughout the year 1910.

When Mahler had to break off his New York concerts, the doctor treating him discovered the presence of streptococci in his blood. Fearing that septicaemia might set in, he advised an immediate return to Europe for consultation with the relevant specialists in Paris. In April 1911 Mahler, now mortally ill, arrived in Paris. A noted bacteriologist confirmed the diagnosis of the New York doctor. At a sanatorium in Neuilly on the outskirts of Paris a course of treatment was attempted, but it was unsuccessful and merely led to a worsening of Mahler's condition. Desperately afraid, Alma

Mahler cabled to a distinguished doctor in Vienna, begging him to come. He arrived, but only to confirm that the case was hopeless. It was decided to transport Mahler to Vienna, where he arrived on the morning of 12 May. The doctors at the sanatorium where he lay issued bulletins, first daily, then at shorter intervals, that marked the rapid deterioration in his state. On 18 May 1911, shortly before midnight, Mahler died.

The public was able to follow the course of Mahler's painful and hopeless struggle, the details of which were described in the press with tactless precision. There were also cloyingly sentimental newspaper articles, whose very titles betray their vulgarity. One writer, in an article entitled 'Yearnings of the stricken heart' went so far as to hold the 'big shareholders' of American musical life responsible for Mahler's heart disease.

Mahler was buried at the Grinzing cemetery. On the tombstone, as he had wished, there is nothing but his name. 'Those who seek me know who I was, and the others do not need to know.'

[9]

The Heritage

Two works which Mahler was able to complete became known only after his death: *Das Lied von der Erde*, a composition for two solo voices and orchestra, the first draft of which went back to the summer of 1907, was completed in October 1909 at the latest; the Ninth Symphony was finished in fair copy, probably in New York, some time before April 1910. A tenth symphony remained as a fragment.

In 1907 Mahler came into possession of a newly published book of the Leipzig Insel-Verlag, *Die chinesische Flöte* (*The Chinese Flute*), consisting of free renderings of Chinese poems by the German poet Hans Bethge. Bethge was no sinologist and had no direct access to Chinese poetry, and the models he used for his sensitive poems were not the original texts but existing versions in German, English and French. We need not consider here whether he was successful in catching the spirit of Chinese lyric verse. What attracted Bethge to these poems was some echo of his own voice, and some of his original poems might indeed find a place in *The Chinese Flute*.

> *Ich kenne Knaben, die zur Mandoline*
> *Dir von Verbrechen reden, dass dir graut.*
> *Ich kenne Mädchen, die mit süsser Miene*
> *Ins Dunkel gehn . . .*

> [I know boys who to the mandolin
> Will talk of crimes that make your blood run cold.
> I know girls who with the sweetest look
> Will go into the dark . . .]

It was this cadence which Bethge thought to recapture in Chinese poetry: 'What graceful lyrical art confronted me here! I felt a shy, transient tenderness of lyrical utterance; I gazed into a verbal art wholly taken up with telling images, sending shafts of light into the melancholy riddle of existence.' Mahler, who knew Bethge's introduction to the eighty-odd poems of the collection, selected seven:

1. Das Trinklied vom Jammer der Erde (after Li Tai-po)
2. Der Einsame im Herbst (after Chang Tsi)
3. Der Pavillon aus Porzellan (after Li Tai-po)
4. Am Ufer (after Li Tai-po)
5. Der Trinker im Frühling (after Li Tai-po)
6. In Erwartung des Freundes (after Mong Kao-jen)
7. Der Abschied des Freundes (after Wang Wei)

Originally Mahler wanted to give the work the general title *Das Lied vom Jammer der Erde* (*The Song of Earthly Woes*). In the end he chose the less gloomy title of *Das Lied von der Erde* (*The Song of the Earth*), nor was it the only change he made. For the purposes of composition, he dealt very freely with Bethge's poems. He transposed passages, changed some titles and contracted the sixth and seventh poems of his choice (*In Erwartung des Freundes* and *Der Abschied des Freundes*) into one movement which he called *Der Abschied* (*The Farewell*). The six movements of this 'song symphony' were eventually entitled:

1. Das Trinklied vom Jammer der Erde (Drinking Song of Earthly Woes)
2. Der Einsame im Herbst (The Lonely Man in Autumn)
3. Von der Jugend (Youth)
4. Von der Schönheit (Beauty)
5. Der Trunkene im Frühling (The Drunken Man in Spring)
6. Der Abschied (The Farewell)

It is instructive to pursue this transformation from the particular to the general: from 'Pavilion' to 'Youth', from 'Beach' to 'Beauty'. By turning the 'Drinker' of the original into a 'Drunken man' and giving him an entirely new line (*Aus tiefstem Schauen lauscht' ich auf*) (From deepest contemplation I emerged), Mahler made him a being remote from the world. Even more telling is the textual change in the last movement of the symphony. Bethge has:

> Ich werde nie mehr in die Ferne schweifen, –
> Müd ist mein Fuss, und müd ist meine Seele,
> Die Erde ist die gleiche überall,
> Und ewig, ewig sind die weissen Wolken . . .

> [Never more shall I wander far abroad, –
> My foot is weary, weary is my soul;
> The earth is everywhere the same,
> And endless, endless the white clouds . . .]

Mahler changes this to:

> Wohin ich geh'? Ich geh', ich wand're in die Berge.
> Ich suche Ruhe für mein einsam' Herz.
> Ich wandle nach der Heimat, meiner Stätte!
> Ich werde niemals in die Ferne schweifen.
> Still ist mein Herz und harret seiner Stunde.
> Die liebe Erde allüberall
> blüht auf im Lenz und grünt aufs neu'!
> Allüberall und ewig blauen licht die Fernen.
> Ewig . . . Ewig . . .

> [Where do I go? I leave, I'm going to the mountains.
> I seek peace for my lonely heart.
> I journey to my homeland, to my resting place.
> Never more shall I wander far abroad.
> My heart is quiet, waiting for its hour.
> Everywhere the dear earth
> Blossoms in springtime and burgeons again!
> Everywhere and evermore the blue distance beckons,
> Evermore . . . Evermore . . .]

'Dying away to nothing' is written above the last bars of the score. The major triad vanishes softly in its colouring of trombones, celestas, harps and strings, released from earthbound tonality by the added sixth of flutes and oboe. This final dying fall ('Ewig . . . Ewig . . .') is the best approach to appreciating the specific character of the *Song of the Earth*. There is all the difference in the world between it and the mighty, spacious E flat major chord of the full orchestra concluding the Eighth. *The Song of the Earth* is conceived more intimately, more like chamber music. Certainly there are also homophonic passages, expressionist orchestral outbursts (as for instance at the beginning) and climaxes of that special kind of polyphony Mahler had cultivated particularly since the Fifth Symphony. But on the whole, a transparent, introspective clarity prevails.

In this context Paul Bekker speaks of Mahler's 'late style', a style that is 'full of astringent fantasy and prophetic of the future, like the late style of every great artist'. Such a statement may sound like a poetic turn of phrase which one may accept or reject as one wishes, but the wisdom of age and intimations of the future can be traced in the written music. Ludwig Schiedermair, who in 1900 had published the first biography of Mahler, in 1932 set one of his students at Bonn University the task of investigating 'Gustav Mahler's orchestration'. In his dissertation, published in 1945, Anton Schäfers has many illuminating things to say about Mahler's late style, as manifested in *The Song of the Earth*. He comes to the conclusion that in this style Mahler was using all three basic forms of orchestral treatment concurrently: the mature form of polyphony, homophony, and a special kind of 'constructive-colouristic' orchestration.

The 'prophetic element' in Mahler's late style has also been the subject of a musicological dissertation, submitted to the University of Hamburg by Helmut Storjohann in 1952. This points out a new creative method, reminiscent of Schönberg's manner of construction. In Mahler's late style, according to Storjohann, inventiveness expresses itself 'in the way he develops new thematic formations from the evolving stream of the basic motif. No longer is there a mere succession of different ideas, but the initial theme determines a series of different ideas which are in some way or other based on it.' The most obvious instance is the beginning of *The Song of the Earth* where the horns establish a series of notes (A-G-E-D-C) which, as in Schönberg, 'gives rise to various formations of motif and theme'.

It is this method of development on the basis of a fundamental structure that lends unity to the six movements of *The Song of the Earth*. It is a method of integration which does not advertise itself, but can be felt even by those who know nothing about Mahler's anticipation of Schönberg's principles. Integration is also the key word for an understanding of Mahler's treatment of the human voice. The tenor (in numbers 1, 3 and 5) and the contralto (in numbers 2, 4 and 6) have cantabile lines which do not go their own way above the orchestra, but appear incorporated in it. The timbre of the voice and the variants of this timbre become in their turn an element of the constructive-colouristic orchestration. Mahler will specify: 'in narrative tone, without expression', and then again, 'very gently and expressively', or 'meditatively', 'hesitantly', 'dolce', and so forth. These instructions, and others concerned with articulation, all seem to aim at making the human voice into an 'instrument'. In this way, too, Mahler's late style points to the future.

In the autumn of 1910 Mahler gave the score to Bruno Walter to study. 'It was the first time', Walter notes in his autobiography, 'that Mahler did not play me a new work himself – he was probably afraid of the excitement. I studied it, and went through a time of the most terrifying entrancement with this passionate, bitter, resigned and benedictory cry of farewell and evanescence.'

A few months after Mahler's death, the newspapers announced that Bruno Walter would conduct the first performance of the work. Anton Webern, who was then living in Berlin, wrote to his friend Alban Berg: 'The Mahler celebration is in Munich on 19 and 20 November ... Tell me, is it conceivable that we should not be there? For the first time since Mahler's death, here is a new work by him. And are we to miss it?' Reading the last section of the text made Webern expect the greatest musical marvels: 'For heaven's sake, what sort of music will this make? I have a feeling all the time that I should be able to guess it before I actually hear it. Can you bear the suspense? I can't.'

Webern asked his friend to get on to Walter for permission to attend the rehearsals. Soon Berg replied from Vienna.

I've seen Walter; of course he's quite willing to let us come to the rehearsals. So we shall be in each other's company for two or three days on end, I shall hear *The Song of the Earth* twice, and by then I shall already know something of it, since the piano reduction will appear, I am told, on 13 November. In such circumstances, it's good to be alive!

Mahler was a great rallying cry for the young in those days. He meant to them what Wagner had meant to the preceding generation. They welcomed *The Song of the Earth* in Munich, the town which since the 'Symphony of a Thousand' had become Mahler territory. Bruno Walter, who conducted this performance, also directed the first performance of the Ninth Symphony on 26 June 1912. This took place in Vienna, under the aegis of the first Vienna Music Festival of the modern kind. The four-movement work was not readily intelligible. The free sonata form of the first movement opened the gate to the world of Schönberg and his school. The second movement scherzo has been mistaken for a parody. Even in 1955 one biographer of Mahler was still objecting to the whole structure of the third movement (a rondo of a rather ghostly character) and the fourth (an adagio of frightening emotional power). It was given to few to recognise the greatness of the Ninth. Alban Berg in the summer of 1912 called it 'the most marvellous thing Mahler ever wrote'. Schönberg found the Ninth very strange. 'Here the author hardly speaks in the first person. It almost seems as though this work had another, concealed author, who was merely using Mahler as a mouthpiece.' This transcendental theory, which can be neither denied nor proved, was advanced by Schönberg in his famous memorial address on Mahler in 1912. Schönberg considered Mahler a saint and a martyr. That Mahler had in his lifetime been misunderstood, attacked and positively reviled, seemed to Schönberg the most natural thing in the world. 'I find this quite fair. After all, the great artist must be punished somehow during his lifetime for the veneration he will later enjoy.'

In this context, Schönberg mentioned one reproach that was levelled against Mahler in an obituary, namely, that he had written 'gigantic symphonic potpourris'. Patient research could unearth a hundred similar taunts set down by Mahler's detractors both before and after 1911, and indeed down to the present day. The list begins with the term *Strudelteigsymphonien* (strudel-pastry symphonies), which as reported in Prague was already current in Vienna by 1900, and ends with the more genteelly worded reservations to be met with even today in musical reference books and histories with pretensions to objectivity. H. J. Moser's *Musiklexicon* (4th edition, Berlin 1955) states that Mahler was mainly important as an influence, that his musical creed is no longer relevant, and that his music 'is no longer an immediate experience to us'. Against the single page this encyclopaedia allocates to Mahler, there are more than two devoted to Hans Pfitzner, who is credited with 'sublimity', 'depth' and 'an everlasting place in German music'. The position of the opponents of Mahler has, to be sure, become somewhat precarious of late. One could almost feel sorry for them; how can they, who rally to the standard of Hans Pfitzner, get over the painful fact that the composer of *Die Rose vom Liebesgarten*, despite the aid Mahler extended to him, is today less esteemed even in German-speaking countries than Mahler himself? Mahler's world renown must have a disheartening effect on some people.

The popularity enjoyed by Mahler's music today is the result of a process that is not easy to describe or explain. In the decades since his death there have always been disciples of Mahler and groups propagating his work. They have usually been local and isolated, only occasionally attaining regional or national significance. It was not until half a century after his death that his reputation at last, and, as it were, independently, gained worldwide currency. One is inclined to find the explanation for this victory in the untiring efforts of his disciples.

The first important move was made by Willem Mengelberg after the 1914–18 war. He celebrated his twenty-fifth anniversary as conductor of the Amsterdam Concertgebouw Orchestra with a Mahler Festival. In May 1920 he directed nine concerts which for the first time offered the entire opus of Mahler. In an epilogue written for this festival, Egon Wellesz says: 'The Amsterdam Mahler Festival marks a beginning for all participants. Now Mahler and his work are no longer the concern of a small group of enthusiasts, but have become of general interest.' Amsterdam has provided a tower-ing pedestal for Mahler's work, and the memorial stone bearing reliefs of Mahler and Mengelberg that has been erected at the Concertgebouw is a tangible symbol of this.

Holland, a neutral country, was eminently suitable as a meeting-place for the Mahler enthusiasts of Europe. The Amsterdam 'peace conference', as one Paris critic called Mengelberg's Mahler Festival, really seemed to give an uplift to the international cultivation of Mahler's music. In Vienna, too, he was now played more frequently. In the two postwar winters of 1918–19 and 1919–20, *The Song of the Earth* could be heard no less than twelve times in the concert hall, and there were thirty performances of various symphonies. In the autumn of 1920 Oskar Fried, encouraged by the Amsterdam Festival, conducted a whole Mahler cycle which included all the symphonies except the Eighth. One reviewer offered this explanation for the vogue: 'There can be no more doubt that Mahler is the composer of our age. Our troubles, our misery, all the intolerable elements of an unpalatable reality, have tremendously increased our metaphysical need, making us want to leave the horrors of everyday life for the solitudes of the great god Pan.'

This interpretation, of course, allowed for the possibility of a decline in the enthusiasm. What had been taken for a genuine understanding among wider circles indeed soon turned out to have been a mere fashion. Only a few found an instinctively musical and at the same time historically compelling approach to Mahler's work. They were helped on their way by Paul Bekker in his book *Gustav Mahler's Symphonies*, published in 1921. This German writer on music was the first to analyse the development of the Austrian symphony proper, and thus the descent of Mahler from Bruckner and Schubert. Austria itself was not ready for this discovery. The little republic did not wish to be reminded of its individuality. The Austrians liked to speak of their country as 'not viable'; how could they then believe in the lifegiving autonomy of their modern music? Pusillanimity gave rise to the *Anschluss* mentality: affiliation to the German Reich, or affiliation to world revolution, or even sentimental affiliation to the ideology of a lost Old Austria. There were thus three ways of understanding Mahler's music: as music of the old Empire (Habsburg monumentality, as it were, shot through with debilitating fatigue); or as 'German music' (did it not draw inspiration from Goethe and Rückert and from the demotic *Wunderhorn*?); or again as 'revolutionary music' (heard by some in the trumpet calls and march rhythms).

Those who disliked the sound of Mahler had a fourth view at their disposal. It is the one that has been most frequently advanced, and not only in Hitler's Greater Germany. This view maintains the 'artistic impotence' of Mahler, deriving it from his Jewish origin. When in 1926 the society of the Vienna Tonkünstlerorchester planned to do another complete cycle of Mahler's œuvre, the question was raised in the *Wiener Neueste Nachrichten*, organ of the Austrian Pan-German Party, whether a Jew like Mahler could ever have been capable of 'participating in the national artistic life of a people'.

The answer the Pan-German State gave to this question is well known. The decadent and destructive attitude behind it was already restricting the social potential of Mahler's music in Austria around 1930.

In America, however, there arose at that time a new understanding for Mahler. In New York 4 January 1931 saw the founding of the Bruckner Society of America, an organisation which in its statutes undertook to uphold the cause of Bruckner and Mahler. From that time onwards, conductors of European origin increasingly put the latter's symphonies on their programmes. Fritz Reiner conducted the Seventh Symphony in March 1931 at Cincinnati; two months later Eugene Goossens performed the Eighth in that town; in the autumn of 1931 Koussevitsky gave the first American performance of the Ninth; Artur Rodzinski conducted the Fourth in Los Angeles on 31 December 1931, and in February 1932 Bruno Walter performed the Fifth in New York on four consecutive days. We owe to the Bruckner Society the publication of the first American biography of Mahler, by Gabriel Engel. The popularisation of Mahler in America was also greatly aided by Otto Klemperer, who took over the direction of the Philharmonic Orchestra of Los Angeles in 1933 and in December 1936 conducted a performance of the Second Symphony in New York about which the critic Olin Downes wrote in the *New York Times*: 'The performance was one of the historic musical occasions that will not be forgotten and will always appear significant in the musical annals of the city.'

Mahler's symphonies steadily strengthened their position in the American concert repertoire. A statistical survey by the sociologist John F. Muller shows that in the year 1950 Mahler's music accounted for 2·5 per cent of the repertoire of the leading American orchestras. After the Second World War, Mahler took seventh place, jointly with Schumann, in the all-American 'popularity pyramid'; in the statistics of the New York Philharmonic Symphony Orchestra he even holds the third place, with Tchaikovsky – surpassed only by Beethoven and Brahms. The ascending movement, initiated in the thirties, has continued unbroken into the present.

As in America, so in Russia, too, conductors who had been personal friends of Mahler's contributed to the spread of his music. Oskar Fried introduced the Second Symphony to St Petersburg in 1906; further evidence of his energetic propagation of Mahler in Russia may be found in the columns of *Russkaya muzykalnaya gazeta*. After the Revolution of 1917 Mahler's music became even more popular in Russia, and at first there was no noticeable tendency to reject it on ideological grounds. Political scruples could still be dispelled, as is shown in Bruno Walter's account of a concert he conducted in Moscow in 1923:

I had put Mahler's Fourth Symphony in one of my programmes, and had handed the text of the last movement, dealing with 'Heavenly Life', to the organisers for translation and reproduction on the printed programme. It was returned to me with a request to change the words: in the new Russia one must not sing of heaven and angels, St Peter or any other saints. I refused, of course, to alter a thing, and eventually I carried my point by persuading the pedantic representative of atheism that the poem was meant 'symbolically'.

In the 1920s, the official Soviet cultural administration still favoured contacts with the West. For the twenty-year-old Dimitri Shostakovich, meeting Bruno Walter proved decisive. In Leningrad in 1926 Shostakovich played his First Symphony to Walter, who made up his mind to perform this music, strongly reminiscent of Mahler, soon afterwards in Berlin. About that time Shostakovich also met Ivan Ivanovich Sollertinsky, a few years older than himself and a fervent admirer of Mahler. Indeed, he wrote a book on Mahler, which was published in Moscow in 1932. Sollertinsky exerted a strong influence on Shostakovich – zealous party-line critics called it 'a harmful influence', as Shostakovich mentions in his autobiographical study. This accusation was due to the change in Soviet musical politics which took place in the thirties and made life difficult for Shostakovich among others. The effect of the new policy on the performance of Mahler in the Soviet Union at that time has not been investigated: we do not even know whether Oskar Fried, who emigrated to the Soviet Union in 1934 and died in Moscow in 1941, had any further chances to promote the work of his beloved friend.

After the war, changing political directives led to an explicit rejection of Mahler's work. An article on 'The culture of Austria' which appeared in the *Great Soviet Encyclopaedia* (2nd edition, 1949) states that his symphonies 'reflect the collapse of petit-bourgeois illusions in the imperialistic era' and that *The Song of the Earth* was typical of the 'reactionary character of Mahler's music'.

Even without knowing the details, we can imagine the effect of such declarations of principle on Soviet concert practice. All the more welcome is the change that came about in the fifties. On the occasion of the centenary of Mahler's birth (July 1960) the Moscow periodical *Sovetskaya muzyka* printed some much more thoughtful essays on the composer. Neither Shostakovich nor his distinguished son Maxim misses any opportunity of affirming their admiration for Mahler. Maxim Shostakovitch declared in an interview of 1967: 'Mahler is my favourite composer.' And Yevgeny Svetlanov, conductor of the State Symphony Orchestra of the USSR, went even further: 'I personally consider Mahler the greatest genius of all peoples and all times.' Svetlanov conducted the first Soviet performance of the Seventh Symphony, and, thanks to his initiative, the Moscow Philharmonic arranged to play two cycles of the works of Mahler. David Oistrakh, who is not only a top-flight violin virtuoso but a very fine and inspiring conductor, has recently promoted Mahler's symphonies in both concert performances and gramophone recordings.

In England, interest in Mahler's work began to grow in the fifties. About 1950 Eric Blom told me that he considered the publication of a Mahler biography in England a risky undertaking; in 1955 he published a volume on Bruckner and Mahler by the Austrian-born musicologist Hans F. Redlich, in the series *The Master Musicians*, of which he was the general editor. In 1958 the young English musicologist Donald Mitchell produced his meritorious study of Mahler's youth, *Gustav Mahler – the early years*. Neville Cardus, who had been writing about Mahler for many years – mainly in the columns of the *Manchester Guardian* – paid tribute to him in a publication of the Royal Festival Hall on the centenary of Mahler's birth. In concert halls and on the air, all the works are increasingly heard. In the sixties Otto Klemperer recorded his versions of *The Song of the Earth* and Symphonies Nos 2, 4 and 9. To this great Mahler conductor Neville Cardus dedicated his comprehensive work on Mahler's symphonies, the first volume of which appeared in 1965.

The musical establishment in Austria has been slow to join the international Mahler movement. The exhibition 'Gustav Mahler and his time', shown during the Vienna *Festwochen* of 1960 at the Secession building, was, however, admirable. The exhibition catalogue, edited by Franz Hadamovsky, made an important contribution towards creating some order in the still rather neglected realm of Mahler research. Bruno Walter conducted a Festival performance of the Fourth Symphony in Vienna in 1960. The return of Walter, who was much moved by the exhibition of documents at the Secession, called up memories of this conductor's endeavours, begun more than fifty years ago, to convert Vienna to Mahler's music. The climax came in May 1936, when Walter conducted at the great Musikvereinssaal a performance of *The Song of the Earth* which was also recorded on gramophone records. The seven discs which were needed for a work of such dimensions before the invention of the long-playing record were subsequently treasured by Mahler enthusiasts all over the world. In 1936 Walter also issued through a Vienna publisher his beautiful essay *Gustav Mahler – a portrait*.

Walter's devoted work in the composer's homeland was interrupted by the annexation of Austria by Germany in 1938. In 1949 Bruno Walter's book appeared in English in New York. In a preface Ernst Křenek, an Austrian composer who had also emigrated to America, stressed the importance of the American sanctuary for European art, threatened and persecuted as it was at home. In 1957 Walter's tribute to Mahler at last became available again to German-speaking readers in a reprint. Only then did a Mahler movement emerge in Austria, led by the survivors of the 'Mahler clique' of long ago, and happily supported by the unprejudiced younger generation which came out more and more strongly for him. During the Festival weeks of 1967, the Vienna Konzerthaus Society put on a complete cycle of Mahler's works, led by prominent conductors such as Karl Böhm, Rafael Kubelik, Leonard Bernstein and Hans Swarowsky, as well as by younger men like Claudio Abbado and Carlos Kleiber.

But the strongest boost to the Mahler renaissance came from the long-playing record. As late as 1951 the international gramophone catalogues contained no more than four symphony recordings, of which only one was generally obtainable, the rest having to be ordered specially from the manufacturer. A few years later I was able in my *Book of Long-playing Records* (Vienna, 1956) to list recordings of all the symphonies. True, Mahler's music was not yet 'big business' for the recording firms, but a matter of prestige for which an occasional risk is worth taking. In Europe the change occurred in the sixties. Catalogues today list numerous stereo recordings of varying technical and musical quality. We owe to Leonard Bernstein a complete Mahler cycle in stereo; Rafael Kubelik is in the process of recording such a cycle. This does not stop other conductors and other recording firms from plunging into the Mahler adventure. Nor is it, financially, a gamble nowadays to record a Mahler symphony, despite the expense of such a recording: a Mahler record pays for itself. Radio transmissions may be going out into a listenerless void; concert promotions may have to be underpinned by subsidies and free tickets; but the demand for discs is incontrovertible evidence for the extraordinary scope and the intensity, surprising even to enthusiasts, of the Mahler renaissance.

Is this renaissance to be ascribed to the work of enthusiasts, to a change in the tastes of the musical public, or to the influence of the record-player? The unremitting efforts of those who have championed Mahler's music should certainly not be underestimated, but on their own they could not have worked the transformation. The attempt to explain it by a supposed awakening of interest in monumental music of the late-Romantic period as such misfires when statistics of record sales show that, though there is a growing demand for Mahler, interest in Richard Strauss records is falling.

'My time will come.' Mahler's prophecy has been fulfilled in the 1960s. Many diverse factors have contributed to this, but perhaps the most decisive of all was the advent of the technically perfected stereo record. Mahler's time had come when it became possible to store and reproduce spatial sound. Advances in technique played a large part in the onset of the new Mahler epoch. One might think that Mahler could not have foreseen this. Who would be bold enough to assert that he could have imagined the technique of manipulated stereo-space in recording, of skilful microphone positioning and the regulation of orchestral balance by the sound engineer at his mixer? Who would venture to make prosaic technique responsible for the victory of a musical dreamer?

But Mahler was no dreamer. He had a very clear idea of the technical requirements necessary for the unconditional surrender of the public to his music. As an expert technician of the opera house and concert hall, he possessed a more precise concept of orchestra and acoustic space than, for instance, Schönberg, Berg and Webern. His tenets on this subject were more prophetic and realistic than most 'spatial sound' ideas of the presentday avant-garde. In this respect, too, Mahler proved the contemporary of the future. We can adduce evidence in support of that.

Mahler's attempts to arrive at a considered patterning of spatial sound emerge from the scores of his symphonies. 'Off-stage orchestras', or individual instruments meant to sound 'as from afar', were integral elements of his music. In his early years he even applied these ideas to the works of the masters of the past. Bruno Walter tells of a performance of Beethoven's Ninth Symphony in Hamburg where Mahler tried out the following space structure:

He had the B flat major march in the finale played by an off-stage orchestra, while the tenor and the male chorus sang on the rostrum, the main orchestra re-entering with the start of the subsequent fugato. This was no mere whim. He thought he had discovered Beethoven's intention, as prefigured in Schiller's text: namely, that the winged progress of the young men should, from the hesitant pianissimo of its start, through the crescendo to the ultimate fortissimo, make its way as though from a vast distance into a victorious presence. To this effect he employed means which Beethoven, hampered by the restrictions of his time, would not have dared to use.

Bruno Walter adds that Mahler was, of course, 'on the wrong track' in this case. Yet Walter emphasises that this questionable experiment had suggested to him an unquestionable basic idea: in order to achieve an authentic interpretation, one must argue back from the fixed notation of a musical work of art to the flux of its inception.

In his Vienna period, Mahler attempted such patterning of sound chiefly in the sphere of opera. To the singer in the title role of Rubinstein's opera *The Demon*, he made a strange suggestion during the rehearsal for the beginning of the second act. The Demon makes an entrance here, but is supposed to be invisible to all the other characters, who only hear his voice. Mahler asked the singer to sing this scene from the prompt-box. 'People must believe it is a call from another world.' The singer protested. He wanted to be seen by the public. For Mahler, who put artistic effect above operatic convention, this was a sufficient reason not to employ the refractory singer in any further productions.

Sound patterns of this kind – concealed sound, and sound from afar – were not Mahler's invention. Wagner not only demanded, but himself constructed special orchestral acoustics for the *Ring des Nibelungen*. The covered orchestra in the 'mystic abyss' of the Bayreuth Festspielhaus is part of the authentic sound picture of the *Ring*, which doubtless becomes falsified in any conventionally built opera house. Nevertheless, some expert musicians and experienced critics have found fault with Wagner's Bayreuth sound – Eduard Hanslick did, and even Richard Strauss.

Mahler was of a different opinion. His efforts were always directed at carrying out the composer's original intentions. So he hit on the idea of having the pit of the Vienna Court Opera Theatre lowered, and this technical alteration was duly carried out in the summer of 1903. There are conflicting reports in the newspapers of the day about the acoustic results achieved. However, none of the critics, as far as one can judge, is concerned with the motives for Mahler's reform. Mahler himself explained them in an interview that appeared on 6 September 1903 in the *Fremdenblatt*. As his views are of great importance, for present-day performing practice as well, they are here reproduced in full:

My considered intention was to deepen the orchestra pit by one and a half metres. The plans were designed so that the floor of the pit could be lowered or raised hydraulically, according to the needs of the work performed. Thus I would put the orchestra at the lowest possible level for certain of Wagner's works, but would keep the small Mozart orchestra at a normal height, and so on, as suits the work in question and as is suggested by constant observation. There are strong arguments for the practice of placing the Wagner orchestra as low as possible: in some of his works, the orchestra is meant to sound as from a nebulous distance; in this way, too, the singers' voices can stand out effectively. To be sure, some passages of Wagner I can imagine better with a completely open orchestra – for instance, the Prelude to the third act of *Lohengrin*. But all in all, the public should gladly welcome the lowering of the pit for the Wagner orchestra. For I think it cannot be very pleasant during an orchestral storm for the people in the stalls to hear the cymbals above anything else, until they feel like stopping up their ears. All this will be changed once the music comes up from a great depth.

Mahler's care for the authentic sound of the *Ring* orchestra at the Vienna Opera shows how seriously he took his duty to a work of art, and how superior he was to his contemporaries who criticised both his experimental spirit and Wagner's original conception. Incidentally, it is surprising that Mahler was so determined to convey the orchestral blur of 'nebulous distance'. As a rule, in his own work, he valued clarity more than anything.

Anyhow, he pioneered the 'removable' orchestra for opera. Historically speaking, this was the beginning of the transition from actual, unchangeable sound space to manipulated, artificial sound space.

Every work of music – this is the gist of Mahler's statement – demands the space appropriate to it. He was always concerned with giving his own works the right acoustical settings. In a letter to Fritz Steinbach, who planned a performance of the Third Symphony at the Cologne Theater am Habsburgerring, Mahler wrote: 'I must say frankly, I am rather uneasy about exposing my symphony to the acoustics of a theatre (moreover, one that has apparently not been tried out). I would have felt happier, honoured master, if you had put my work on an ordinary Gürzenich programme.' With similar anxiety, he had written a year before to Bruno Walter in Berlin: 'What are the acoustics like in the Kroll Hall? Strauss wants to do my Third there. With the orchestra on the stage! Is that possible?'

Mahler's ceaseless revisions of orchestration, his avowed wish to reshape his own scores 'every five years', spring above all from the endeavour to make the orchestral sound image independent of the acoustic conditions. His friends report with astonishment that he frequently changed the orchestration of his symphonies in the course of rehearsals. Egon Wellesz, a most trustworthy expert witness, tells us how at a rehearsal of the Second Symphony Mahler was dissatisfied with the passage *O Schmerz, du Alldurchdringender*, because the line did not come through clearly. He solved the problem by eliminating the trombone-chords in the score, thus making the voice audible. He then said to the orchestra: 'Clarity is my chief concern. All power to the conductor who alters my scores where the acoustics of the hall or the quality of the orchestra demand it, to carry out my intentions.'

Mahler's symphonies, to a greater degree than most works of his contemporaries, are dependent on space. A reverberating hall with a strong echo in the lower sound ranges can all but kill their effect. The transparent acoustics of many modern concert halls, on the other hand, are apt to make them appear 'over-orchestrated' in places. Mahler was aware of these facts, and that is why he tried as often as possible to handle the realisation of his compositional ideas himself: there were few conductors to whom he felt able to entrust even the partial solution of this problem. He trusted Mengelberg, Fried and Walter, for instance. But who among these most faithful of the faithful would dare to meddle with his orchestration, even where adaptation to particular spatial conditions seemed essential to the spirit of Mahler?

Numerous passages in the symphonies are distorted by unsuitable concert halls even though conductor and orchestra observe the instructions on the score most scrupulously. In nineteenth-century halls of the type of the Leipzig Gewandhaus or the Vienna Musikverein the strings often struggle in vain for minutes on end to put their parts across against the unfettered brass. It is easier to achieve the desired balance in many modern halls, such as the Royal Festival Hall in London or the Stuttgart Liederhalle. Strictly speaking, every performance of a Mahler symphony should be preceded by suitable sound-editing if the polyphony, homophony and instrumental timbres are to be preserved intact.

Studio-recording the music largely removes the risks of particular concert hall acoustics. For recording purposes a suitable space can be chosen which can then be further adapted to the special requirements of the score by movable screens or partitions (as in the studios of the Hessische Rundfunk). It becomes unnecessary to make adjustments to the score, as Mahler himself used to do. If the strings threaten to be overpowered by the rampant brass, the balance can be restored by careful placing of microphones and by sensitive sound-editing at the mixer.

The best stereo recordings of recent times can at last give us a sound image closer to Mahler's intentions than almost any concert performance. Nothing prevents the juxtaposing of distant, echoing sound with close, precise sound. For the musically trained technicians of sound recording, directional mixers and intensity compensators, artificial reverberation and tape editing make it possible to realise all the demands of the score without resorting to Mahler's risky invitation to make changes in his music. Thanks to the techniques of electro-acoustic recording and reproduction, textual purity can be preserved and Mahler's original intention, as manifested in his notation, fulfilled. The stereo record has been the salvation of these works.

In 1906 Mahler completed his Eighth Symphony. In 1910 he performed it in Munich. Between 1906 and 1910 Robert von Lieben developed his amplifying valve, without which electro-acoustic recording would have remained an impossibility. Not that Mahler was thinking specifically of this when he said that his time was yet to come. But everything he composed cries out for electro-acoustic realisation, for independence from pre-established sound space, for the free availability of all technical resources.

In the service of art, recording technique can help us over obstacles that previously seemed insuperable. There is a stereo recording of the Eighth Symphony in which the sound of a church organ in Switzerland is combined with the voices of singers and the strains of an orchestra that were recorded under Leonard Bernstein's direction in a London studio. The synthesis we hear from the loudspeakers was never an actual sound, either in England or on the continent – yet now it exists, a technological realisation of the directives preserved in Mahler's musical notation.

The growing number of concert performances, gramophone recordings and broadcasts of Mahler's works makes the question of the scores and parts used particularly important. Corrupt material which runs counter to the composer's intentions could create a false picture of his work at the very time when public interest in it has reached its height. The scores used until recently have left much to be desired.

Fortunately the International Mahler Society, formed in Vienna in 1955 under the chairmanship of Bruno Walter, made the publication of a critical collected edition its principal task. Thanks to the indefatigable labours of Erwin Ratz, acting president of the International Mahler Society, a considerable number of volumes were published in a relatively short time. Up to 1968 the following works had appeared in the critical collected edition: Symphonies Nos 1, 4, 5, 6 and 7, *Das Lied von der Erde*, and the adagio of the unfinished Tenth Symphony.

About the relation of the new edition to the versions previously used, Erwin Ratz has said:

With the exception of *Das Lied von der Erde*, which Mahler was never able to perform, these volumes for the first time present the text authorised as definitive by Mahler. Hitherto, although negotiations for new agreements had been going on, only the old versions had been used. It is common knowledge that Mahler, when directing performances of his own works, made more or less farreaching changes in the orchestration, in order to attain the utmost clarity in the presentation of his musical ideas. Once the fair copy was completed, he never changed anything in the musical structure; his retouchings are concerned purely with the realisation of the sound. They are, however, exceedingly illuminating, and a comparison of the various versions is a most impressive experience.

Although the compositional structure of the older editions agrees with that of the critical collected edition, yet the individual changes do sometimes make a crucial difference. Thus the Fifth Symphony in the version of the collected edition, which must now be considered authentic, contains more than 250 passages that differ from the older version. In the Sixth Symphony, moreover, Erwin Ratz settles the order of the individual movements. Mahler at first put the scherzo second and the andante third, subsequently decided to switch them round, and in the end reverted to the original order.

The adagio of the unfinished Tenth Symphony attracted attention even at a time when performances of the completed works were rather infrequent, exerting the fatal fascination of the incomplete. A facsimile print of the draft score appeared in 1924, with the adagio 'in an extremely faulty version, furnished with impossible retouchings'. The critical collected edition at last reproduces the unretouched original form. The preface to this edition also comes out against ill-fated attempts to reconstruct the other four movements of the Tenth. Only Mahler himself, it points out, could have shaped the existing draft into a finished work of art.

In this collected edition Erwin Ratz has produced a worthy memorial to the composer, and laid a reliable foundation for the performance of Mahler's music in our time. The volumes of the collected edition have incidentally facilitated the task of this biographer, who has otherwise suffered much from the unbelievably neglected state of Mahler research. For the adventures of a biographer in the jungle of documents and reports, eye-witness accounts and legends, see below.

I have spent over thirty years preparing to write this biography. To qualify oneself for such a task it is vital not merely to study documents, letters and reports, but above all to familiarise oneself with Mahler's music. This includes going to concerts, but also close reading of the scores, and constant attempts to perform the piano transcriptions of the symphonies in an intimate circle. Music enthusiasts today, with the whole range of gramophone recordings at their disposal for home performance, may feel sorry for the older generation, who had to try and get the feel of works rarely performed in the concert hall by mentally investing the sound four hands could coax out of a piano with all the richness of Mahler's orchestral writing. But we were not as badly off as one might think, for by using our imagination to build up the orchestra we in a way relived some of the difficulties he must have encountered in conceiving his works. In our far from effortless playing we could, within our modest powers, pursue Mahler's struggles with a new orchestral language. Today music lovers can put on a gramophone record and enjoy the more or less perfect result of interpretative labours without any effort on their part. Yet our hard-won appreciation in the old pre-

recording days makes us rejoice all the more over the liberation of
Mahler through electronic technique.

My love for Mahler was not constant. There were years when I
turned away from his music. The detachment gained by this – which
arose partly from a misunderstanding of Mahler and partly from a
change in my inclinations – proved useful in the end, for it enabled
me to understand the fickleness of public favour. The musicologist
has little interest in this phenomenon. He is concerned with the
history of compositions, with biographical data, and the accumu-
lated evidence about Mahler's creative work. The sociologist, however, is fascinated by the interplay between artist and society, and by
the changing position of the work of art in its social context. Understanding these variables will ultimately deepen his understanding of
the work itself.

The existing Mahler literature gives no adequate account of these
fluctuations. Leaving aside a few venomous pamphlets, its bulk
consists of a collection of eulogies. Mahler is glorified, sometimes
with understanding for his music and in intelligible language, but
more often in a flood of meaningless verbiage. Even Paul Bekker's
perceptive book on *Gustav Mahler's Symphonies* is not free from such
phrasemongering. All this makes it difficult for a wouldbe biographer
to penetrate to the facts. His work becomes an explorer's adventure.

I confess that in the course of this work I have never ceased to be
amazed. There is a well-established tradition of presenting Mahler,
and the saying 'tradition is slackness' could well be applied to it.
Clichés linger on that were coined largely by Mahler disciples, some
in Mahler's lifetime. One might think that modern musicology
would have discredited these either factually incorrect or distorted,
details of the sentimental Mahler legend by setting them against the
true facts, but this has not happened.

Even elementary biographical facts are assiduously put into dis-
torting contexts. One continually comes across the assertion that
in his first three engagements as a young conductor Mahler suffered
from the inadequate resources of the theatres. With a strange
ignorance of conditions prevailing under the Austrian Empire, the
pathetic little summer rep theatre at Bad Hall is put on the same

level, not only as the Stadttheater at Olmütz, but as the distinguished Landestheater at Laibach, the capital of the duchy of Krain. In an otherwise commendable book on Mahler (Berlin, 1960) Hans Christoph Worbs maintains that Mahler, in Laibach as at Bad Hall, had at his disposal 'only the most meagre resources for his artistic activity', and Hans Ferdinand Redlich states in his brief biography (London, 1955) that conditions in Laibach were 'no less ridiculous' than at the wretched summer theatre.

If Laibach in 1881 and 1882 had really been ridiculous in the artistic sense, how was it possible for Mahler there to acquire a conducting technique that caused a musical sensation at Olmütz? Only a miracle could explain such an advance, and Mahler's life is rich enough in genuine miracles to do without fictitious ones. The true situation at Laibach is made quite clear by a study which Professor Dragotin Cvetko, a musicologist working in Ljubljana (present-day Laibach) has most generously made accessible to me in advance of publication. The account of Gustav Mahler in Laibach in the present biography is based on Professor Cvetko's essay which is to appear under the above title in the series *Musik des Ostens* (Kassel).

Until recently there was similar uncertainty about Mahler's work at the Olmütz Stadttheater. The distinguished Czech musicologist Zdenek Nejedly even asserted in his biography (Prague, 1958) that Mahler was active in Olmütz not just for a few weeks, but from 1883 to 1885. Fortunately I discovered a musicologist in Olmütz itself who had carefully collected and analysed the documents on Mahler's work at that time. In her hitherto unpublished dissertation ('Gustav Mahler v Olomouci') Dagmar Kučerová presents the results of her investigation, making a contribution to research from which this book has profited.

I got on to Dagmar Kučerová, who was about to disclose these important documents, by a stroke of luck while searching for Mahler's personal file in the archives of the Staatstheater in Kassel. Herr Hans Joachim Schaefer, literary adviser at the theatre, drew my attention to enquiries that had for some time been reaching him from researchers in Europe and America; among these was an enquiry from Olmütz. This concentration of interest on Kassel since about 1960 is quite understandable, for Schaefer had announced in the periodical *Musica* that Mahler's personal file had been preserved among the documents of the former Court Theatre.

Going through this file proved just as useful as consulting the relevant dossiers in the Court and State Archives in Vienna. Study of these documents together with the published letters seems to demolish the legend of Mahler's 'expulsion' from more than one responsible post. This applies not only to his departures from Kassel, Leipzig, Hamburg and Vienna, but also to his leaving Budapest. In their book on Mahler (in Hungarian, Budapest, 1965), Tibor Gedeon and Miklós Máthé made the contents of important documents accessible. Michael Meixner was able to publish some of the material in German, in the *Almanac* of the Vienna Festival Weeks of 1967, edited by myself. What is so astonishing is that all these sources – from the Kassel personal file to the standing orders for the Budapest staff and the directives of the Budapest Ministry of the Interior – have received hardly any attention from Mahler researchers. There has even been uncertainty about the repertoire of the Budapest Opera under Mahler. The survey of the repertoire found in the jubilee souvenir publication of the Hungarian State Opera (*A Hetvenötéves Magyar Állami Operaház*, Budapest, 1959) gives full information on that point, and is, moreover, very useful for the approximate dating of some of Mahler's letters which had defied chronological classification. This in turn led to emendations of the previously accepted chronology of his life.

I had a sense of adventure in tapping the sources that touch on Mahler's private life, but I did not enter this intimate sphere just for the sake of it. This kind of quest is only meaningful where private matters have a bearing on the public, artistic life. Hero-worship should not lead one into making any and every event in the life of a genius a subject of investigation, though Arnold Schönberg, in his memorial address on Mahler, expressed the view that with a great man 'nothing is unimportant', and every one of his actions 'somehow productive'; Schönberg said he would even 'have liked to watch Mahler tying a necktie'. On those grounds, there seems no reason why ties that had rather more influence on Mahler's personality than his neckties should be excluded from biographical presentation. However, I have tried to describe these emotional relationships with appropriate reserve. Although the Kassel love affair tempted me to try and discover the young lady who had inspired the *Songs of a Wayfarer*, I swept the laboriously assembled evidence back into my filing cabinet when I realised that knowledge of her identity would contribute little or nothing to our knowledge of Mahler.

Things were different when it came to Mahler's relationship with Anna von Mildenburg. Here the seemingly private sphere overlapped the intellectual and artistic. Discretion might have been equal to downright lying, as deprived of the intensity of that relationship, Mahler's portrait would appear distorted.

The same goes for the meeting between Mahler and Freud, which has been extensively treated in English and American literature. It was not just an encounter between patient and doctor. Their converse which, as I have shown, led to mutual tributes, is surely of general cultural interest.

The fact that in her memoirs (*Gustav Mahler – Erinnerungen und Briefe*, Amsterdam 1940 and Vienna 1949) Alma Mahler quotes the text of Mahler's tribute without explaining that this refers to Freud is one of the minor blemishes of her account. She is always, or nearly always, reliable where she speaks of aesthetic judgments or emotional reactions; it becomes risky to trust her in questions of fact or chronology. In the latter respect, the inaccuracy of her edition of the letters (*Gustav Mahler, Briefe 1879 bis 1911*, Vienna, 1925) is particularly irritating. Wrong dating can lead to wrong conclusions. I have carried out some investigations with a view to rectifying these errors, and it soon became apparent that a new critical edition of Mahler's letters is highly desirable. It should include a number of further letters, by no means unimportant, which have come to light in the course of the years and have only to a limited extent been published in newspapers and periodicals.

It is not only Alma Mahler who falsifies chronology, but also more than one publication with a claim to musicological standing. Thus,

H. F. Redlich is of the opinion that Mahler could not have begun *The Song of the Earth* in 1907, because Hans Bethge's volume of poems *Die chinesische Flöte* had not been yet published. To prove this he does not, as one might have expected, quote a primary source, but a remark in an essay by Paul Stefan (*Gustav Mahler – Eine Studie über Persönlichkeit und Werk*, 4th edition, Munich 1912). He could have consulted Bethge himself: the anthology *Deutsche Lyrik seit Liliencron*, edited by Bethge, gives 1907 as the year of publication of *Die chinesische Flöte*. In this particular case, Alma's memoirs can be trusted, for she reports that Mahler was working on these poems 'after the death of our child, after the doctor's terrible diagnosis' – that is, in the summer of 1907.

Doubtless I am beginning to tire the reader with such minutiae. This is done deliberately, for I should like to arouse his sympathy for the despondency which sometimes overtook me during this work. There were all too few facts I could consider safely established; nearly every document I took up produced doubts. I was particularly suspicious of certain sentences which recur almost verbatim in a variety of publications, as, for instance, the statement that in America Mahler conducted 'a complete cycle' of Bruckner's symphonies. American documentation does not support this. A survey of the programmes of the concerts Mahler directed there (published by Irving Kolodin in 1960) shows no more than that Bruckner's Fourth Symphony was included. What is the point of these legends, perpetuated uncritically by successive biographers? Does Mahler's genuine feeling for Bruckner's work – admittedly less manifest in the last years of his life – really demand these fairy-tales?

Another recurrent myth is the story of the 'new orchestra' supposedly created for Mahler in New York in 1909, which in fact turns out to be none other than the venerable orchestra of the New York Philharmonic Society, founded in 1842. The only new thing about it was the change in its legal constitution, enforced by the sponsors in 1909 in order to give Mahler absolute power. Nor was Mahler a 'guest conductor' in the United States: his status with the New York Philharmonic was more closely defined and legally secure than his connection with any European orchestra had ever been.

America gave him what he had always wanted. It seems that his European biographers are reluctant to accept this unpalatable fact.

Legends are also cherished which purport to account for Mahler's early death: America had been a torment to him, undermining his health; the everyday cares of the Vienna Opera had made him unhappy, because he could pursue his inner destiny of being a composer only during his holidays. None of this is borne out by the facts of Mahler's life. His dedicated work on the staging of operas, particularly in the period from 1903 onwards, is sufficient proof of his genuine creative interest in the problems of the musical theatre. Very few writers have studied this aspect of his activities. There are significant allusions to it in the writings of Paul Stefan and Richard Specht, and in the essays of Alfred Roller. Erwin Stein deals more thoroughly with Mahler's operatic work in Vienna (in *The Opera Bedside Book*, edited by Harold Rosenthal, London, 1965). Insufficient attention has so far been given to several essays by Ludwig Hevesi (*Altkunst-Neukunst*, Vienna, 1909), which contain exceptionally vivid accounts of Mahler's and Roller's stage productions.

A useful starting point for the biographer is an article by Mahler's friend Guido Adler, professor of music at Vienna University, which was published in 1914 in the *Biographisches Jahrbuch und Deutscher Nekrolog* (German biographical yearbook and death-roll); the article subsequently appeared as a separate publication: *Gustav Mahler* (Vienna, 1916). There is also important information in Natalie Bauer-Lechner's *Erinnerungen an Gustav Mahler* (Reminiscences of Gustav Mahler; Vienna, 1923), and in Ludwig Karpath's essays published under the title *Begegnung mit dem Genius* (Encounters with Genius; Vienna, 1934). Karpath, who was trained as an opera singer but soon turned to music criticism, met Mahler in Budapest, and for some years kept in close contact with him in Vienna. After Karpath's death in 1936, his extensive archives, which contained some original documents and many informative copies, came into the possession of Dr Willi Reich, to whom my sincere thanks are due for his kindness in putting this material at my disposal and thus greatly facilitating my work.

[261]

The material I have collected and studied in preparing this biography does not fill me with satisfaction: it seems, on the contrary, to show up the dismal state of Mahler scholarship. The informed reader of this biography will perhaps miss some favourite anecdotes about Mahler; nor will it escape the critical reviewer that certain events are presented otherwise than in previous accounts. If I were to corroborate all that has been said, or left unsaid, in true scholarly fashion, I would have to produce a separate volume with the title *Gustav Mahler – documents regarding his life and work*. Such a book will certainly be written one day when biographical research on Mahler attains a standard commensurate with the subject.

Register of Works

This survey is based on the *Register of works* published by the International Gustav Mahler Society. Figures in italics indicate the pages on which the works are discussed.

SYMPHONIES

First Symphony in D major (1888). *Pages 73–78 passim*, 81, 84, 95–6, 101, 102, 110, 111, 119, 223, 227, 254

Second Symphony in C minor (1894), with soprano and alto solo and mixed choir, words by Klopstock and from *Des Knaben Wunderhorn*. *Pages 87, 96–103 passim*, 110, 111, 112–14, 118–19, 122, 130, 151, 159, 160, 191, 193, 217, 225, 228, 244, 246, 251–2

Third Symphony in D minor (1896) with alto solo, women's and boys' choir, words by Friedrich Nietzsche and from *Des Knaben Wunderhorn*. *Pages 110, 119–128 passim*, 141, 159, 160, 167, 182, 191, 212, 251

Fourth Symphony in G major (1900) with soprano solo, words from *Des Knaben Wunderhorn*. *Pages 158–61*, 182, 183, 243, 244, 246, 254

Fifth Symphony in C sharp minor (1902). *Pages 77*, 165, 167, 181, 182–3, 185–8 *passim*, 189–90, 191, 194–5, 197, 238, 243, 254

Sixth Symphony in A minor (1904). *Pages 77*, 181–2, 183–8 *passim*, 189–90, 191, 203, 210, 212, 254

Seventh Symphony in E minor (1905). *Pages 77*, 181, 186–7, 188, 189–90, 191, 203, 223, 243, 245, 254

Eighth Symphony in E flat major (1906) for three sopranos, two contraltos, tenor, baritone, bass, boys' choir, two mixed choirs and large orchestra. *First Part:* Hymn, *Veni, creator spiritus; Second Part:* Final scene of Goethe's *Faust Part II*. *Pages 8*, 191, 210, 211, 217, 229–32, 238, 240, 242, 243, 253

Das Lied von der Erde (Song of the Earth) (1908). A symphony for tenor and alto (or baritone) solo and orchestra, words from Chinese poems translated by Hans Bethge. *Pages 191*, 198, 223, 235–40, 242, 245, 246–7, 254, 259, 260

Ninth Symphony in D major (1909). *Pages 77*, 191, 226, 235, 240, 243, 246

Adagio from the unfinished tenth Symphony in F sharp major (1910).
Pages 9, 226, 235, 254–5

CHOIR AND ORCHESTRA

Das klagende Lied (1880, revised 1898) for soprano, alto and tenor solo,
mixed choir and orchestra, on an original text. *Pages* 44, 45, 46–48, 64,
102 (cf. also Symphonies No. 2, 3 and 8)

VOICE AND ORCHESTRA

Lieder eines fahrenden Gesellen (Songs of the Wayfarer) (1884?) on original
texts and on words from *Des Knaben Wunderhorn*. *Pages* 60–64, 105,
119

Twelve Songs from *Des Knaben Wunderhorn* (1892–95). *Pages* 105–9

Ten songs were published by Mahler in 1905 in the form of a cycle; two
songs are parts of symphonies: '*Es sungen drei Engel*' of the Third
Symphony, and '*Urlicht*' of the Second

Kindertotenlieder (1901–4) on poems by Friedrich Rückert and from
Des Knaben Wunderhorn. *Pages* 20, 165, 197–9, 227

Sieben Lieder aus letzter Zeit (1899–1903) on poems by Friedrich Rückert
and from *Des Knaben Wunderhorn*. *Page* 197

VOICE AND PIANO

Fourteen *Lieder und Gesänge aus der Jugendzeit*. *Page* 104

Also mentioned

Song: *Erinnerung*. *Page* 77

Early Works—not preserved

Operas: *Herzog Ernst von Schwaben*. *Pages* 20–1, 25
         Rübezahl. *Pages* 25, 44, 45–6

Score to Scheffel's *Der Trompeter von Säckingen*. *Page* 58

Not specified: *Die Argonauten*. *Page* 25

N.B. The works listed in the section 'Voice and Orchestra' exist also in
versions for voice and pianoforte.

Select Bibliography

Adler, Guido, *Gustav Mahler*, Vienna-Leipzig, 1916

Adorno, Theodor W., *Mahler. Eine musikalische Physiognomik*, Frankfurt, 1960

Bauer-Lechner, Natalie, *Erinnerungen an Gustav Mahler*, Vienna, 1923

Bekker, Paul, *Gustav Mahlers Sinfonien*, Berlin, 1921

Cardus, Neville, *Gustav Mahler: his mind and his music*, vol. 1 (The first five symphonies), London, 1965

Engel, Gabriel, *Gustav Mahler, Song-symphonist*, New York, 1932

Gedeon, Tibor and Mathé, Miklós, *Gustav Mahler*, Budapest, 1965

Hadamowsky, Franz (ed.), *Gustav Mahler und seine Zeit*, catalogue of the Vienna Festival Exhibition, Vienna, 1960

Klemperer, Otto, *Meine Erinnerungen an Gustav Mahler*, Zürich, 1960

Kučerová, Dagmar, 'Gustav Mahler v Olomouci', *Hudebni Veda*, no. 4, Prague (1968)

Mahler, Alma, *Gustav Mahler, Erinnerungen und Briefe*, Amsterdam, 1940. (English edition, translated by Basil Creighton, entitled *Gustav Mahler, Memories and Letters*, London 1946; enlarged edition, revised and edited and with an introduction by Donald Mitchell, London, 1968); *And the Bridge is Love*, New York, 1958

Mahler, Gustav, *Briefe, 1879–1911*, edited by Alma Maria Mahler, Vienna-Leipzig, 1924

Matter, Jean, *Mahler. Le démoniaque*, Lausanne, 1959

Mitchell, Donald, *Gustav Mahler: the early years*, London, 1958

Neisser, Arthur, *Gustav Mahler*, Leipzig, 1918

Nejedly, Zdenek, *Gustav Mahler*, Prague, 1958

Ratz, Erwin, *Von Leben und Werk* and *Zum Formproblem*, in *Gustav Mahler* (a collection of essays and speeches by Theodor W. Adorno, Ernst Bloch, Otto Klemperer, Hans Mayer, Erwin Ratz and Arnold Schoenberg), Tübingen, 1966

Redlich, Hans Ferdinand, *Gustav Mahler. Eine Erkenntnis*, Nuremberg, 1919; *Bruckner and Mahler*, London, 1955

Reich, Willi (ed.), *Gustav Mahler. Im eigenen Wort – im Wort der Freunde*, Zürich, 1958

SELECT BIBLIOGRAPHY

Ritter, William, *Souvenirs sur Gustave Mahler*, in *Schweizerische Musikzeitung*, vol. 101 (1961), no. 1

Roller, Alfred, *Die Bildnisse von Gustav Mahler*, Vienna, 1922

Schaefer, Hans Joachim, 'Gustav Mahlers Wirken in Kassel', *Musica*, vol. 14 (1960), no. 6

Schaefers, Anton, *Gustav Mahlers Instrumentation*, Düsseldorf, 1935

Schibler, Armin, *Zum Werk Gustav Mahlers*, Lindau, 1955

Schiedermair, Ludwig, *Gustav Mahler, eine biographisch-kritische Würdigung*, Munich, 1900

Specht, Richard, *Gustav Mahler*, Berlin, 1913

Stefan, Paul, *Gustav Mahler, eine Studie über Persönlichkeit und Werk*, Munich, 1910; English edition, trans. by T. E. Clark, entitled *Gustav Mahler. A study of his personality and work*, New York, 1913.

Stein, Erwin, 'Mahlers Instrumentationsretuschen', *Pult und Taktstock*, vol. 4 (1928); 'Mahler and the Vienna Opera', *The Opera Bedside Book*, ed. Harold Rosenthal, London, 1965

Vignal, Marc, *Mahler*, Paris, 1966

Walter, Bruno, *Gustav Mahler*, Vienna-Leipzig-Zürich, 1936. (English edition, trans. by James Galston, London, 1937, new edition, London, 1958); *Theme and Variations. An Autobiography*, London, 1947

Wellesz, Egon, *Die neue Instrumentation*, Berlin, 1928–29; 'Mahlers Instrumentation', *Musikblätter des Anbruch*, vol. 12 (1930), no. 3; 'The Symphonies of Gustav Mahler', in *The Music Review*, vol. 1 (1940)

Index

INDEX

Humperdinck, Engelbert, 111, 145
Hungarian National Theatre, 82

Ibsen, Henrik, 121, 159, 166
Iglau, 17, 19, 22, 25, 29, 57, 64,
  88, 97, 187; Gymnasium, 31;
  Municipal Theatre, 22–3, 31
Iglauer Sonntagsblatt, 22
Illustriertes Extrablatt, 174
Imperial October Manifesto *see*
  Oktoberdiplom
International Mahler Society, 254
Ischl, 130

Jahn, Wilhelm, 129–31 *passim*,
  134, 136, 142, 143, 145, 148–9,
  180
Jalowetz, Heinrich, 218
Jauner, Franz, 37
Joachim, Joseph, 72
Jones, Ernest, 8, 12

Kahn, Otto, F., 222
Kainz, 220
Kalbeck, Max, 47, 173, 210
Kališt, 16, 19
Karlsbad Stadttheater, 116
Karlsruhe, 72
Karpath, Ludwig, 117, 129, 130,
  135, 175–6, 261
Kassel, 62, 64; Court Theatre,
  57–60 *passim*, 65–7 *passim*, 105;
  Musikfest, 65, 66, 115;
  Staatstheater, archives of, 56,
  57, 58, 200, 257–8
Klafsky, Katharina, 93, 115
Kleiber, Carlos, 247
Klemperer, Otto, 230, 243–4, 246

Klimt, Gustav, 138, 162, 163–4,
  165, 168, 181, 218, 220
Klinger, Max, 163–4, 167
Klopstock, Friedrich Gottlieb,
  Auferstehn, 97, 98–101
Knote, Heinrich, 222
Kolodin, Irving, 221, 260
Korngold, Julius, 211, 212–3
Koussevitsky, Sergei, 243
Kovarović, Karel, 162
Krancsevics String Quartet, 83
Kraus, Clemens, 191
Krefeld, 167
Krenek, Ernst, 247
Krenn, Frenz, 30, 35
Krisper, Anton, 31, 48, 51
Krzyzanowski, Rudolf, 31, 32, 35
Kubelik, Rafael, 247
Kučerová, Dagmar, 54, 257
Kunstwart, Berlin, 191
Kurz, Selma, 210, 212

Labor, Josef, 166
Laibach (Ljubljana), 48, 51, 53,
  56, 58; Landestheater, 49–51,
  257; Philharmonic Society, 49,
  50, 51
Laibacher Zeitung, 49, 51
L'Allemand, Captain, 141
Lalo, Edouard, 158
Lalo, Pierre, 158
Lammasch, Heinrich, 137
Langbehn, Julius, 120–1, 122
Laue, Max von, 207–8
L'Aurore, 138
Lecocq, Alexandre Charles, 50
Lehár, Franz, 196–7
Lehmann, Lilli, 219
Leiden, 8, 10, 11

[271]

THOR HEYERDAHL
Sea Routes to Polynesia

WHO WERE THE POLYNESIANS?

When Thor Heyerdahl first suggested that the Polynesian Islands could have been colonised in prehistoric times by South American Indians who crossed the Pacific on wooden rafts, many of the experts remained sceptical. How, they asked, could the frail reed and balsa wood rafts of the South American Indians have spanned such enormous distances?

The *Kon-Tiki* expedition proved that it was possible: now, in *Sea Routes to Polynesia*, Thor Heyerdahl explores the theories behind his epic voyage, describes his subsequent discoveries and provides a fascinating insight into the islands, peoples and customs of the Pacific from the Malay peninsular to the coast of Ecuador, from the aborigines of the Galapagos to the statues of Rano-Raraku on Easter Island.

THE PALLISERS Anthony Trollope

THE PALLISERS

Set amid the swirl of London's social and political life in the 1860's, Anthony Trollope's sequence of six parliamentary novels follows the fortunes of Plantagenet Palliser, dedicated politician, heir to the greatest dukedom in Britain, and his beautiful, extrovert wife, Glencora. Interwoven with their story are those of 'Planty Pall's' colleagues and Glencora's social allies and rivals, from wily Lizzy Eustace, obsessed by her famous family diamonds, to the naif Irishman Phineas Finn and his four loves.

This saga of romance, intrigue, blackmail and even murder, originally amounted to more than a million and a half words, written for leisured Victorian readers. For modern readers Michael Hardwick has produced this single volume edition, skilfully abridged to preserve the spirit and intention of Trollope's great work.

NIGEL NICOLSON
PORTRAIT OF A MARRIAGE

Portrait of a Marriage tells the story of Harold Nicolson's forty-nine-year marriage to Vita Sackville-West, a union based on mutual trust, shared interests, deepening love, total frankness and reciprocal infidelity. It is also the journal of Vita's love affair with Violet Trefusis, the crisis which nearly broke the Nicolsons' unconventional, but extraordinarily successful marriage.

'Vita's . . . journal will earn an honoured place in the records of confessional literature.'
THE TIMES

'Excels for intensity and unexpectedness anything of its kind in fiction.'
FINANCIAL TIMES

'Mr Nicolson's good faith is patent . . . the tone perfect.'
Sybille Bedford, THE LISTENER

'THE MOST CONVINCING AND ENTHRALLING OF LOVE STORIES.'
ECONOMIST

The Lost Continent of Mu

James Churchward

MU: the Empire of the Sun, a lost culture which dominated the world 25,000 years ago. A vanished continent which sent Colonel James Churchward on a lifetime's search, from the vaults of an Indian temple to Australia, from Siberia to the South Seas.

For in 1868, while serving with the British Army in India, Churchward became close friends with a high priest who taught him how to decipher some stone tablets, hidden for centuries in the temple vaults. They told of a civilization which had emerged, flourished and decayed long before our own: the continent of Mu.

This is Churchward's story of how he followed the trail of Mu literally to the ends of the earth and of how he eventually pieced together a picture of a civilization lost in the mists of time.